CONTENTS

plan graphics

SECOND EDITION

DRAWING • DELINEATION • LETTERING

THEODORE D. WALKER

Additional copies may be ordered from: **P D A PUBLISHERS**
Box 3075
West Lafayette, Indiana
47906

Library of Congress Catalog Card Number: 75-12051
ISBN 0-914886-07-X (cloth)
ISBN 0-914886-12-6 (paper)

Printed in the United States of America

INTRODUCTION

This book resulted from a need which became apparent following the publication of *Perspective Sketches* in 1972. Professionals and students alike requested additional visuals beyond the sketches for reference. Even though the central focus of this book is on plans it also includes elevations and sections.

Good graphics are impressive to clients whether we like it or not. Sharp, clean, crisp work creates a more positive impression than work which is dull and sloppy.

Graphic skills, in the language of the educator, are *perceptual motor skills*. They are easiest to learn when an individual is young and such skill development is easiest to achieve. The many hours of effort spent early in life will provide many rewards, including self satisfaction and a sense of achievement, later in one's career.

There is very little text in this book as *perceptual motor skills* are almost impossible to describe in words. One who has these skills can demonstrate them to another, after which the latter must practice to master them. The approach in this book is to provide many different examples which can be used by anyone as he experiments with the development of his own skills. To master any *perceptual motor skill* whether it is graphics, surgery, or performing on a musical instrument, many long patient hours of practice are required. Some will find it easier and quicker to learn than others as we are all different.

In its organization, this book begins with several different graphic techniques for site analysis. In sequence this chapter is followed by design concepts, master plans of various sizes and scale, plans drawn completely freehand, and a chapter of plans at full size or unreduced which will be explained later. Other chapters include elevations and sections, and lettering. The final chapter lists the sources and credits for all the plans shown and in some cases additional information is provided.

The process of reducing plans photograph-

ically (as was done for most of those in this book) reduces the width of the lines, eliminates some white space and fuzziness, and makes the drawings sharper and crisper than at their full size. Chapter Six, a group of full size drawings, includes work in ink, pencil and felt tip. These have been provided to illustrate work not reduced. You may wish to refer to this chapter frequently as you review plans in other chapters in order to observe the contrast and change created during reduction. The following pages may be helpful in this review:

FULL SIZE	REDUCTION
166	60
167	88
168	53
169	57
172	90
173	94

David Linstrum has prepared the following illustrations especially for this book to compare pencil, marker, and ink techniques side by side. He suggests testing various media, techniques, and paper in this manner before launching a final presentation drawing to insure getting the results you want.

INK

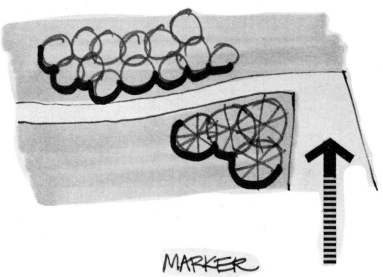

PENCIL

MARKER

4

SECOND EDITION

Added to the first edition are several more plans in black and white and a group of plans in color. These form Chapter Nine. The color plans vary in scale, character, technique, and colors to provide as much diversity as possible under the economic restraints of reproduction.

PLEASE NOTE

Since the principal intent of this book is to serve as a reference for graphic techniques, no design should be copied. The rights to each illustration herein belong to the individual or firm who originally designed it.

ACKNOWLEDGEMENTS

The author gratefully acknowledges the assistance and generosity of many individuals and offices who contributed examples for this book. Each is listed below his work. In most cases these individuals and firms are landscape architects unless otherwise identified. Where the name of a firm is followed by the name of an individual, the latter prepared the drawing for that firm.

SITE ANALYSIS

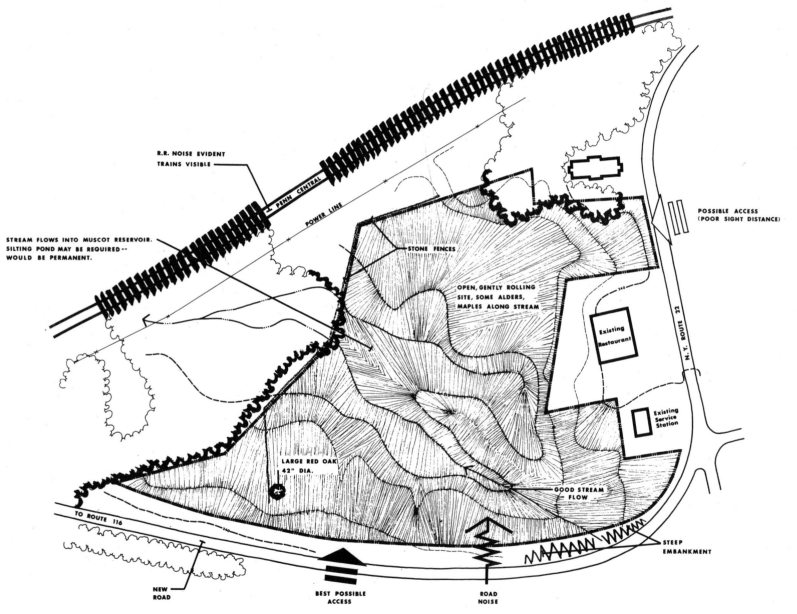

R.R. NOISE EVIDENT
TRAINS VISIBLE

PENN CENTRAL

POWER LINE

STREAM FLOWS INTO MUSCOT RESERVOIR.
SILTING POND MAY BE REQUIRED --
WOULD BE PERMANENT.

STONE FENCES

OPEN, GENTLY ROLLING
SITE, SOME ALDERS,
MAPLES ALONG STREAM

POSSIBLE ACCESS
(POOR SIGHT DISTANCE)

N. Y. ROUTE 22

Existing
Restaurant

Existing
Service
Station

LARGE RED OAK
42" DIA.

GOOD STREAM
FLOW

TO ROUTE 116

STEEP
EMBANKMENT

NEW
ROAD

BEST POSSIBLE
ACCESS

ROAD
NOISE

Site Analysis, North Salem, UDC. The Saratoga Associates.

8

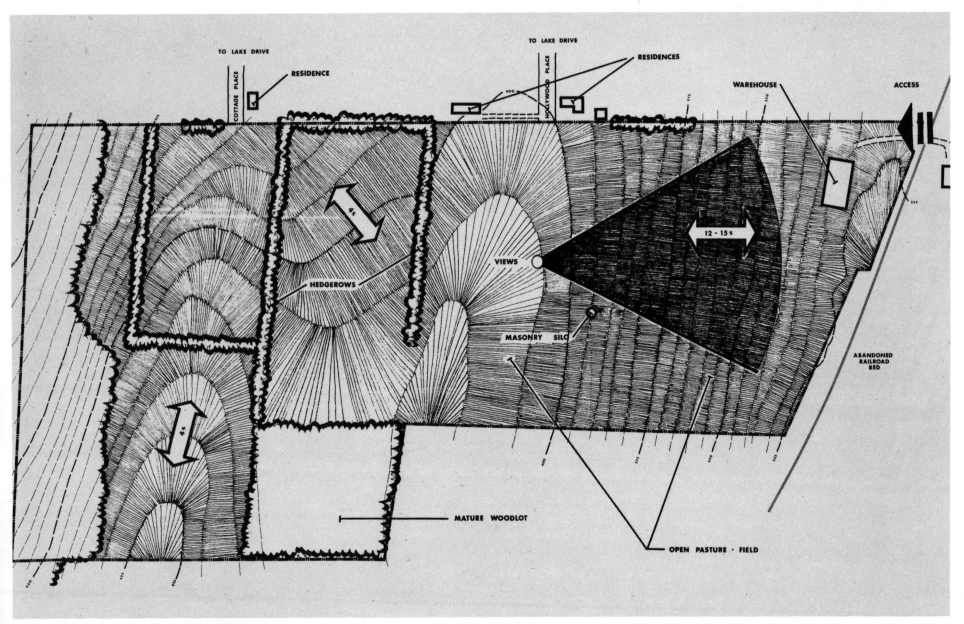

Site Analysis, Somers, UDC. The Saratoga Associates.

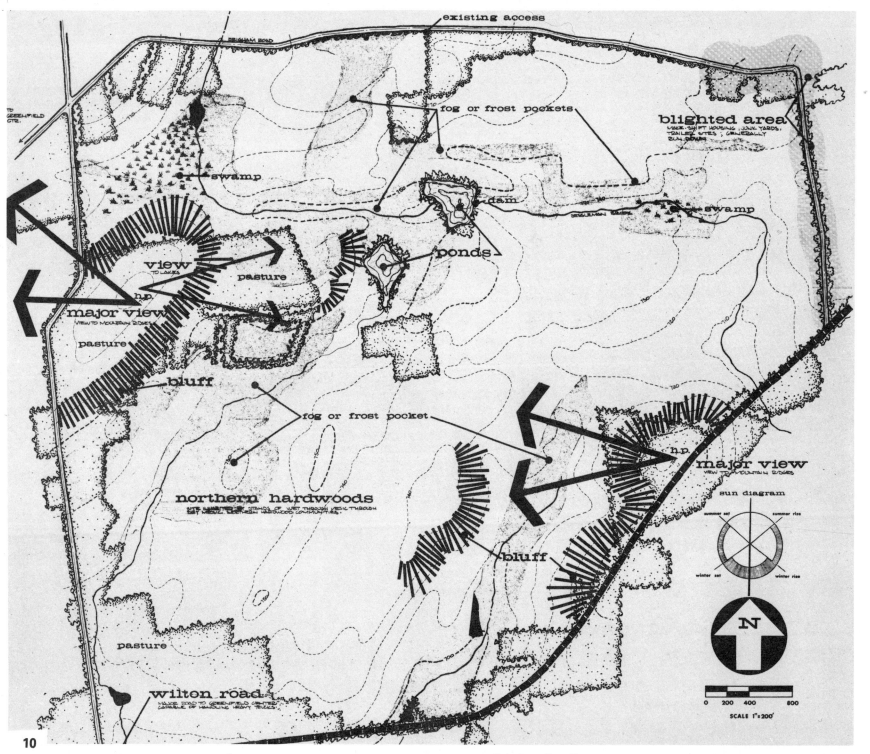

existing access

BRIGHAM ROAD

TO
GREENFIELD
CTR.

fog or frost pockets

blighted area

MAKE-SHIFT HOUSING ; JUNK YARDS ;
TRAILER SITES ; GENERALLY
RUN DOWN.

swamp

dam

swamp

ponds

view

TO LAKES

pasture

h.p.

major view

VIEW TO MOUNTAIN RIDGES

pasture

bluff

fog or frost pocket

h.p.

major view

VIEW TO MOUNTAIN RIDGES

sun diagram

summer set   summer rise

winter set   winter rise

northern hardwoods

bluff

N

pasture

wilton road

MAJOR ROAD TO GREENFIELD CENTER
CAPABLE OF HANDLING HEAVY TRUCKS.

SCALE 1"=200'

0   200   400   800

10

Existing Site Features, New Town. The Saratoga Associates.

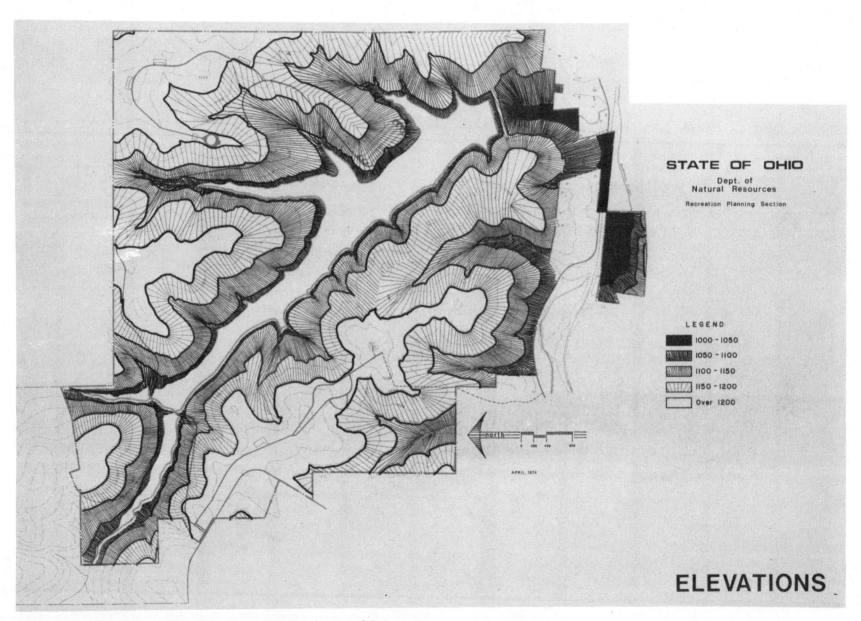

STATE OF OHIO
Dept. of
Natural Resources
Recreation Planning Section

LEGEND
1000 - 1050
1050 - 1100
1100 - 1150
1150 - 1200
Over 1200

north

APRIL, 1974

ELEVATIONS

Plans contracted by State of Ohio, Department of Natural Resources.

11

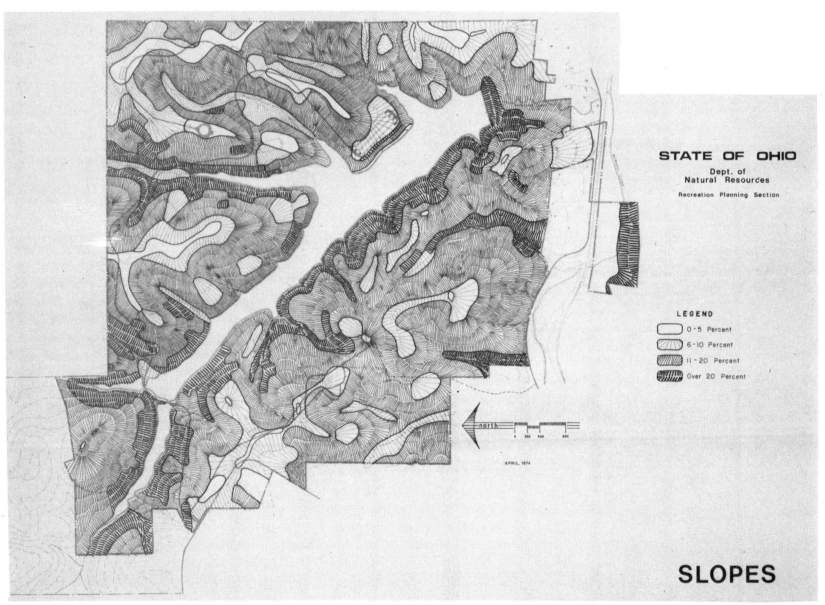

STATE OF OHIO
Dept. of
Natural Resources
Recreation Planning Section

LEGEND
0 - 5 Percent
6 - 10 Percent
11 - 20 Percent
Over 20 Percent

north
0   200   400   600

APRIL, 1974

SLOPES

Plans contracted by State of Ohio, Department of Natural Resources.

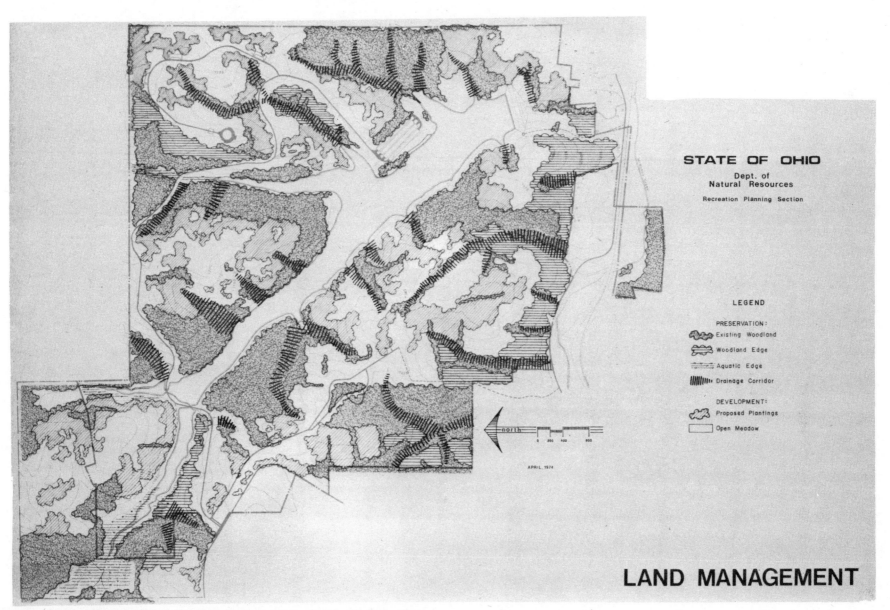

STATE OF OHIO
Dept. of
Natural Resources
Recreation Planning Section

LEGEND

PRESERVATION:
Existing Woodland
Woodland Edge
Aquatic Edge
Drainage Corridor

DEVELOPMENT:
Proposed Plantings
Open Meadow

north   0   200   400   800

APRIL 1974

LAND MANAGEMENT

Plans contracted by State of Ohio, Department of Natural Resources.

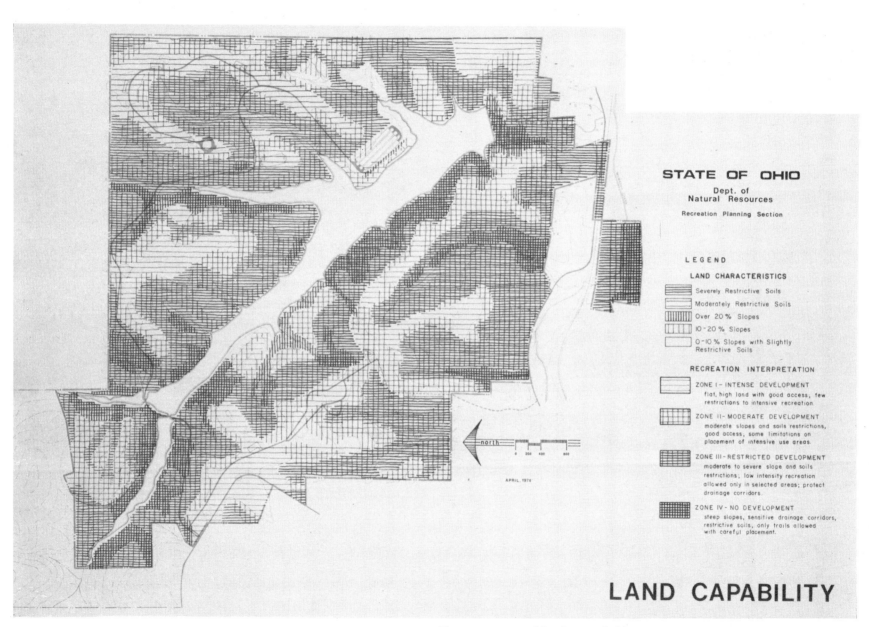

STATE OF OHIO
Dept. of
Natural Resources
Recreation Planning Section

LEGEND
LAND CHARACTERISTICS

Severely Restrictive Soils
Moderately Restrictive Soils
Over 20% Slopes
10-20% Slopes
0-10% Slopes with Slightly Restrictive Soils

RECREATION INTERPRETATION

ZONE I- INTENSE DEVELOPMENT
flat, high land with good access, few restrictions to intensive recreation.

ZONE II- MODERATE DEVELOPMENT
moderate slopes and soils restrictions, good access, some limitations on placement of intensive use areas.

ZONE III- RESTRICTED DEVELOPMENT
moderate to severe slope and soils restrictions; low intensity recreation allowed only in selected areas; protect drainage corridors.

ZONE IV- NO DEVELOPMENT
steep slopes, sensitive drainage corridors, restrictive soils, only trails allowed with careful placement.

north

0   200   400   800

APRIL, 1974

LAND CAPABILITY

Plans contracted by State of Ohio, Department of Natural Resources.

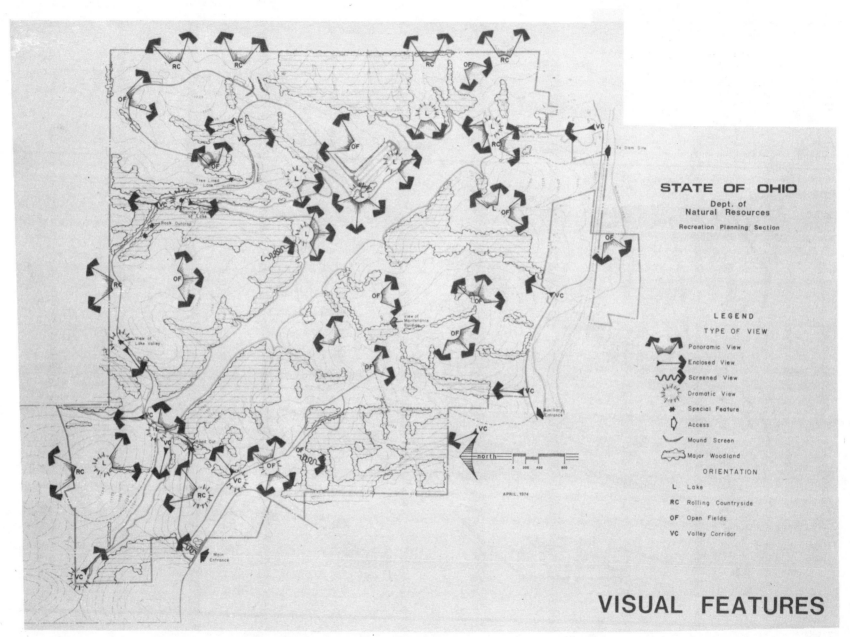

LEGEND

TYPE OF VIEW

Panoramic View

Enclosed View

Screened View

Dramatic View

Special Feature

Access

Mound Screen

Major Woodland

ORIENTATION

L   Lake

RC   Rolling Countryside

OF   Open Fields

VC   Valley Corridor

north

0   200   400   600

APRIL, 1974

VISUAL FEATURES

Plans contracted by State of Ohio, Department of Natural Resources.

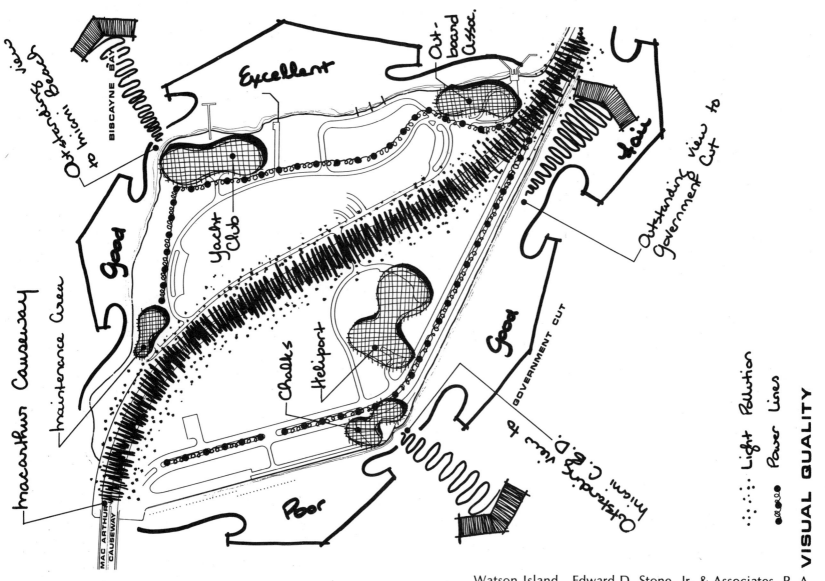

Watson Island.   Edward D. Stone, Jr. & Associates, P. A.

VISUAL QUALITY

16

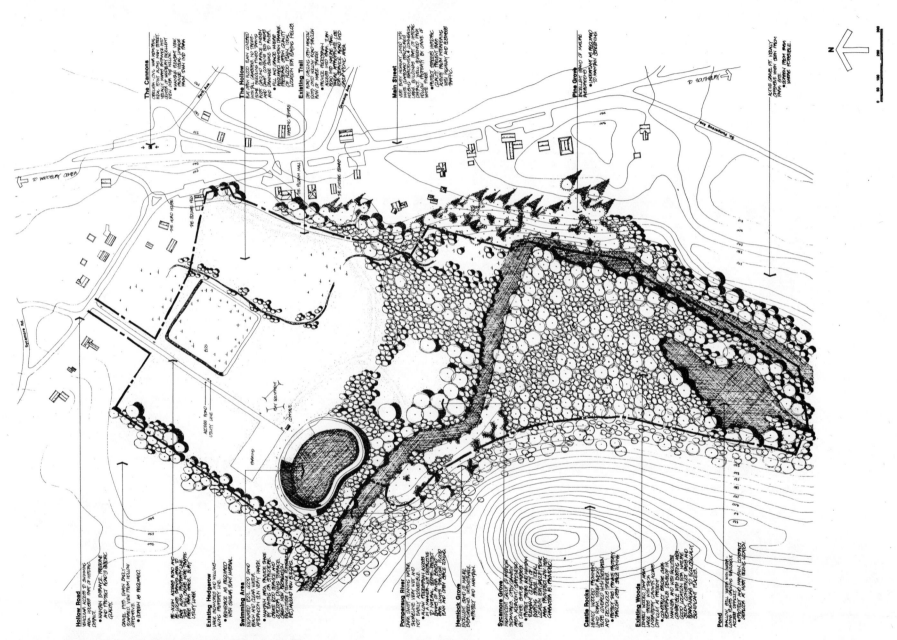

Site Analysis — Land Use. Miceli, Weed, Kulik.

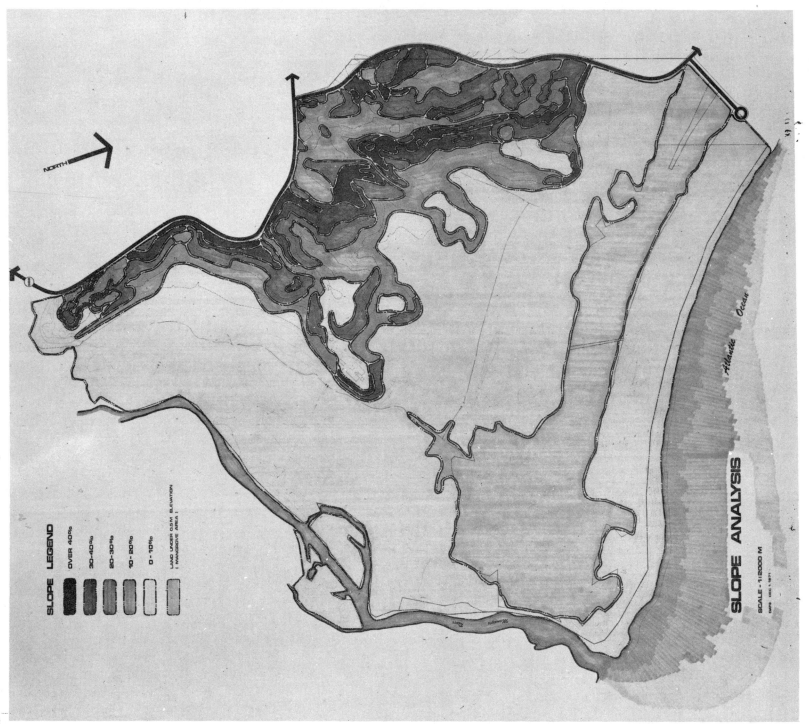

SLOPE LEGEND

OVER 40%
30-40%
20-30%
10-20%
0-10%
LAND UNDER 0.5M ELEVATION
(MANGROVE AREA)

NORTH

SLOPE ANALYSIS

SCALE - 1:12000 M

DATE: DEC 1, 1971

Atlantic Ocean

Palmer Resort.   Edward D. Stone, Jr. & Associates, P. A.

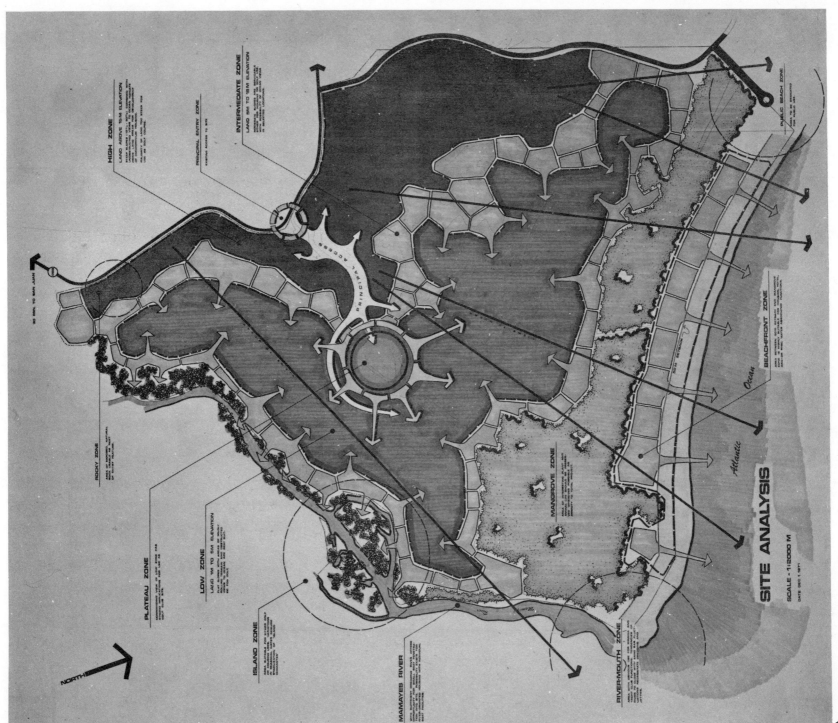

SITE ANALYSIS

SCALE - 1:12000 M

DATE DEC 1 1971

Palmer Resort. Edward D. Stone, Jr. & Associates, P. A.

0–5
5–10
10–15
15–30

PERCENT OF SLOPE

Western Connecticut State College. CR3, Inc., by Jeffrey A. Gebrian.

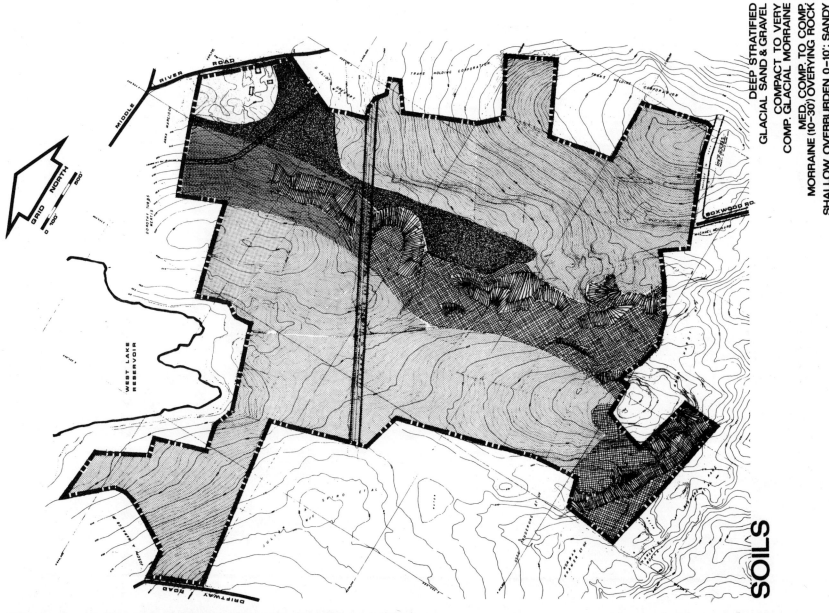

SOILS

Legend:
- DEEP STRATIFIED GLACIAL SAND & GRAVEL
- COMPACT TO VERY COMP. GLACIAL MORRAINE
- MED. COMP. TO COMP. MORRAINE (10-30') OVERYING ROCK
- SHALLOW OVERBURDEN 0-10'; SANDY LOAM & LOOSE GLACIAL MORRAINE
- POORLY DRAINED MINERAL SOILS - PEAT & MUCK BOGS
- EXPOSED ROCK

GRID NORTH

0 100' 500'

WEST LAKE RESERVOIR

Western Connecticut State College. CR3, Inc., by Jeffrey A. Gebrian.

DRAINAGE – ELEVATIONS

Western Connecticut State College. CR3, Inc., by Jeffrey A. Gebrian.

BELOW 600

600 – 650

650 – 700

ABOVE 700

PEAT BOG

STREAM

22

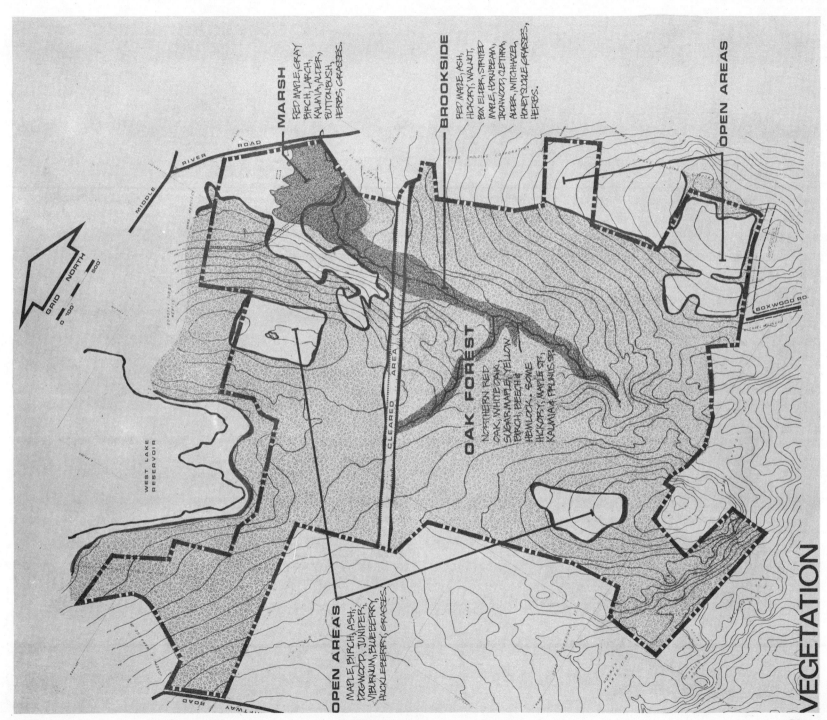

MARSH

RED MAPLE, GRAY BIRCH, LARCH, KALMIA, ALDER, BUTTONBUSH, HERBS, GRASSES.

BROOKSIDE

RED MAPLE, ASH, HICKORY, WALNUT, BOX ELDER, STRIPED MAPLE, HORNBEAM, IRONWOOD, CLETHRA, ALDER, WITCHHAZEL, HONEYSUCKLE GRASSES, HERBS.

OPEN AREAS

OAK FOREST

NORTHERN RED OAK, WHITE OAK, SUGAR MAPLE, YELLOW BIRCH, BEECH, HEMLOCK, SOME HICKORY, MAPLE SP., KALMIA & PRUNUS SP.

OPEN AREAS

MAPLE, BIRCH, ASH, DOGWOOD, JUNIPER, VIBURNUM, BLUEBERRY, HUCKLEBERRY, GRASSES.

MIDDLE RIVER ROAD

WEST LAKE RESERVOIR

GRID NORTH
0 100   500'

BOXWOOD RD.

PUTWAY ROAD

VEGETATION

Western Connecticut State College.   CR3, Inc., by Jeffrey A. Gebrian.

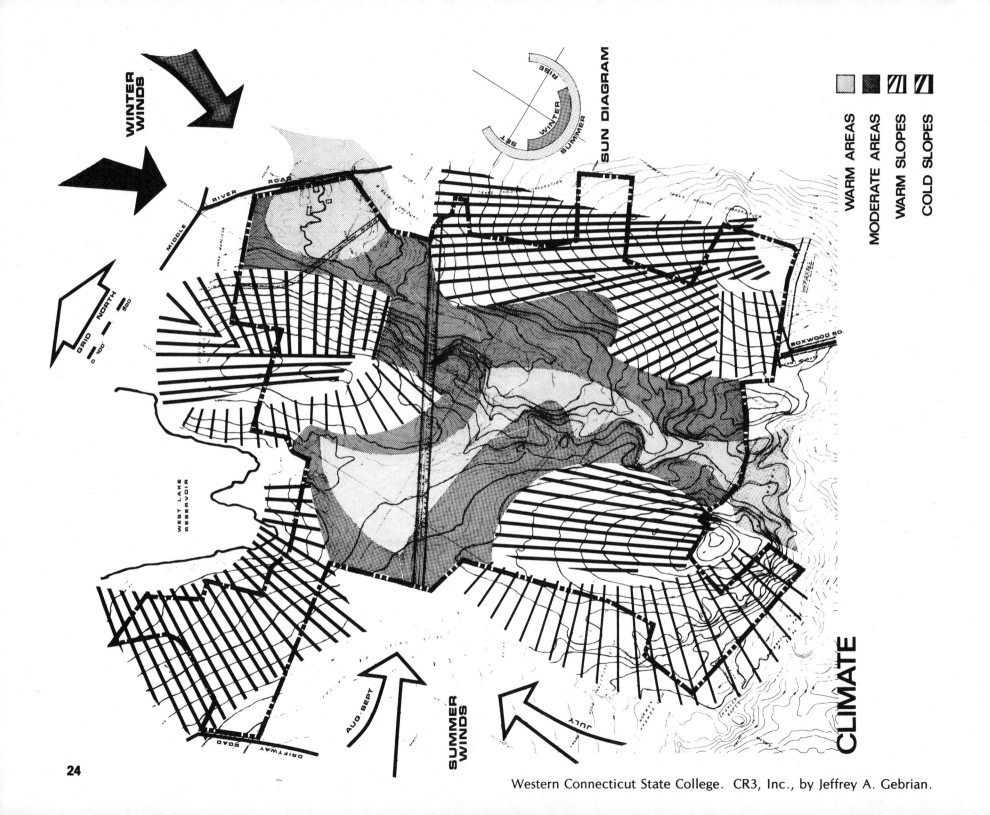

WINTER WINDS

SUN DIAGRAM

RIDGE
WINTER SET
SUMMER

WARM AREAS
MODERATE AREAS
WARM SLOPES
COLD SLOPES

GRID NORTH

0 100' 500'

MIDDLE RIVER ROAD

WEST LAKE RESERVOIR

DRIFTWAY ROAD

BOXWOOD RD.

SUMMER WINDS

AUG-SEPT

JULY

CLIMATE

Western Connecticut State College. CR3, Inc., by Jeffrey A. Gebrian.

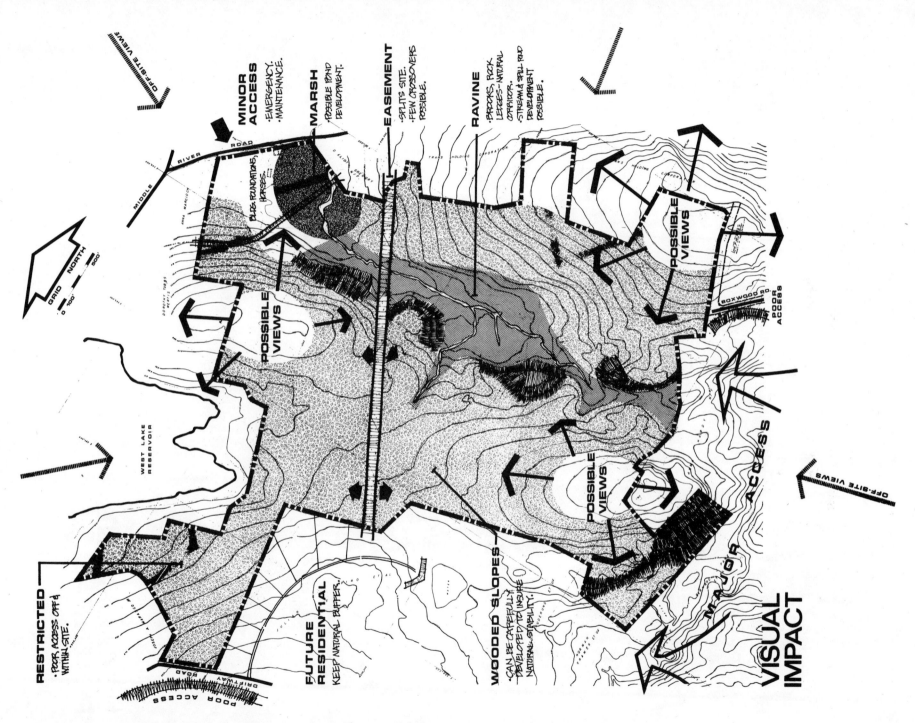

MINOR ACCESS
· EMERGENCY.
· MAINTENANCE.

MARSH
POSSIBLE POND DEVELOPMENT.

EASEMENT
· SPLITS SITE.
· FEW CROSSOVERS POSSIBLE.

RAVINE
· BROOKS, ROCK LEDGES-NATURAL CORRIDOR.
· STREAM & SPILL POND DEVELOPMENT POSSIBLE.

OFFSITE VIEW

GRID NORTH
0 100   500

WEST LAKE RESERVOIR

POSSIBLE VIEWS

POSSIBLE VIEWS

BOXWOOD RD.

POOR ACCESS

POSSIBLE VIEWS

OFF-SITE VIEWS

RESTRICTED
· POOR ACCESS OFF & WITHIN SITE.

POOR ACCESS

FUTURE RESIDENTIAL
KEEP NATURAL BUFFER.

WOODED SLOPES
· CAN BE CAREFULLY DEVELOPED TO INSURE NATURAL STABILITY.

MAJOR ACCESS

VISUAL IMPACT

Western Connecticut State College. CR3, Inc., by Jeffrey A. Gebrian.

25

VERY GOOD

GOOD

FAIR

POOR

DEVELOPMENT
POTENTIAL

GRID NORTH

0   100   200

WEST LAKE
RESERVOIR

MIDDLE   RIVER   ROAD

BOXWOOD RD.

Western Connecticut State College. CR3, Inc., by Jeffrey A. Gebrian.

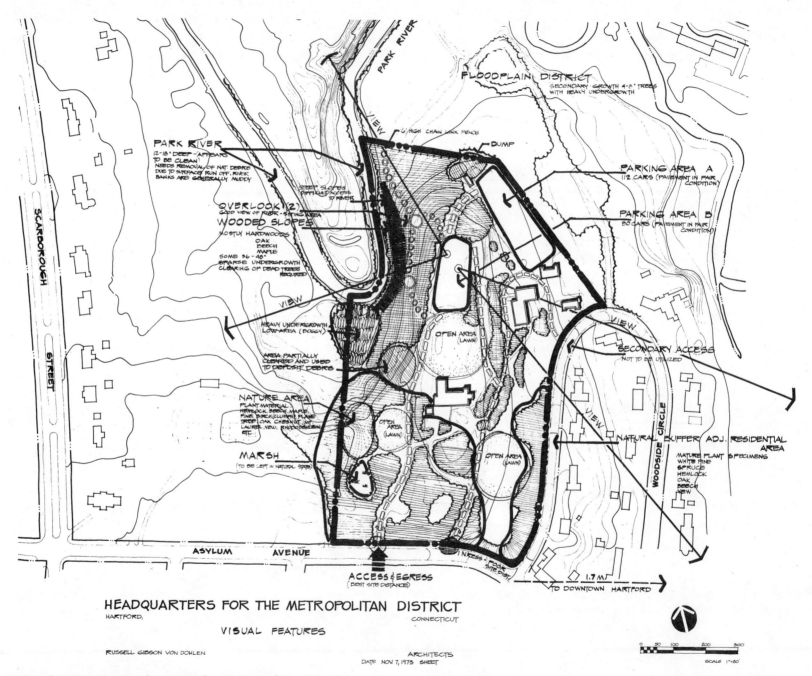

PARK RIVER

PARK RIVER
12-18' DEEP - APPEARS
TO BE CLEAN!
NEEDS REMOVAL OF NAT. DEBRIS
DUE TO SURFACE RUN OFF. RIVER
BANKS ARE GENERALLY MUDDY

FLOODPLAIN DISTRICT
SECONDARY GROWTH 4-8" TREES
WITH HEAVY UNDERGROWTH

6' HIGH CHAIN LINK FENCE

DUMP

PARKING AREA A
112 CARS (PAVEMENT IN FAIR
CONDITION)

PARKING AREA B
80 CARS (PAVEMENT IN FAIR
CONDITION)

STEEP SLOPES
DIFFICULT ACCESS
TO RIVER

OVERLOOK 2
GOOD VIEW OF RIVER - SITTING AREA
WOODED SLOPES
MOSTLY HARDWOODS
OAK
BEECH
MAPLE
SOME 36-48"
SPARSE UNDERGROWTH
CLEARING OF DEAD TREES
REQUIRED

VIEW

OPEN AREA
(LAWN)

HEAVY UNDERGROWTH
LOW AREA (BOGGY)

AREA PARTIALLY
CLEARED AND USED
TO DEPOSIT DEBRIS

SECONDARY ACCESS
NOT TO BE UTILIZED

VIEW

NATURE AREA
PLANT MATERIAL
HEMLOCK, BEECH, MAPLE,
PINE, BIRCH (CLUMPS) FLAME
TREE, OAK, CHESTNUT, MT.
LAUREL, YEW, RHODODENDRON
ETC.

OPEN
AREA
(LAWN)

OPEN AREA
(LAWN)

WOODSIDE CIRCLE

NATURAL BUFFER ADJ. RESIDENTIAL
AREA

MARSH
(TO BE LEFT IN NATURAL STATE)

MATURE PLANT SPECIMENS
WHITE PINE
SPRUCE
HEMLOCK
OAK
BEECH
VIEW

ASYLUM   AVENUE

INGRESS - POOR SITE DIST.

ACCESS & EGRESS
(BEST SITE DISTANCE)

TO DOWNTOWN HARTFORD

1.7 MI.

SCARBOROUGH   STREET

HEADQUARTERS FOR THE METROPOLITAN DISTRICT
HARTFORD,   CONNECTICUT
VISUAL FEATURES

RUSSELL GIBSON VON DOHLEN   ARCHITECTS
                                   DATE NOV. 7, 1973 SHEET

SCALE 1"=80'
0   50   100   200   300

Visual Features, Headquarters for Metropolitan District,
Hartford, Connecticut. CR3, Inc., by Dainis Lazda.

DESIGN CONCEPTS

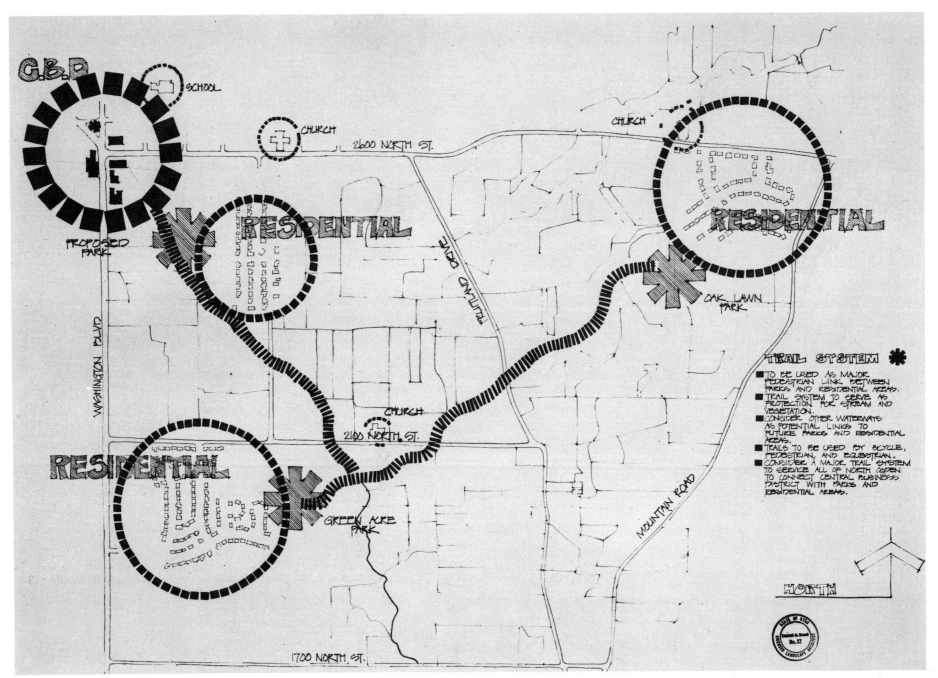

Green Acre Park. Maas and Grassli.

TRAIL SYSTEM ✳

■ TO BE USED AS MAJOR PEDESTRIAN LINK BETWEEN PARKS AND RESIDENTIAL AREAS.

■ TRAIL SYSTEM TO SERVE AS PROTECTION FOR STREAM AND VEGETATION.

■ CONSIDER OTHER WATERWAYS AS POTENTIAL LINKS TO FUTURE PARKS AND RESIDENTIAL AREAS.

■ TRAILS TO BE USED BY BICYCLE, PEDESTRIAN, AND EQUESTRIAN.

■ CONSIDER A MAJOR TRAIL SYSTEM TO SERVICE ALL OF NORTH OGDEN TO CONNECT CENTRAL BUSINESS DISTRICT WITH PARKS AND RESIDENTIAL AREAS.

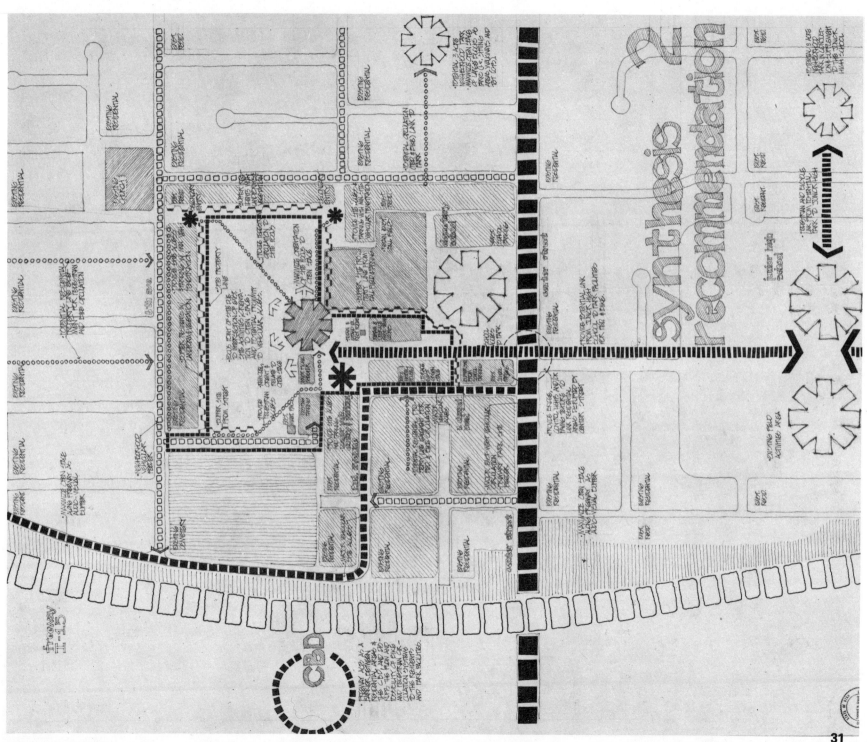

Maas and Grassli.

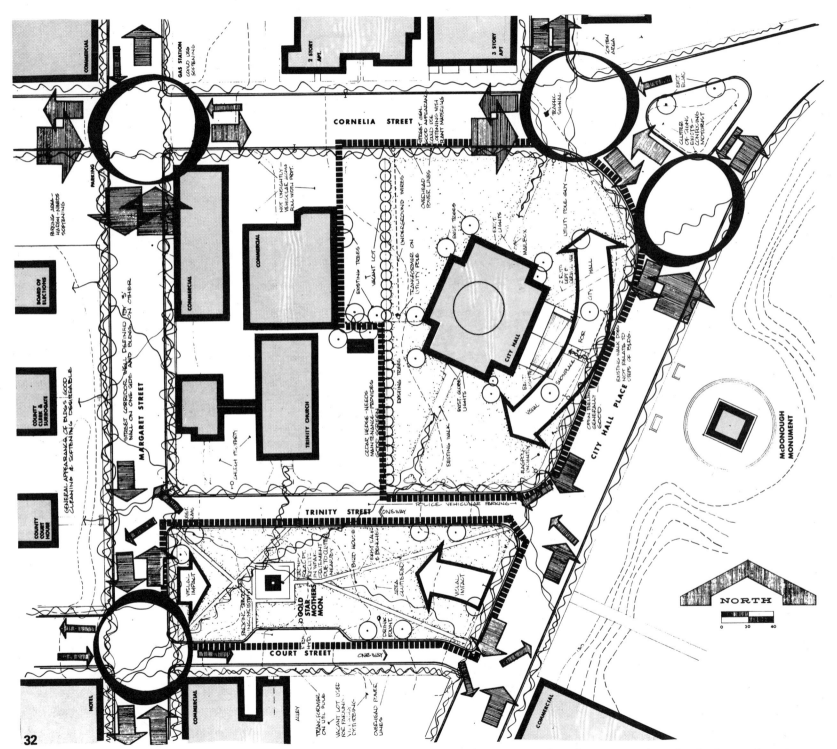

32

Master plan for City Hall and Trinity Park. The Saratoga Associates.

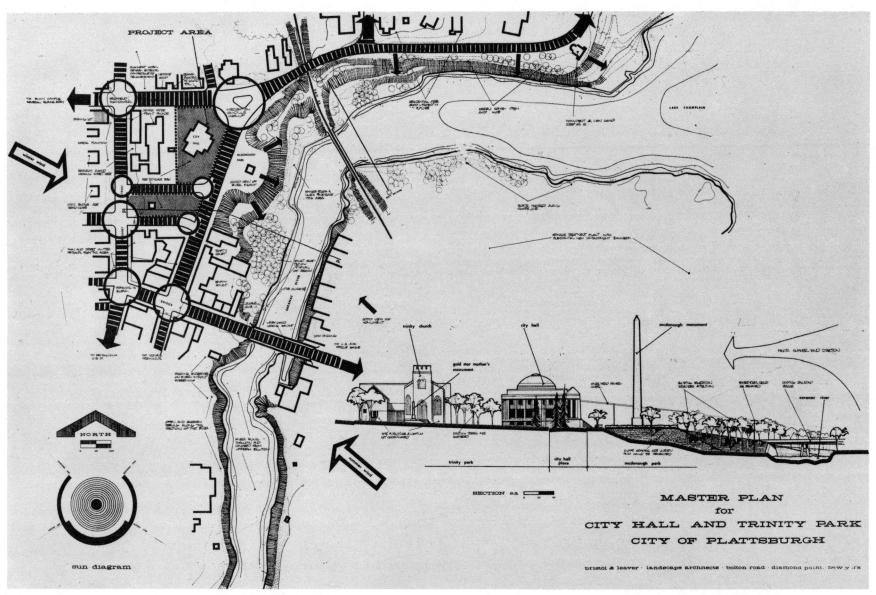

PROJECT AREA

LAKE CHAMPLAIN

NORTH

sun diagram

trinity church

city hall

mcdonough monument

gold star mother's monument

trinity park

city hall place

mcdonough park

SECTION aa

MASTER PLAN
for
CITY HALL AND TRINITY PARK
CITY OF PLATTSBURGH

bristol & leaver · landscape architects · bolton road · diamond point, new york

Master plan for City Hall and Trinity Park. The Saratoga Associates.

33

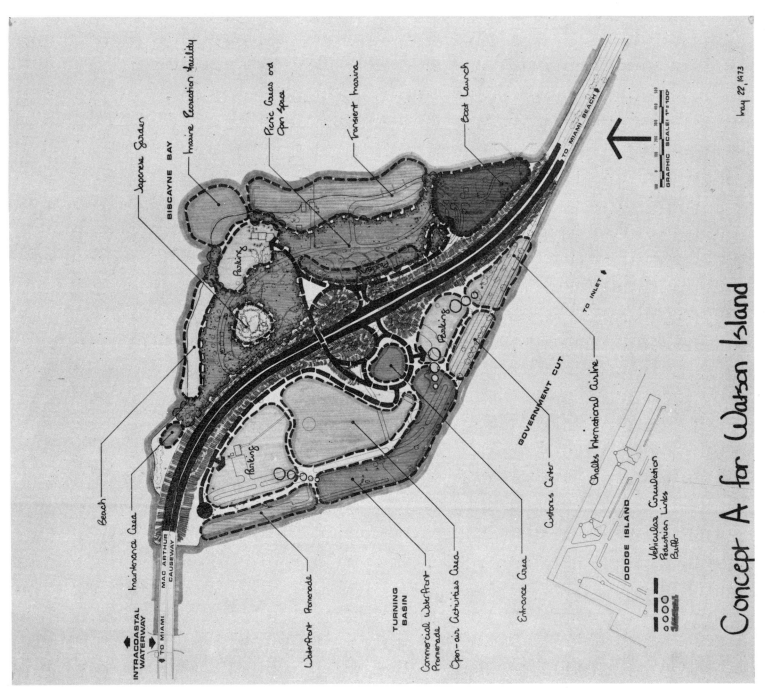

INTRACOASTAL WATERWAY

TO MIAMI

MAC ARTHUR CAUSEWAY

Maintenance Area

Beach

Japanese Garden

BISCAYNE BAY

Marine Recreation Facility

Picnic Areas and Open Space

Transient Marina

Boat Launch

TO MIAMI BEACH

Parking

Parking

Parking

Waterfront Promenade

Commercial Waterfront Promenade

Open-air Activities Area

TURNING BASIN

Entrance Area

Customs Center

Chalks International Airline

GOVERNMENT CUT

TO INLET

may 22, 1973

GRAPHIC SCALE: 1" = 100'

DODGE ISLAND

Vehicular Circulation
Pedestrian Links
Buffer

Concept A for Watson Island

Watson Island. Edward D. Stone, Jr. & Associates, P.A.

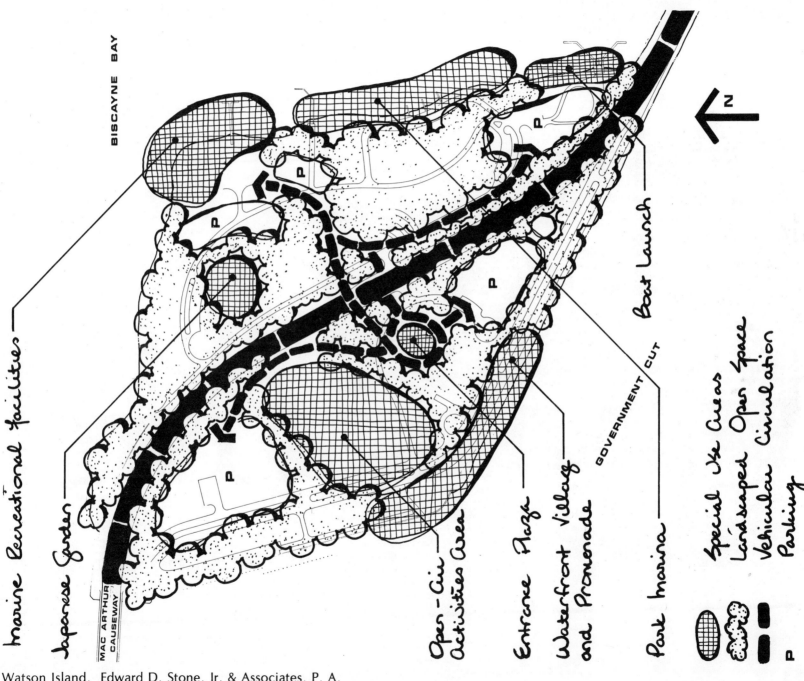

BISCAYNE BAY

N

MAC ARTHUR CAUSEWAY

Marine Recreational Facilities

Japanese Garden

Open-Air Activities Area

Entrance Plaza

Waterfront Village and Promenade

Park Marina

GOVERNMENT CUT

Boat Launch

Special Use Areas

Landscaped Open Space

Vehicular Circulation

P   Parking

LAND USE CONCEPT

Watson Island.   Edward D. Stone, Jr. & Associates, P. A.

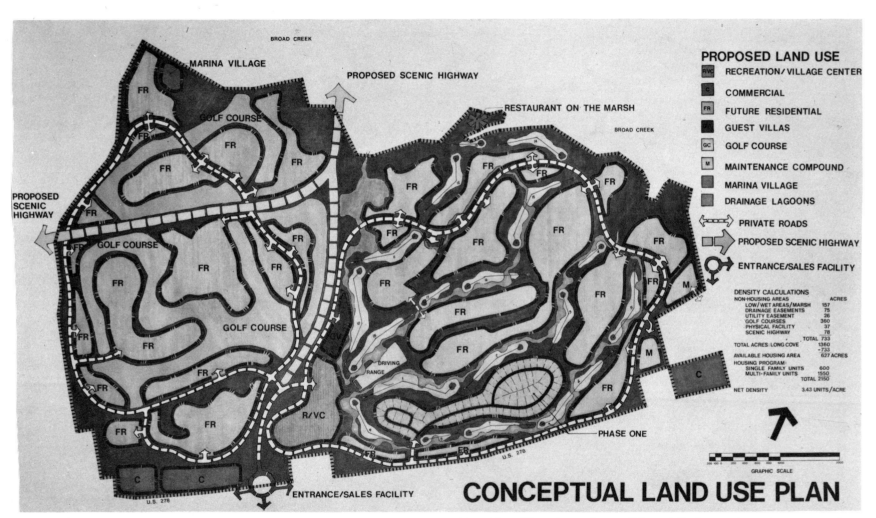

BROAD CREEK

MARINA VILLAGE

PROPOSED SCENIC HIGHWAY

RESTAURANT ON THE MARSH

BROAD CREEK

FR

GOLF COURSE

FR

FR

FR

PROPOSED
SCENIC
HIGHWAY

FR

FR

FR

FR

FR

FR

FR

FR

FR

FR

GOLF COURSE

FR

FR

FR

FR

FR

FR

M

FR

FR

GOLF COURSE

FR

FR

FR

FR

FR

DRIVING
RANGE

FR

R/VC

FR

FR

C

FR

C

C

U.S. 278

PHASE ONE

U.S. 278

FR

FR

ENTRANCE/SALES FACILITY

U.S. 278

PROPOSED LAND USE

RVC	RECREATION/VILLAGE CENTER
C	COMMERCIAL
FR	FUTURE RESIDENTIAL
	GUEST VILLAS
GC	GOLF COURSE
M	MAINTENANCE COMPOUND
	MARINA VILLAGE
	DRAINAGE LAGOONS
⟨┄⟩	PRIVATE ROADS
⟹	PROPOSED SCENIC HIGHWAY
◉	ENTRANCE/SALES FACILITY

DENSITY CALCULATIONS

NON-HOUSING AREAS	ACRES
LOW/WET AREAS/MARSH	157
DRAINAGE EASEMENTS	75
UTILITY EASEMENT	26
GOLF COURSES	360
PHYSICAL FACILITY	37
SCENIC HIGHWAY	78
TOTAL	733

TOTAL ACRES: LONG COVE	1360
	-733
AVAILABLE HOUSING AREA	627 ACRES

HOUSING PROGRAM:	
SINGLE FAMILY UNITS	600
MULTI-FAMILY UNITS	1550
TOTAL	2150

NET DENSITY   3.43 UNITS/ACRE

GRAPHIC SCALE

CONCEPTUAL LAND USE PLAN

Conceptual Land Use Plan, Long Cove. Edward D. Stone, Jr. & Associates, P.A.

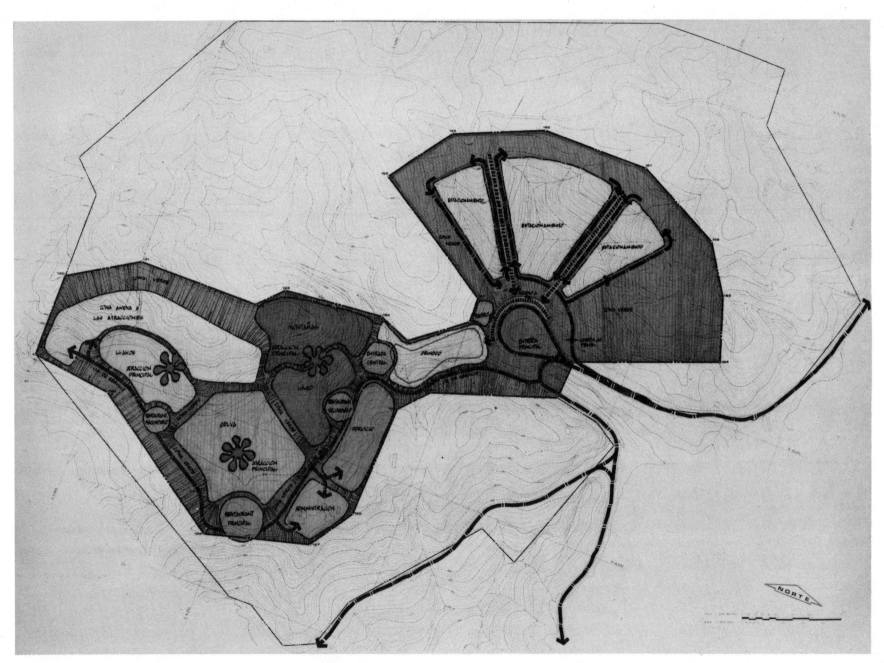

Parque de Motivos. Edward D. Stone, Jr. & Associates, P.A.

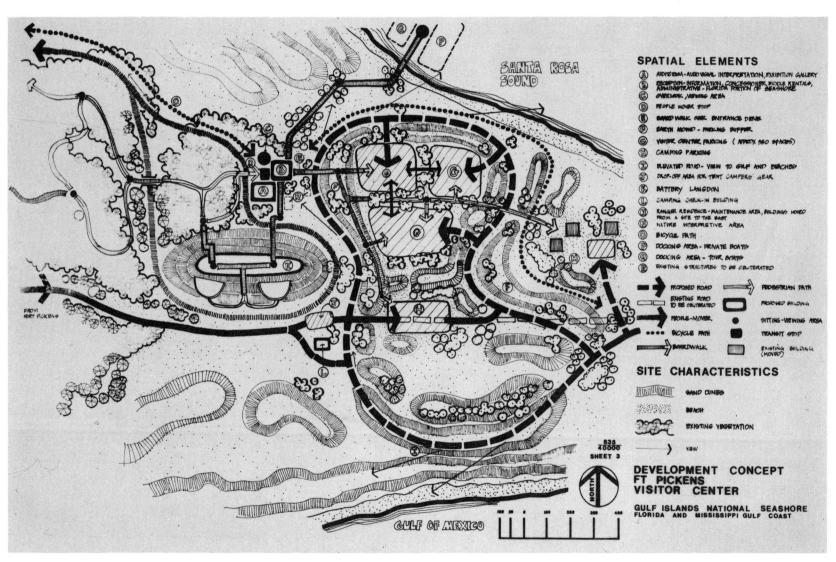

SANTA ROSA SOUND

SPATIAL ELEMENTS

(A) AUDITORIUM-AUDIO-VISUAL INTERPRETATION, EXHIBITION GALLERY
(B) RECEPTION-INFORMATION, CONCESSIONER, BICYCLE RENTALS, ADMINISTRATIVE - FLORIDA PORTION OF SEASHORE
(C) OVERLOOK, VIEWING AREA
(D) PEOPLE MOVER STOP
(E) RAISED WALK OVER ENTRANCE DRIVE
(F) EARTH MOUND - PARKING BUFFER
(G) VISITOR CENTER PARKING (APPROX 350 SPACES)
(H) CAMPING PARKING
(I) ELEVATED ROAD - VIEW TO GULF AND BEACHES
(J) DROP-OFF AREA FOR TENT CAMPERS' GEAR
(K) BATTERY LANGDON
(L) CAMPING CHECK-IN BUILDING
(M) RANGER RESIDENCE-MAINTENANCE AREA, BUILDINGS MOVED FROM A SITE TO THE EAST
(N) NATURE INTERPRETIVE AREA
(O) BICYCLE PATH
(P) DOCKING AREA - PRIVATE BOATS
(Q) DOCKING AREA - TOUR BOATS
(R) EXISTING STRUCTURES TO BE OBLITERATED

PROPOSED ROAD   PEDESTRIAN PATH
EXISTING ROAD TO BE OBLITERATED PROPOSED BUILDING
PEOPLE-MOVER   SITTING-VIEWING AREA
BICYCLE PATH   TRANSIT STOP
BOARDWALK   EXISTING BUILDING (MOVED)

SITE CHARACTERISTICS

SAND DUNES
BEACH
EXISTING VEGETATION
VIEW

FROM FORT PICKENS

635
40000
SHEET 3

DEVELOPMENT CONCEPT
FT PICKENS
VISITOR CENTER

GULF ISLANDS NATIONAL SEASHORE
FLORIDA AND MISSISSIPPI GULF COAST

NORTH

GULF OF MEXICO

Gulf Islands National Seashore. Reynolds, Smith and Hills, Architects-Engineers-Planners, Inc., in consultation with the National Park Service.

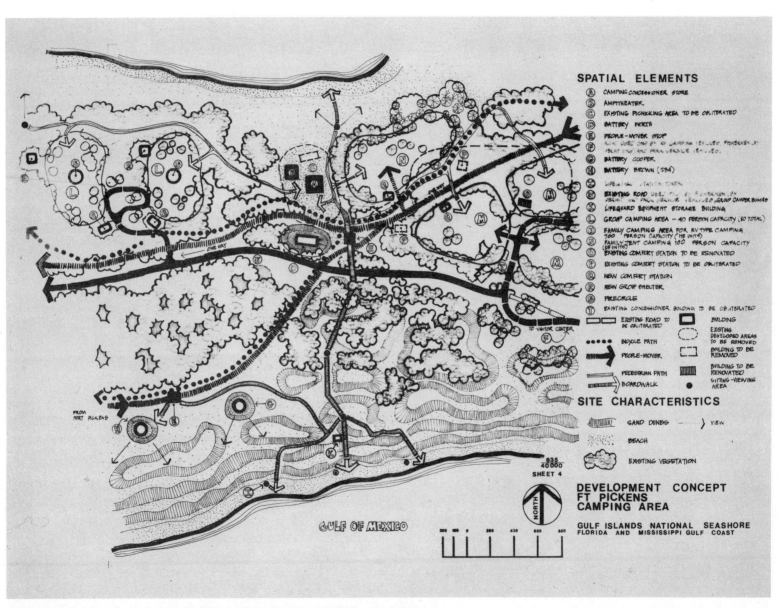

SPATIAL ELEMENTS

(A) CAMPING CONCESSIONER STORE
(B) AMPITHEATER
(C) EXISTING PICNICKING AREA TO BE OBLITERATED
(D) BATTERY NORTH
(E) PEOPLE-MOVER STOP
(F) ROAD USED ONLY BY RV CAMPING VEHICLES, FISHERMEN BY PERMIT AND PARK SERVICE VEHICLES
(G) BATTERY COOPER
(H) BATTERY BROWN (234)
(I) LIFEGUARD STATION TOWER
(J) EXISTING ROAD USED ONLY BY FISHERMEN BY PERMIT AND PARK SERVICE VEHICLES, GROUP CAMPER BUSSES
(K) LIFEGUARD EQUIPMENT STORAGE BUILDING
(L) GROUP CAMPING AREA — 40 PERSON CAPACITY (80 TOTAL)
(M) FAMILY CAMPING AREA FOR RV TYPE CAMPING 700 PERSON CAPACITY (175 UNITS)
(N) FAMILY TENT CAMPING 100 PERSON CAPACITY (28 UNITS)
(O) EXISTING COMFORT STATION TO BE RENOVATED
(P) EXISTING COMFORT STATION TO BE OBLITERATED
(Q) NEW COMFORT STATION
(R) NEW GROUP SHELTER
(S) FIRECIRCLE
(T) EXISTING CONCESSIONER BUILDING TO BE OBLITERATED

▭ EXISTING ROAD TO BE OBLITERATED
●●● BICYCLE PATH
➤ PEOPLE-MOVER
PEDESTRIAN PATH
BOARDWALK

▭ BUILDING
⬭ EXISTING DEVELOPED AREAS TO BE REMOVED
▢ BUILDING TO BE REMOVED
▨ BUILDING TO BE RENOVATED
● SITTING-VIEWING AREA

SITE CHARACTERISTICS

SAND DUNES
BEACH
EXISTING VEGETATION
⟩ VIEW

635 40000
SHEET 4

NORTH

DEVELOPMENT CONCEPT
FT PICKENS
CAMPING AREA

GULF ISLANDS NATIONAL SEASHORE
FLORIDA AND MISSISSIPPI GULF COAST

GULF OF MEXICO

ONE WAY
FROM FORT PICKENS
TO VISITOR CENTER

200 100 0   200   400   600   800

Gulf Islands National Seashore. Reynolds, Smith and Hills, Architects-
Engineers-Planners, Inc., in consultation with the National Park Service.

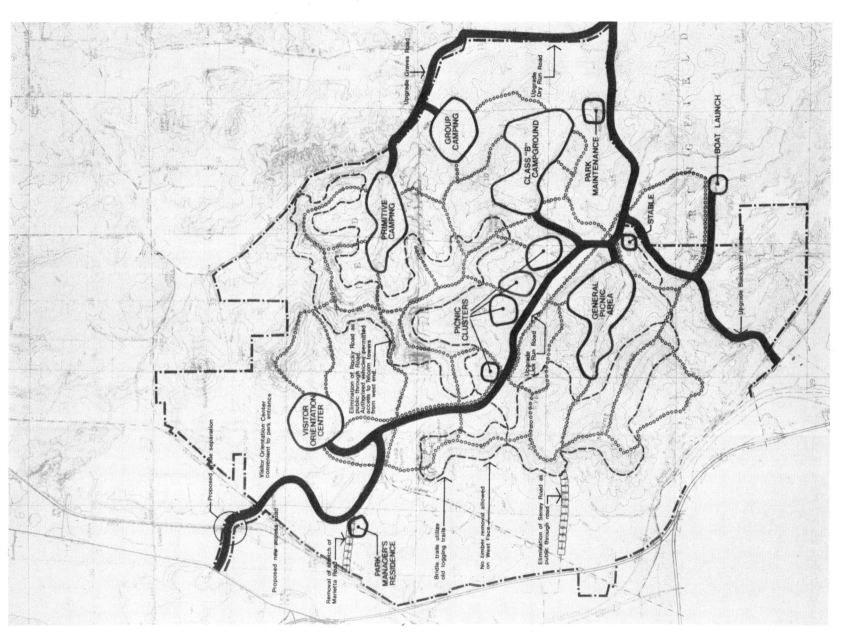

GROUP CAMPING

PRIMITIVE CAMPING

CLASS "B" CAMPGROUND

PARK MAINTENANCE

BOAT LAUNCH

STABLE

PICNIC CLUSTERS

GENERAL PICNIC AREA

VISITOR ORIENTATION CENTER

PARK MANAGER'S RESIDENCE

Upgrade Graves Road

Upgrade Dry Run Road

Upgrade Blacksmith Hill road

Upgrade Lick Run Road

Elimination of Rocky Road as public through Road. Authorized vehicle access permitted to Telecom towers from west end.

Visitor Orientation Center convenient to park entrance

Proposed grade separation

Proposed new access road

Removal of stretch of Marietta Road

Bridle trails utilize old logging trails

No timber removal allowed on West Face

Elimination of Seney Road as public through road

Plans contracted by State of Ohio, Department of Natural Resources.

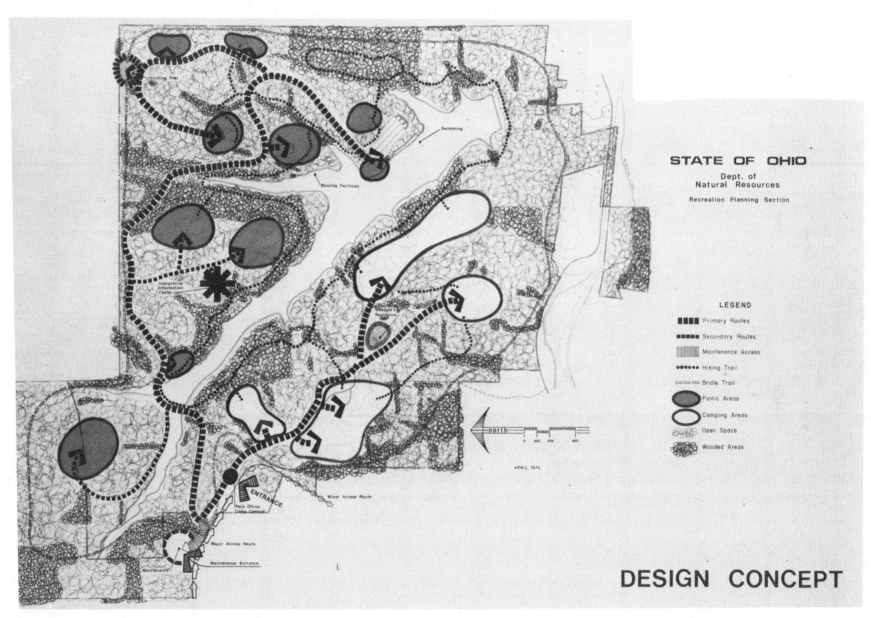

STATE OF OHIO

Dept. of
Natural Resources

Recreation Planning Section

LEGEND

▮▮▮▮ Primary Routes

▬▬▬ Secondary Routes

▥▥▥ Maintenance Access

•••••• Hiking Trail

━ ━ ━ Bridle Trail

⬤ Picnic Areas

◯ Camping Areas

Open Space

Wooded Areas

north   0 200 400 800

APRIL, 1974

DESIGN CONCEPT

Plans contracted by State of Ohio, Department of Natural Resources.

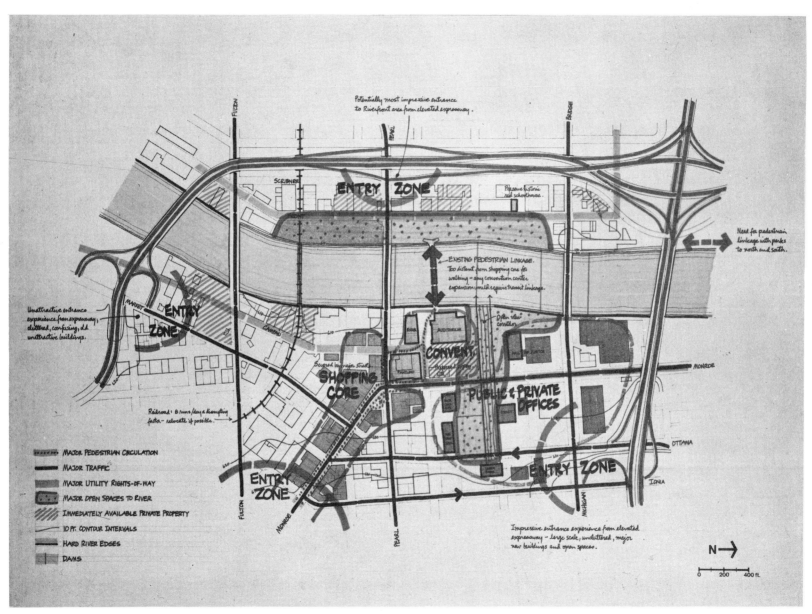

Site Analysis, Grand Rapids Riverfront. Johnson, Johnson & Roy, Inc. Felt-tip marker on sepia.

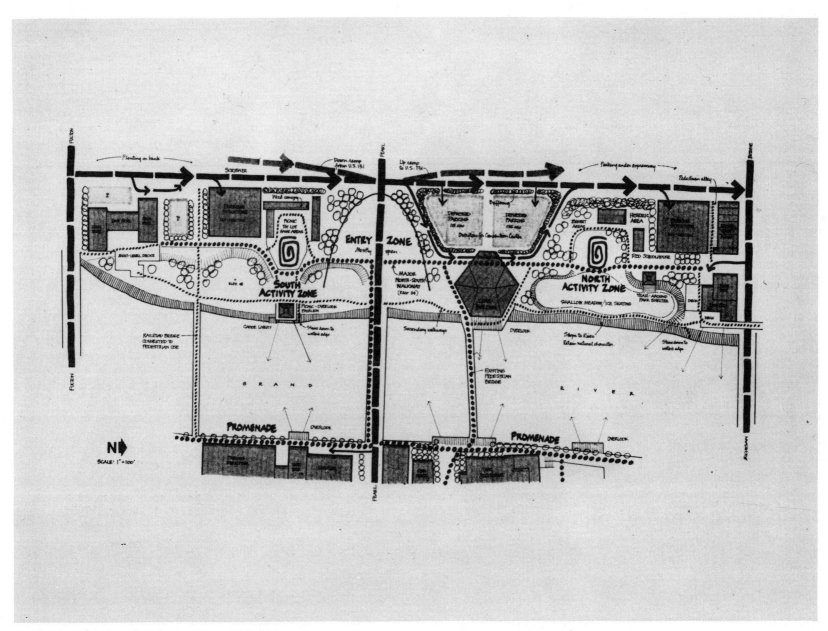

Grand Rapids Riverfront Park Concept. Johnson,
Johnson & Roy, Inc. Felt-tip marker and pencil on vellum.

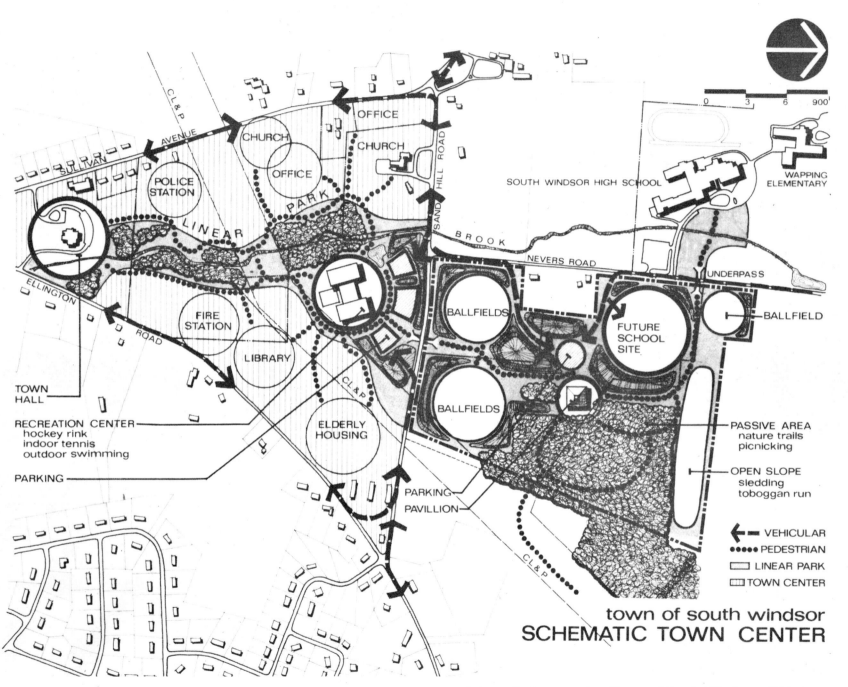

OFFICE

CHURCH

OFFICE

CHURCH

SOUTH WINDSOR HIGH SCHOOL

WAPPING ELEMENTARY

POLICE STATION

PARK

LINEAR

BROOK

NEVERS ROAD

UNDERPASS

FIRE STATION

BALLFIELDS

FUTURE SCHOOL SITE

BALLFIELD

LIBRARY

TOWN HALL

RECREATION CENTER
hockey rink
indoor tennis
outdoor swimming

PARKING

ELDERLY HOUSING

BALLFIELDS

PASSIVE AREA
nature trails
picnicking

OPEN SLOPE
sledding
toboggan run

PARKING

PAVILLION

VEHICULAR
PEDESTRIAN
LINEAR PARK
TOWN CENTER

town of south windsor
SCHEMATIC TOWN CENTER

0 3 6 900'

SULLIVAN   AVENUE

CL & P

ELLINGTON   ROAD

CL & P

CL & P

SAND HILL ROAD

Schematic town center, Town of South Windsor. CR3, Inc.,
by Jeffrey A. Gebrian. Client: Gregory Louis Montana, Architect.

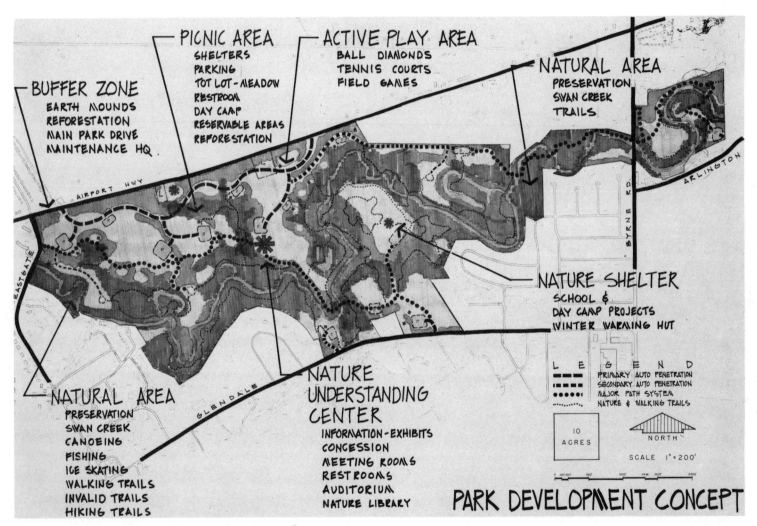

BUFFER ZONE
EARTH MOUNDS
REFORESTATION
MAIN PARK DRIVE
MAINTENANCE HQ

PICNIC AREA
SHELTERS
PARKING
TOT LOT - MEADOW
RESTROOM
DAY CAMP
RESERVABLE AREAS
REFORESTATION

ACTIVE PLAY AREA
BALL DIAMONDS
TENNIS COURTS
FIELD GAMES

NATURAL AREA
PRESERVATION
SWAN CREEK
TRAILS

NATURE SHELTER
SCHOOL &
DAY CAMP PROJECTS
WINTER WARMING HUT

NATURAL AREA
PRESERVATION
SWAN CREEK
CANOEING
FISHING
ICE SKATING
WALKING TRAILS
INVALID TRAILS
HIKING TRAILS

**NATURE
UNDERSTANDING
CENTER**
INFORMATION - EXHIBITS
CONCESSION
MEETING ROOMS
RESTROOMS
AUDITORIUM
NATURE LIBRARY

L E G E N D
PRIMARY AUTO PENETRATION
SECONDARY AUTO PENETRATION
MAJOR PATH SYSTEM
NATURE & WALKING TRAILS

10 ACRES

NORTH

SCALE 1" = 200'

PARK DEVELOPMENT CONCEPT

AIRPORT HWY
EASTGATE
GLENDALE
BYRNE RD
ARLINGTON

Swan Creek Metro Park. The Collaborative, Inc.

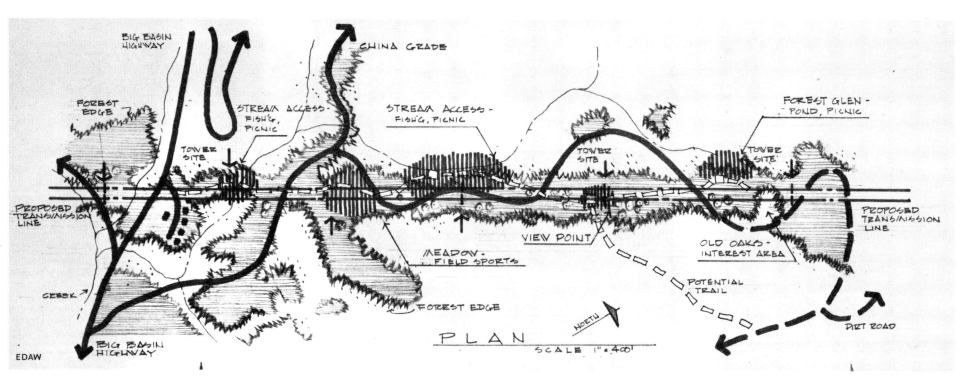

BIG BASIN HIGHWAY

CHINA GRADE

FOREST EDGE

STREAM ACCESS - FISH'G, PICNIC

STREAM ACCESS - FISH'G, PICNIC

FOREST GLEN - POND, PICNIC

TOWER SITE

TOWER SITE

TOWER SITE

PROPOSED TRANSMISSION LINE

PROPOSED TRANSMISSION LINE

VIEW POINT

OLD OAKS - INTEREST AREA

CREEK

MEADOW - FIELD SPORTS

POTENTIAL TRAIL

FOREST EDGE

NORTH

DIRT ROAD

EDAW

BIG BASIN HIGHWAY

P L A N

SCALE 1" = 400'

Pacific Gas and Electric Co. EDAW, Inc., by Herbert Schaal.

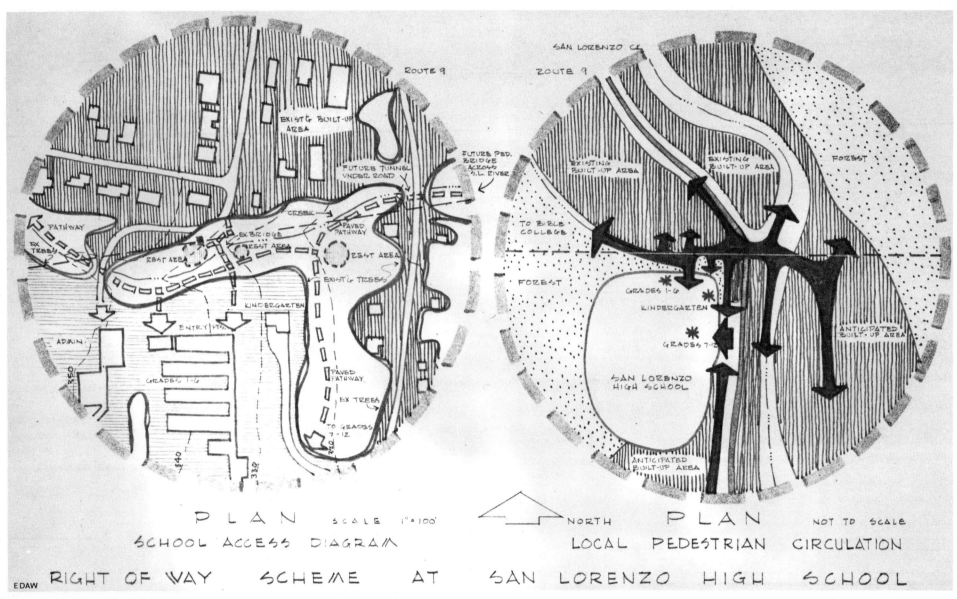

PLAN SCALE 1"=100'

SCHOOL ACCESS DIAGRAM

PLAN NOT TO SCALE

LOCAL PEDESTRIAN CIRCULATION

RIGHT OF WAY SCHEME AT SAN LORENZO HIGH SCHOOL

Pacific Gas and Electric Co. EDAW, Inc., by Herbert Schaal.

47

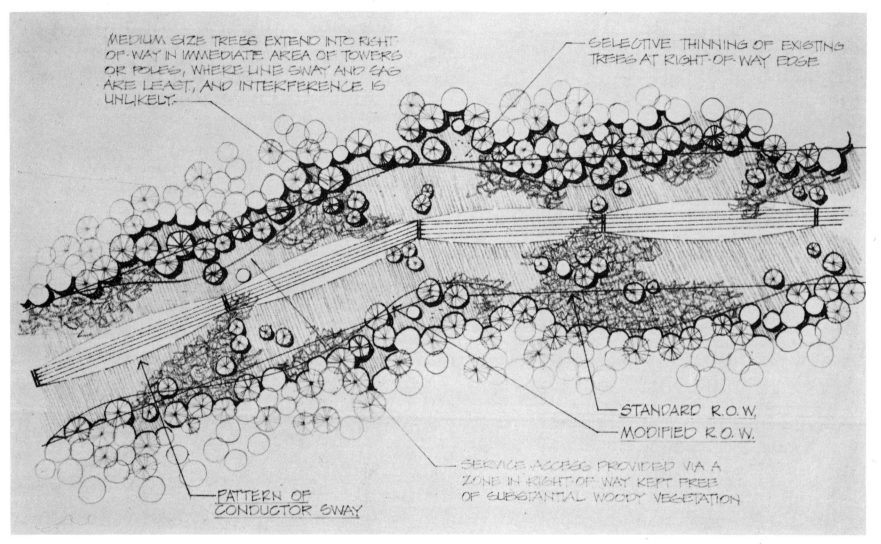

MEDIUM SIZE TREES EXTEND INTO RIGHT-OF-WAY IN IMMEDIATE AREA OF TOWERS OR POLES, WHERE LINE SWAY AND SAG ARE LEAST, AND INTERFERENCE IS UNLIKELY.

SELECTIVE THINNING OF EXISTING TREES AT RIGHT-OF-WAY EDGE

STANDARD R.O.W.
MODIFIED R.O.W.

PATTERN OF CONDUCTOR SWAY

SERVICE ACCESS PROVIDED VIA A ZONE IN RIGHT-OF-WAY KEPT FREE OF SUBSTANTIAL WOODY VEGETATION

Consumers Power Transmission R.O.W. Study. Johnson, Johnson & Roy, Inc.

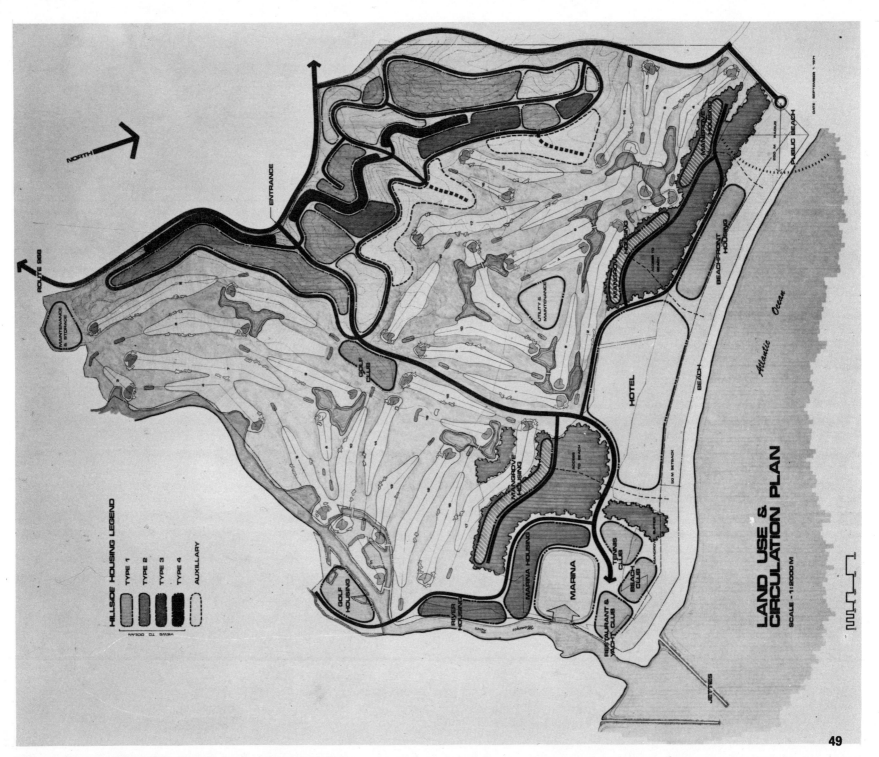

LAND USE & CIRCULATION PLAN

SCALE - 1:2000 M

HILLSIDE HOUSING LEGEND

TYPE 1
TYPE 2
TYPE 3
TYPE 4
AUXILIARY

VIEWS TO OCEAN

NORTH

ROUTE 988

ENTRANCE

MAINTENANCE & STORAGE

GOLF CLUB

UTILITY & MAINTENANCE

MAINTENANCE HOUSING

MANGROVE HOUSING

BEACHFRONT HOUSING

PUBLIC BEACH

500 M RADIUS

Atlantic Ocean

HOTEL

BEACH

50 M SETBACK

MANGROVE HOUSING

ACCESS TO BEACH

MARINA HOUSING

MARINA

TENNIS CLUB

BEACH CLUB

RESTAURANT & YACHT CLUB

GOLF HOUSING

RIVER HOUSING

River

JETTIES

DATE SEPTEMBER 1, 1971

49

Palmer Resort.   Edward D. Stone, Jr. & Associates, P.A.

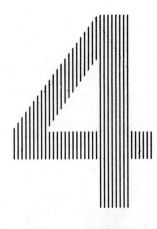

MASTER PLANS

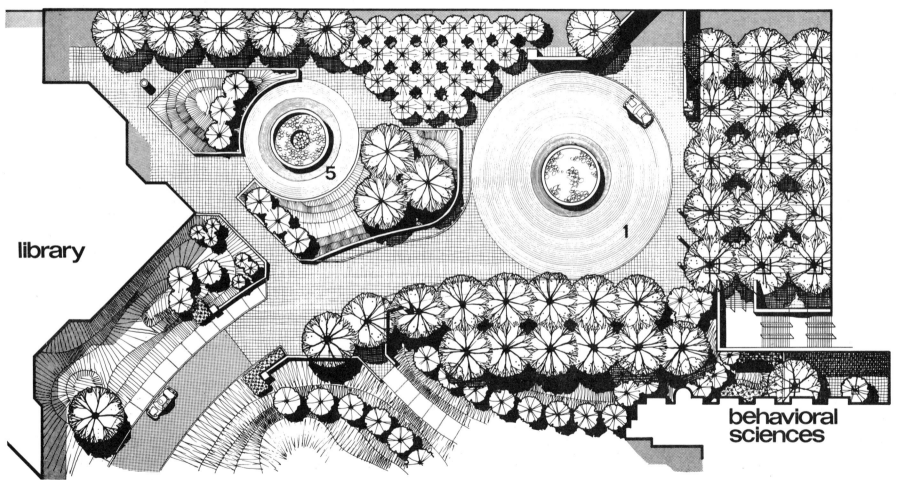

library

5

1

behavioral
sciences

Western Connecticut State College. CR3, Inc., by Kenneth Kay.

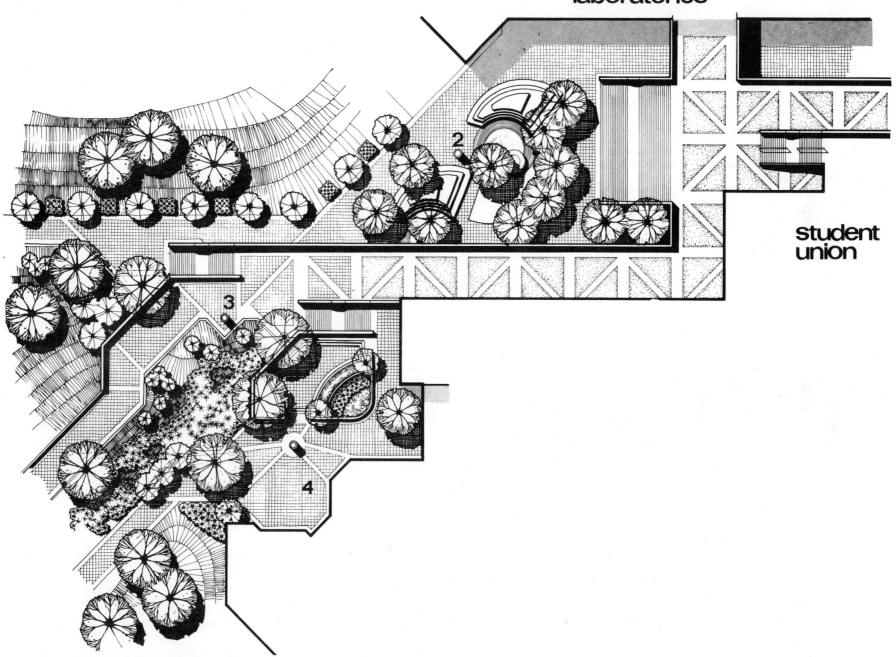

classrooms &
laboratories

student
union

Western Connecticut State College. CR3, Inc., by Kenneth Kay.

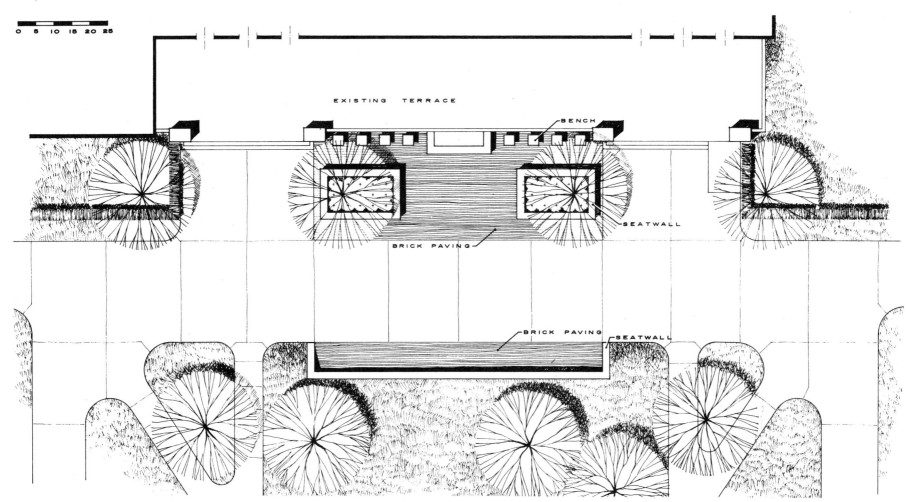

EXISTING TERRACE

BENCH

SEATWALL

BRICK PAVING

BRICK PAVING   SEATWALL

0 5 10 15 20 25

University of Illinois Office for Capital Programs.

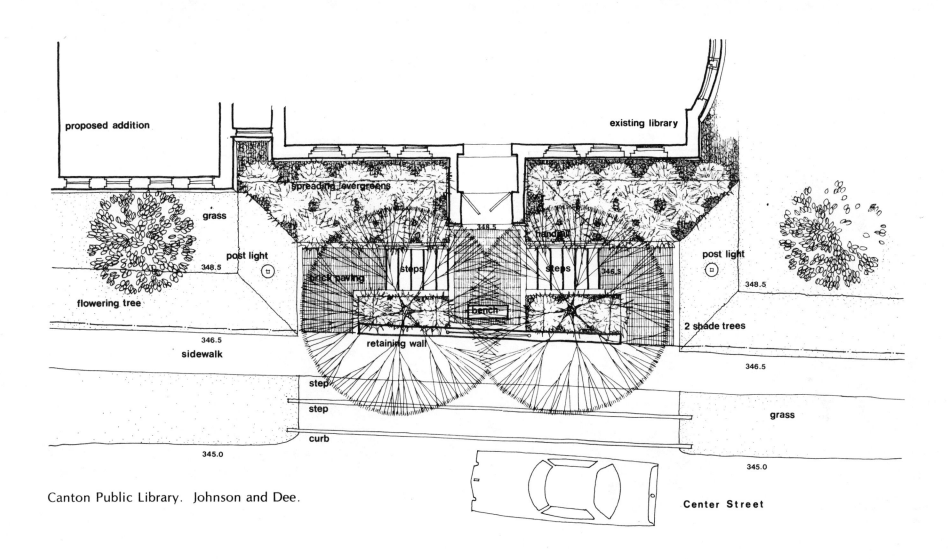

proposed addition

existing library

grass

Spreading evergreens

post light

348.5

flowering tree

brick paving

steps

steps

handrail

post light

348.5

346.5

sidewalk

bench

retaining wall

2 shade trees

346.5

step

step

grass

curb

345.0

345.0

Canton Public Library. Johnson and Dee.

Center Street

Site Plan for A. E. Bye's House. A. E. Bye & Associates; by A. E. Bye, Terry Souders, Lawrence Goldberg, Theodore Geraldi. F-lead pencil on vellum.

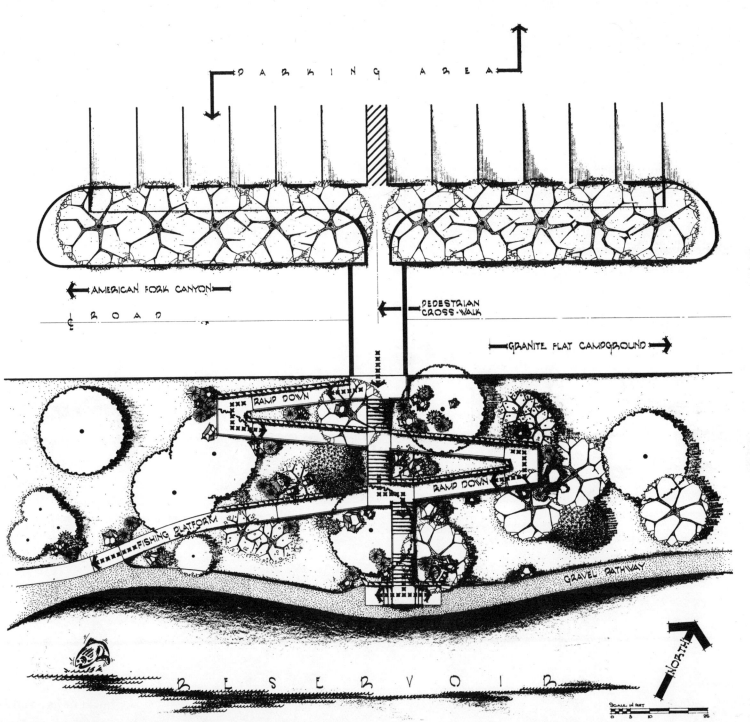

PARKING AREA

AMERICAN FORK CANYON
ROAD

PEDESTRIAN
CROSS·WALK

GRANITE FLAT CAMPGROUND

RAMP DOWN

RAMP DOWN

FISHING PLATFORM

GRAVEL PATHWAY

RESERVOIR

NORTH

SCALE IN FEET
0 5 10 20

Tibble Fork Reservoir Area, Uinta National Forest. Norman Malone.

57

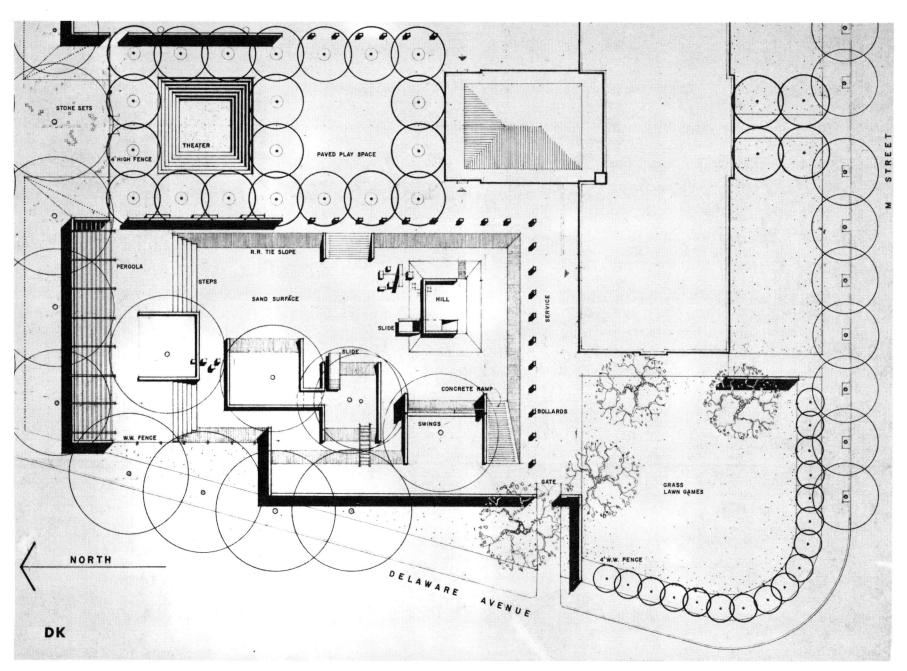

STONE SETS

THEATER

4' HIGH FENCE

PAVED PLAY SPACE

PERGOLA

STEPS

R.R. TIE SLOPE

SAND SURFACE

SLIDE

HILL

SLIDE

SERVICE

CONCRETE RAMP

W.W. FENCE

SWINGS

BOLLARDS

GATE

GRASS LAWN GAMES

NORTH

4' W.W. FENCE

DELAWARE AVENUE

M STREET

DK

Dan Kiley and Partners.

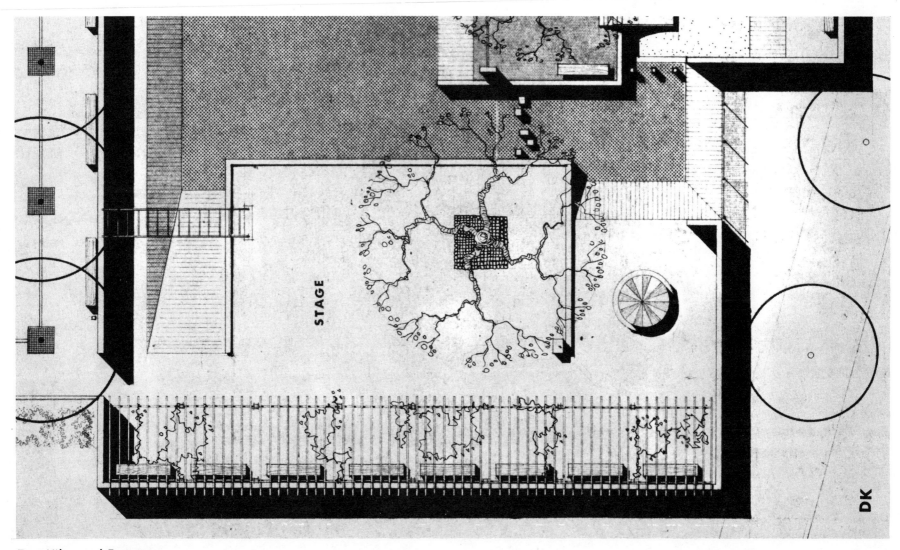

STAGE

DK

Dan Kiley and Partners.

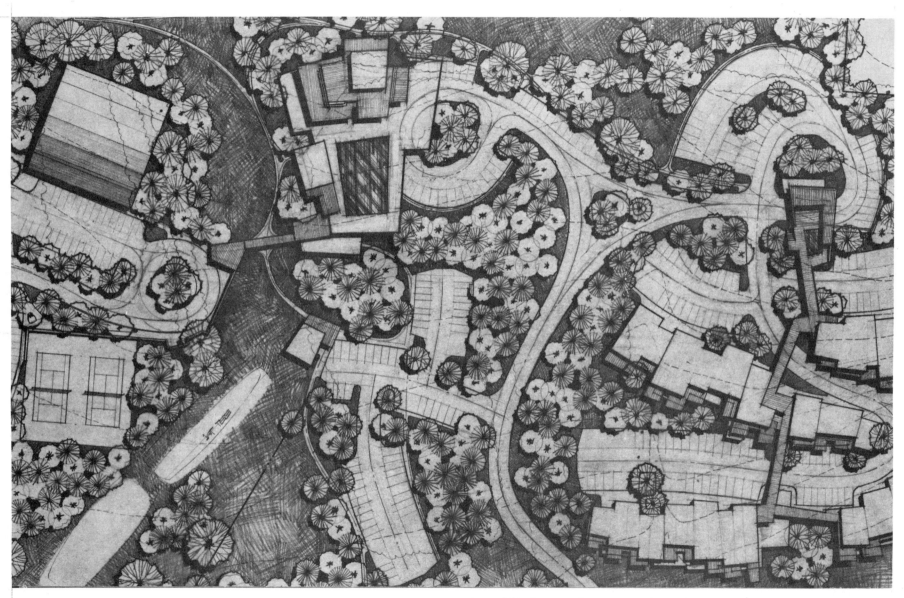

Bristol Harbour. The Reimann-Buechner Partnership by Cortland Read.

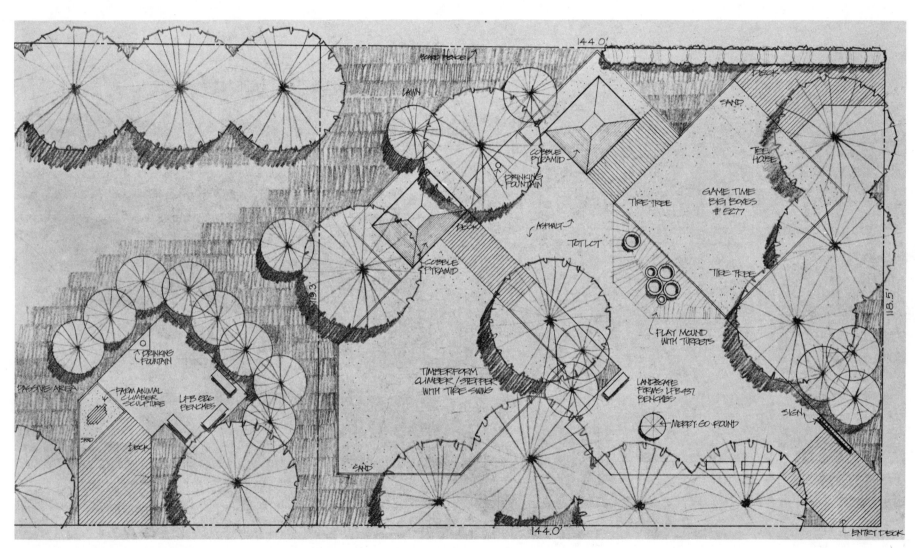

Labels within the plan:
144.0'
BOARD FENCE
LAWN
COBBLE PYRAMID
DRINKING FOUNTAIN
DECK
COBBLE PYRAMID
ASPHALT
119.3'
DRINKING FOUNTAIN
PASSIVE AREA
FARM ANIMAL CLIMBER SCULPTURE
LFB 526 BENCHES
SAND
DECK
TIMBERFORM CLIMBER/STEPPER WITH TIRE SWING
SAND
TIRE TREE
TOTLOT
GAME TIME BIG BOXES #E277
TREE HOUSE
DECK
SAND
TIRE TREE
PLAY MOUND WITH TURRETS
118.5'
LANDSCAPE FORMS LFB 437 BENCHES
MERRY-GO-ROUND
SIGN
144.0'
ENTRY DECK

East Chicago Parks. Perkins & Will, Inc., by David Linstrum.

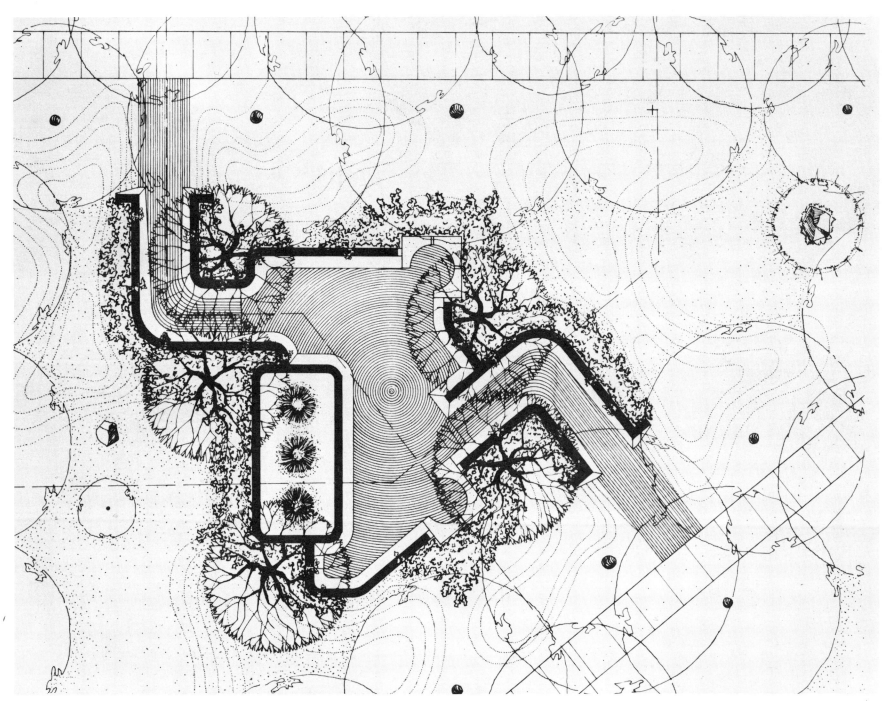

Dauch Memorial Park. William A. Behnke Associates.
James H. Ness, Associated Landscape Architect.

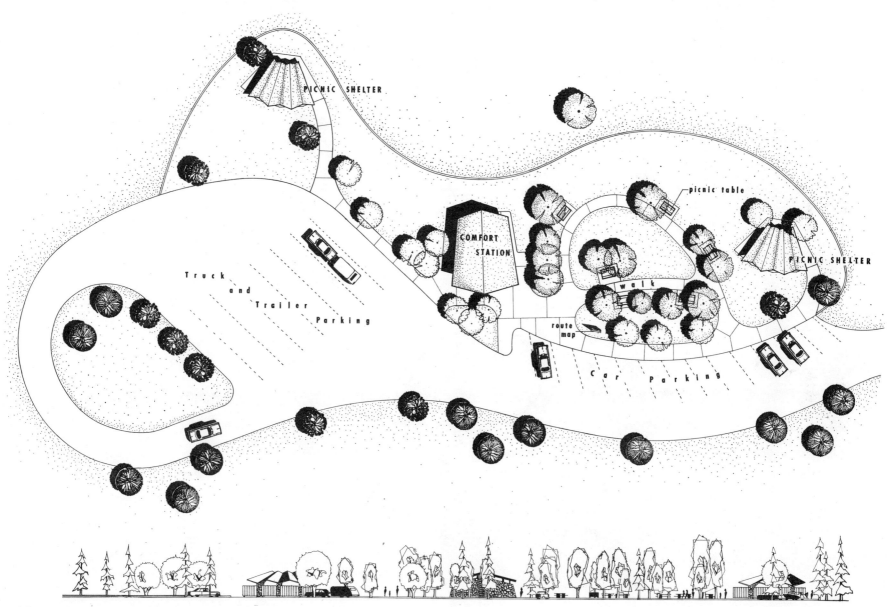

PICNIC SHELTER

COMFORT STATION

Truck and Trailer Parking

picnic table

PICNIC SHELTER

walk

route map

Car Parking

California Department of Transportation.

63

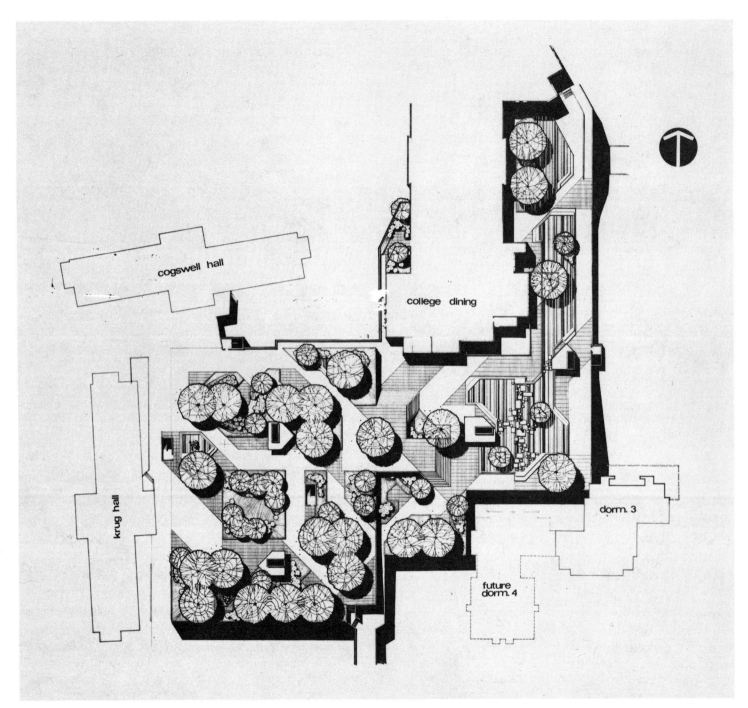

cogswell hall

college dining

krug hall

dorm. 3

future
dorm. 4

Model Secondary School for the Deaf. CR3, Inc.
Client: Hudgins, Thompson & Ball, Architects.

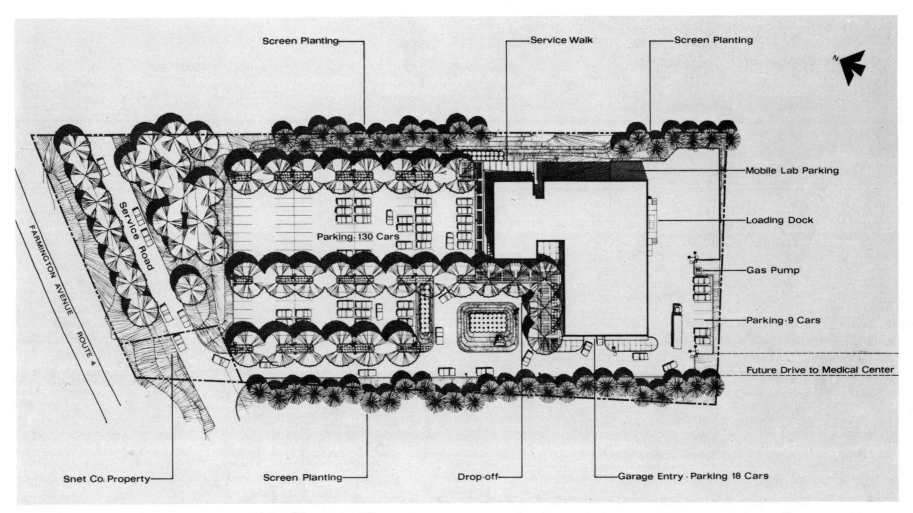

Screen Planting   Service Walk   Screen Planting

N

Mobile Lab Parking

Loading Dock

Gas Pump

Parking·9 Cars

Future Drive to Medical Center

FARMINGTON AVENUE

ROUTE 4

Service Road

Parking·130 Cars

Snet Co. Property   Screen Planting   Drop·off   Garage Entry · Parking 18 Cars

American Red Cross Northeast Regional Headquarters. CR3, Inc.,
by Jeffrey A. Gebrian. Client: Hirsch, Kaestle Boos, Architects.

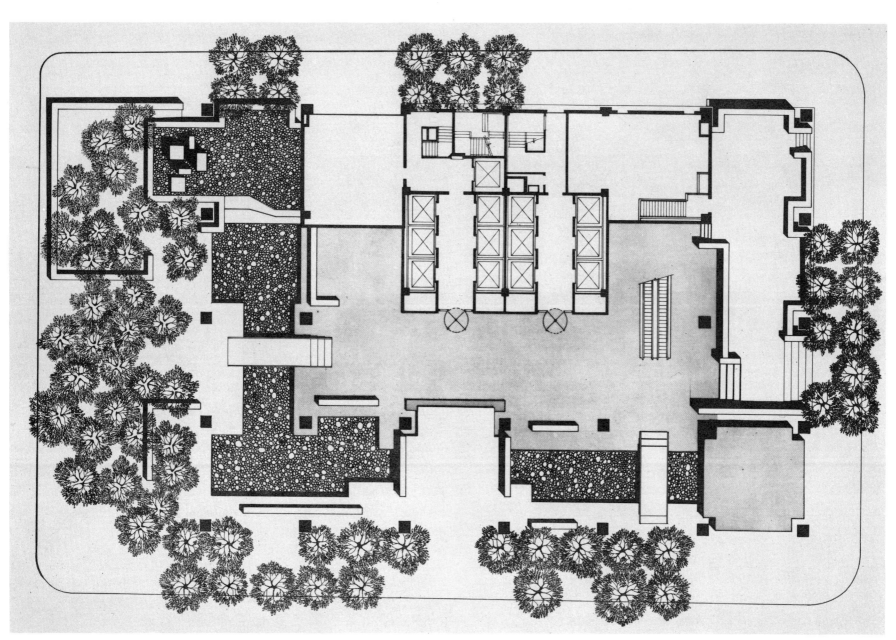

77 Water Street Building; A. E. Bye & Associates by Jane
McGuinness. Architect: Emery Roth & Sons. Ink on mylar.

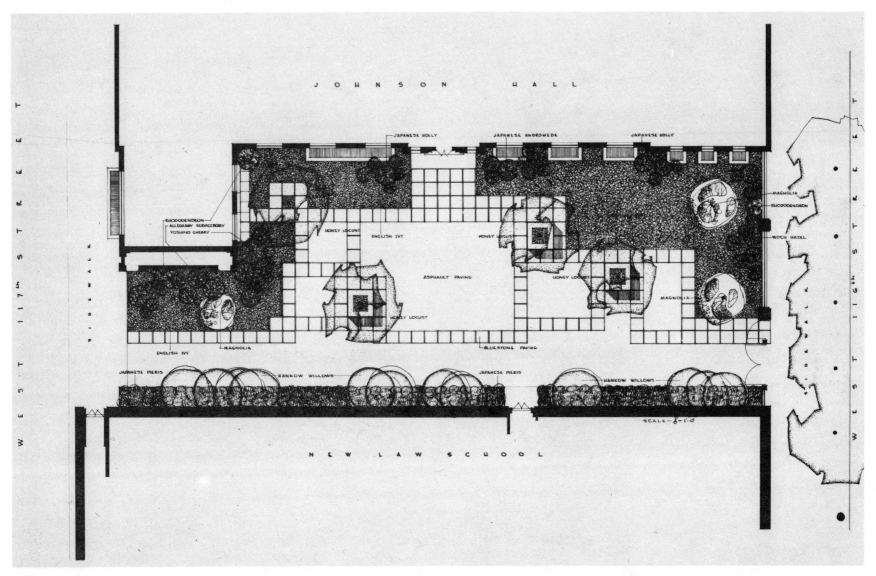

Sulzburger Plaza, Columbia University. A. E. Bye & Associates. Ink on vellum.

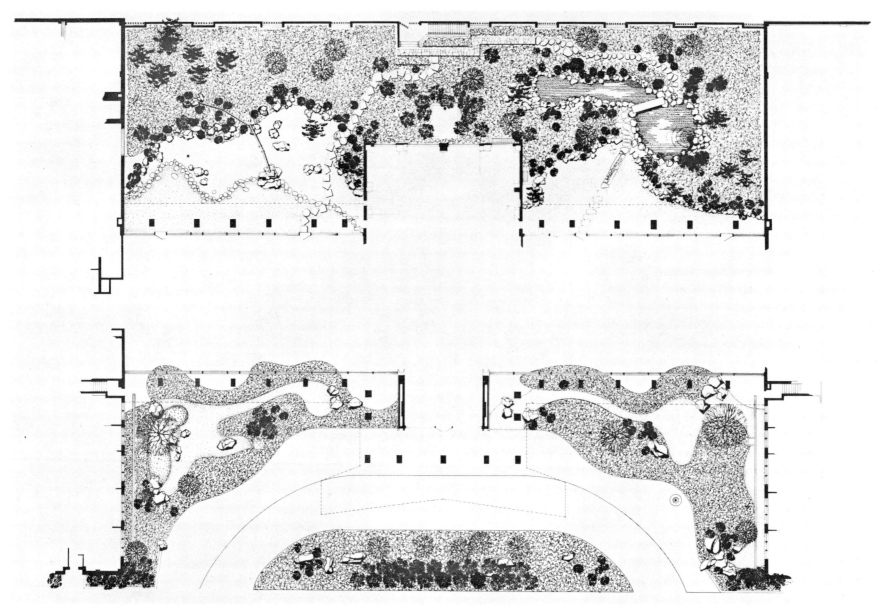

Imperial House. A. E. Bye & Associates by A. E. Bye. Ink on mylar.

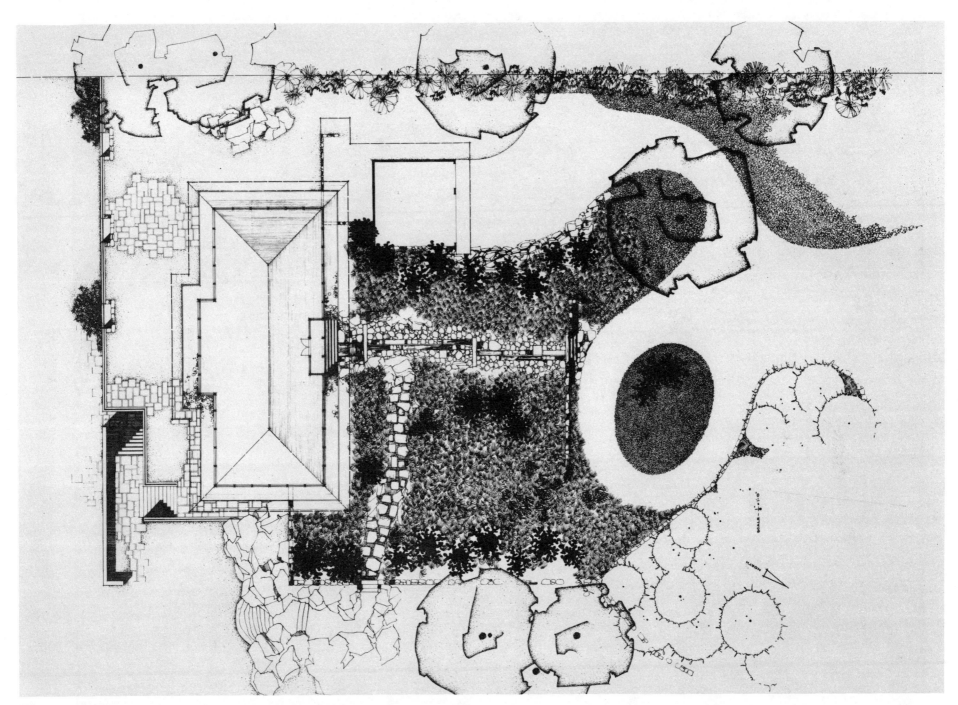

Residence. A. E. Bye & Associates by A. E. Bye. Ink on vellum.

RESIDENCE

Residence. A. E. Bye & Associates by Neal Bastable. Ink on mylar.

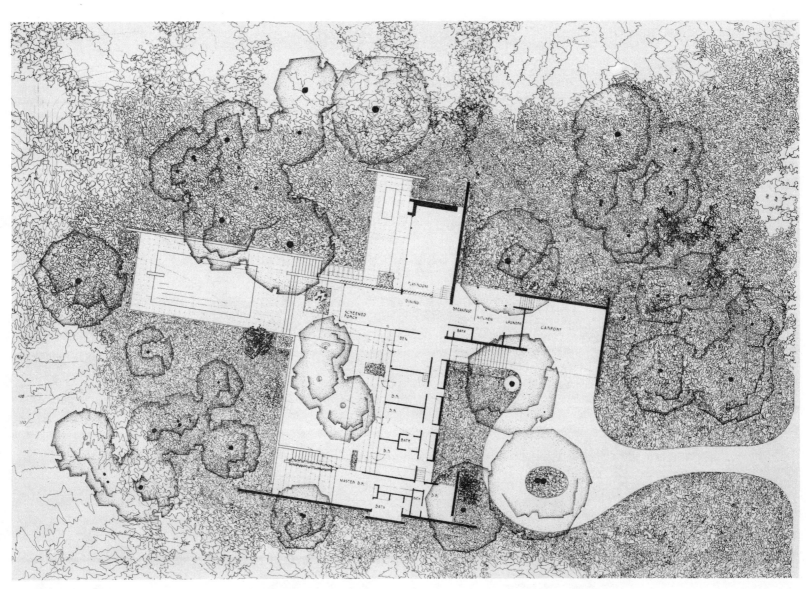

Residence. A. E. Bye & Associates. Ink on vellum.

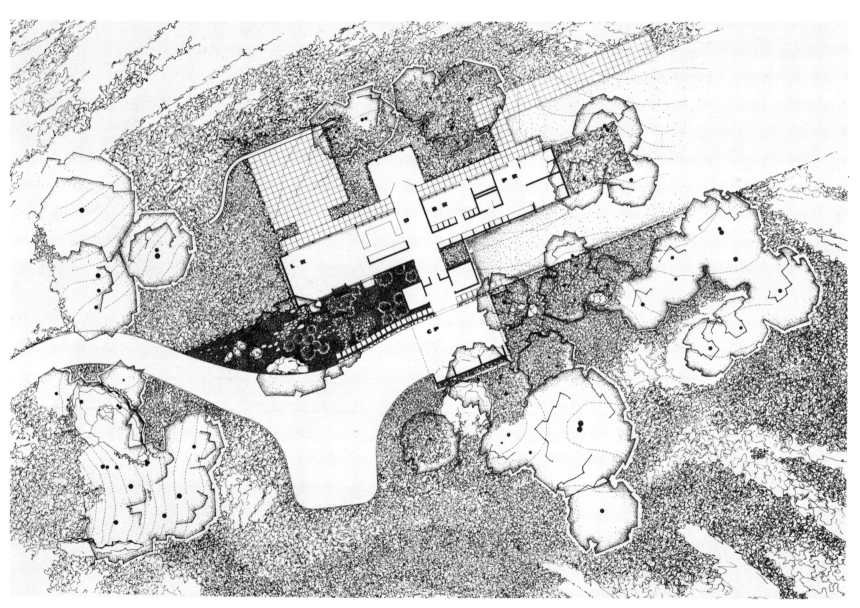

Residence. A. E. Bye & Associates by A. E. Bye. Ink on vellum.

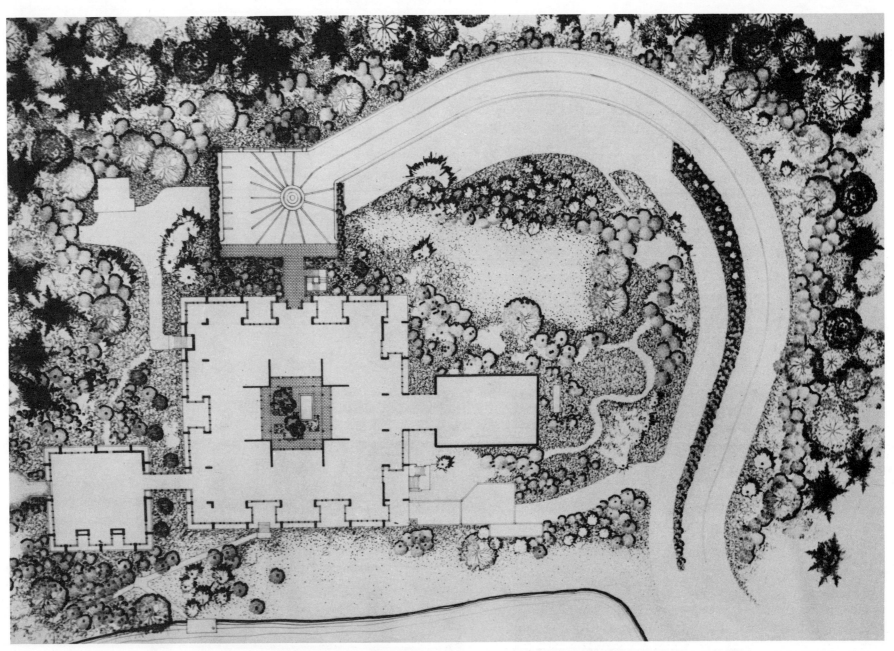

Harvey Hubbell Corporate Headquarters. A. E. Bye & Associates by
Lawrence Goldberg. Architect: Bruce Campbell Graham. Ink on vellum.

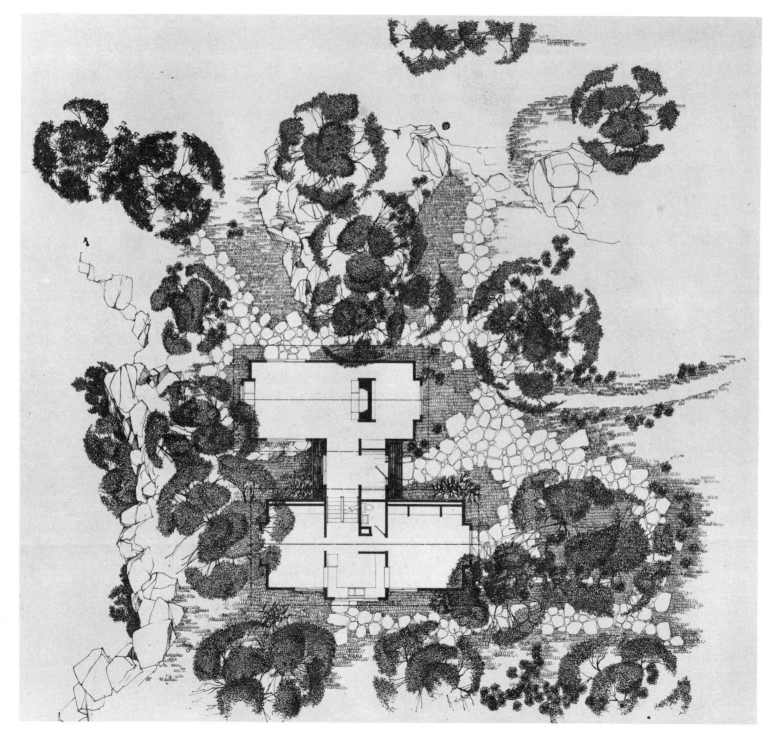

Leitzsch Residence. A. E. Bye & Associates
by James Balsley. Ink on vellum.

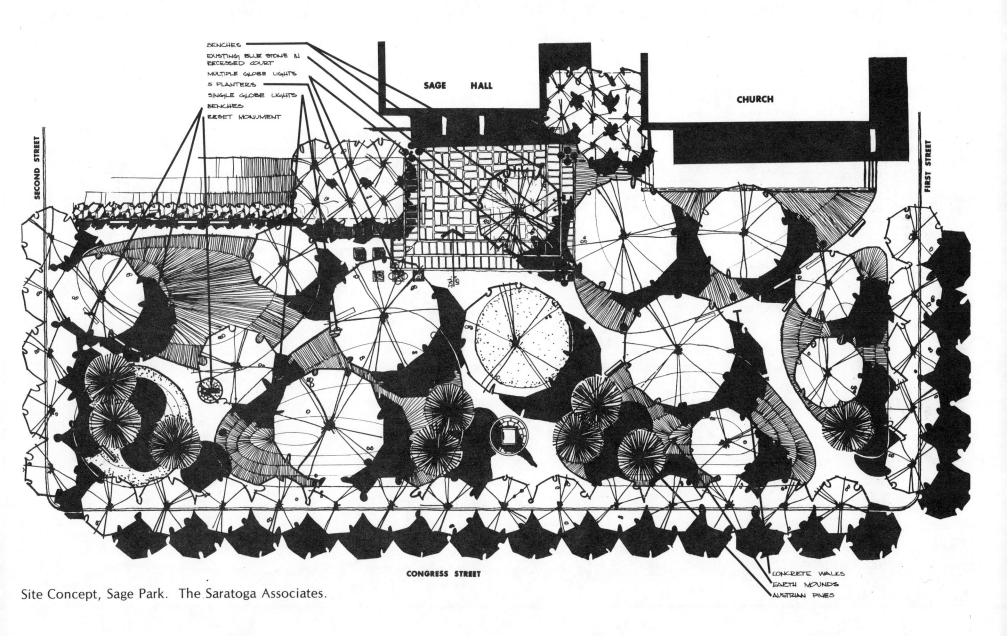

BENCHES
EXISTING BLUE STONE IN RECESSED COURT
MULTIPLE GLOBE LIGHTS
5 PLANTERS
SINGLE GLOBE LIGHTS
BENCHES
RESET MONUMENT

SECOND STREET

SAGE HALL

CHURCH

FIRST STREET

CONGRESS STREET

CONCRETE WALKS
EARTH MOUNDS
AUSTRIAN PINES

Site Concept, Sage Park. The Saratoga Associates.

75

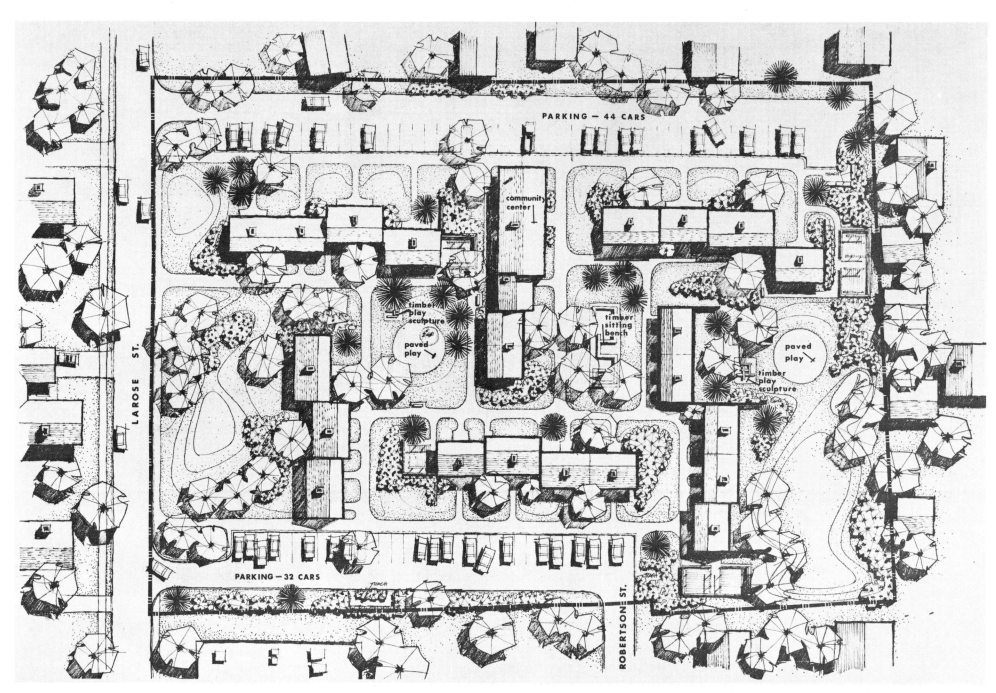

PARKING — 44 CARS

community center

timber play sculpture

paved play

timber sitting bench

timber play sculpture

paved play

LAROSE ST.

ROBERTSON ST.

PARKING — 32 CARS

Larose Gardens. The Saratoga Associates.

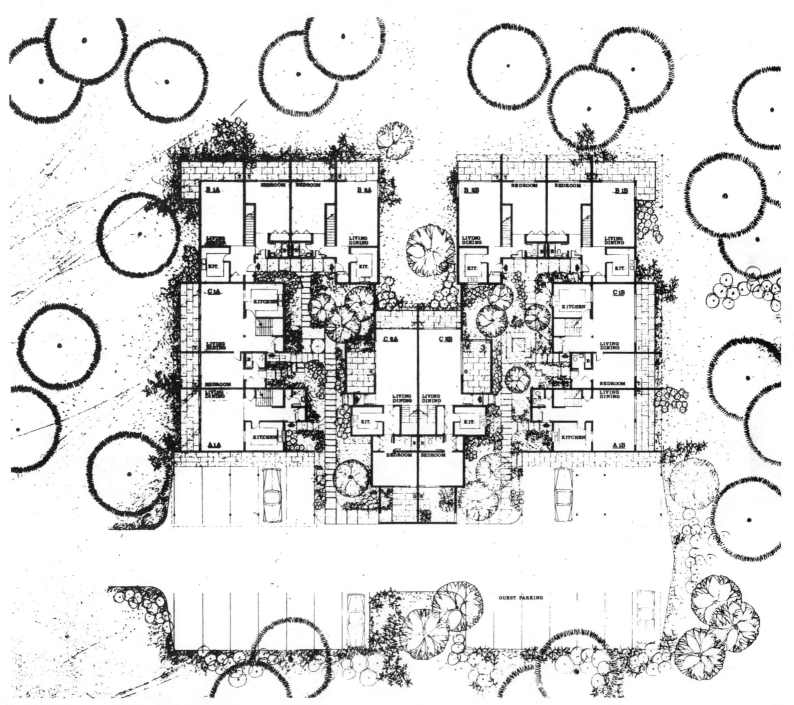

Quail Ridge Townhouse. Sasaki, Dawson, DeMay
Associates, Inc., by Philip Minervine.

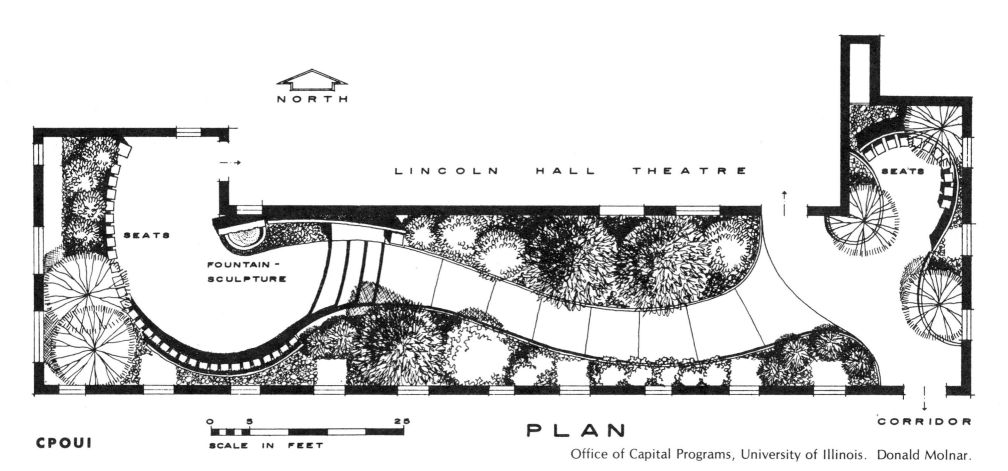

NORTH

LINCOLN HALL THEATRE

SEATS

FOUNTAIN -
SCULPTURE

SEATS

CORRIDOR

CPOUI

0   5   25

SCALE IN FEET

PLAN

Office of Capital Programs, University of Illinois. Donald Molnar.

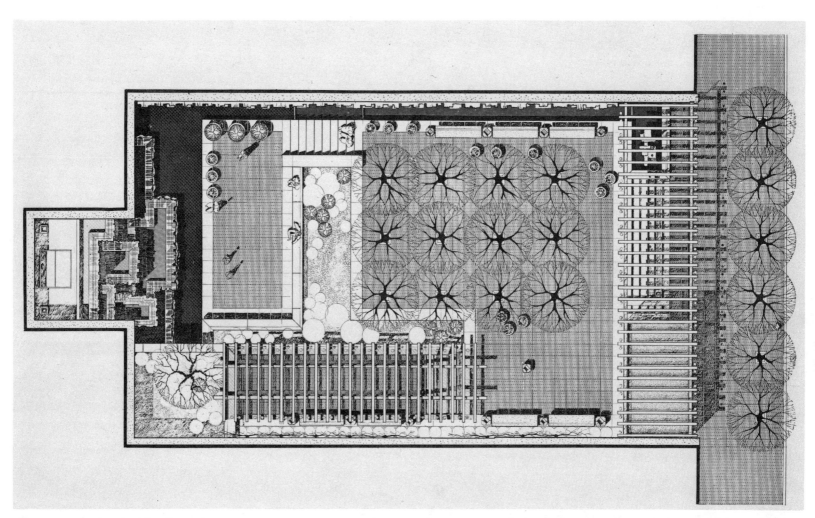

Greenacre Park. Sasaki, Dawson, DeMay Associates, Inc., by Ron Wortman.

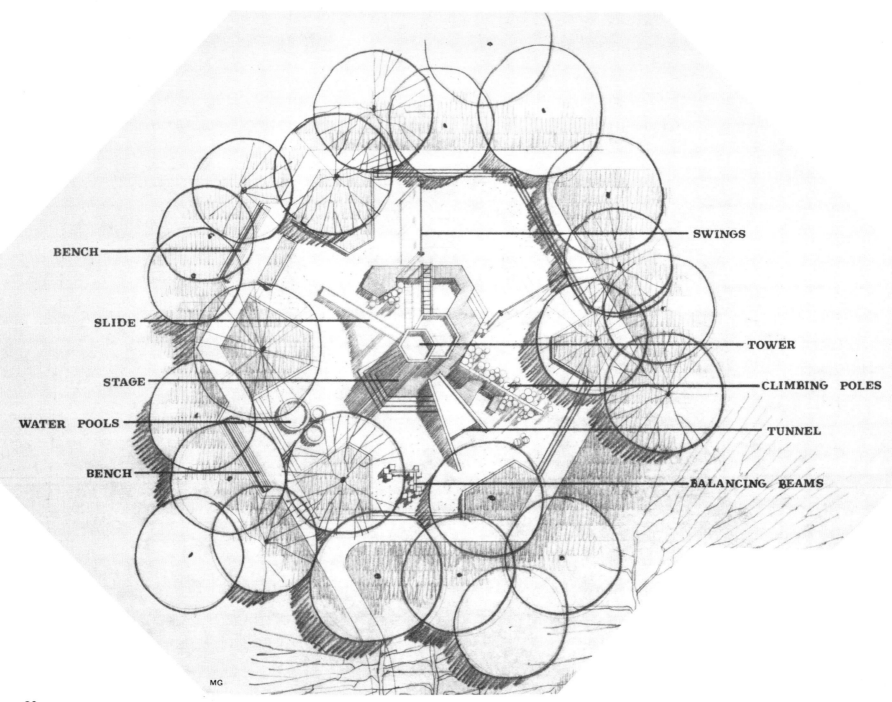

BENCH

SWINGS

SLIDE

TOWER

STAGE

CLIMBING POLES

WATER POOLS

TUNNEL

BENCH

BALANCING BEAMS

MG

80

Maas and Grassli.

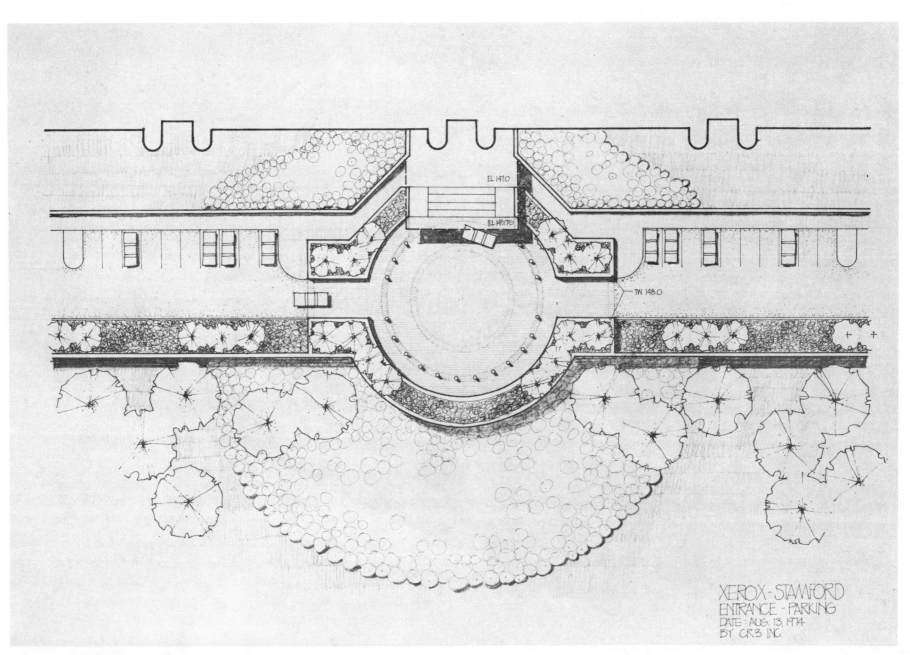

Labels within the drawing:

EL 147.0

EL 145.75

TW. 148.0

Xerox — Stamford entrance parking. CR3, Inc., by
Carl Mueller. Client: Perkins & Will, Architects.

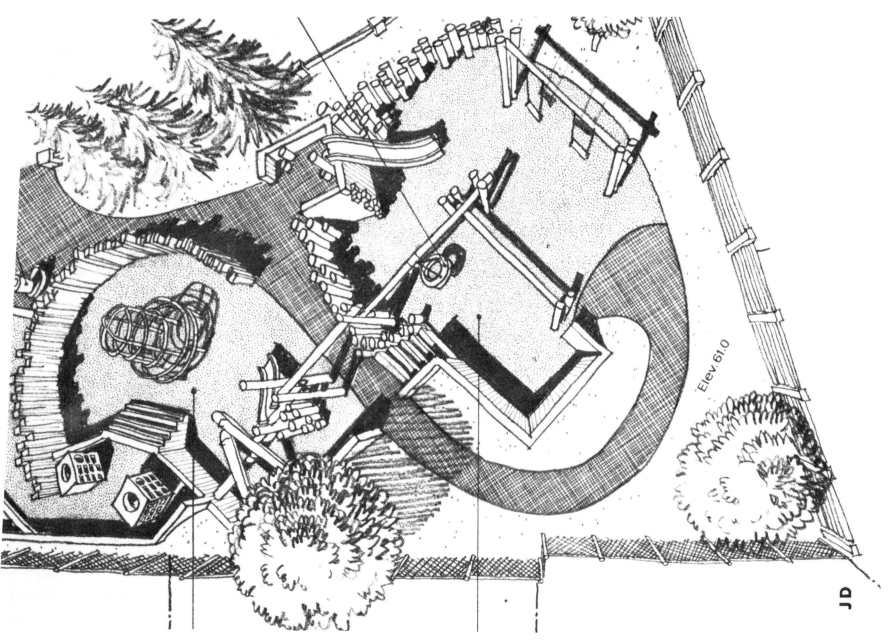

Elev. 61.0

JD

Nelton Court Play Area. Johnson and Dee.

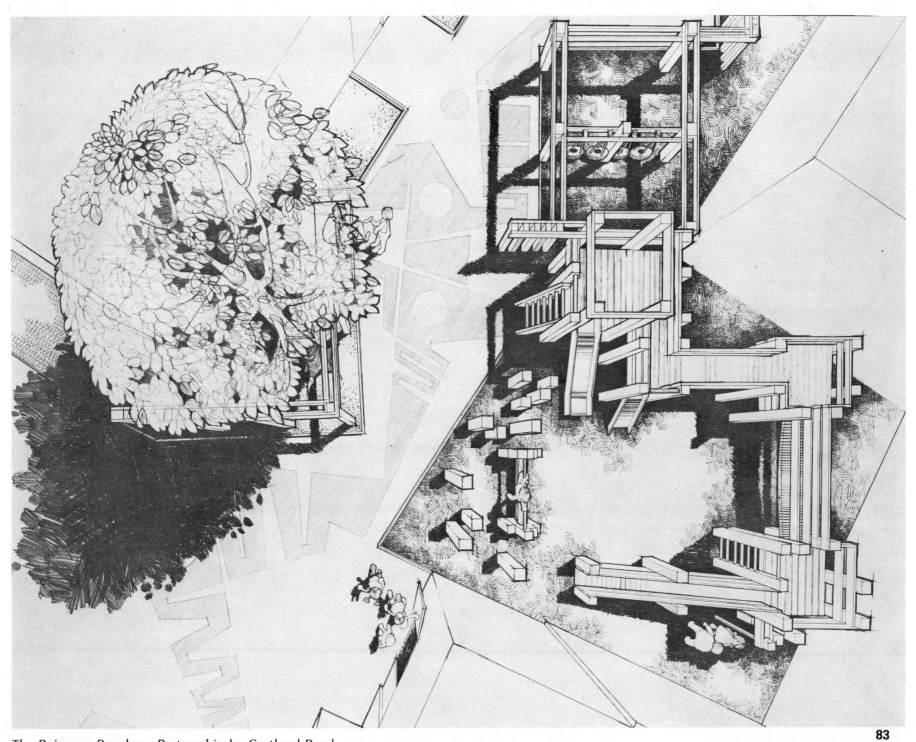

The Reimann-Buechner Partnership by Cortland Read.

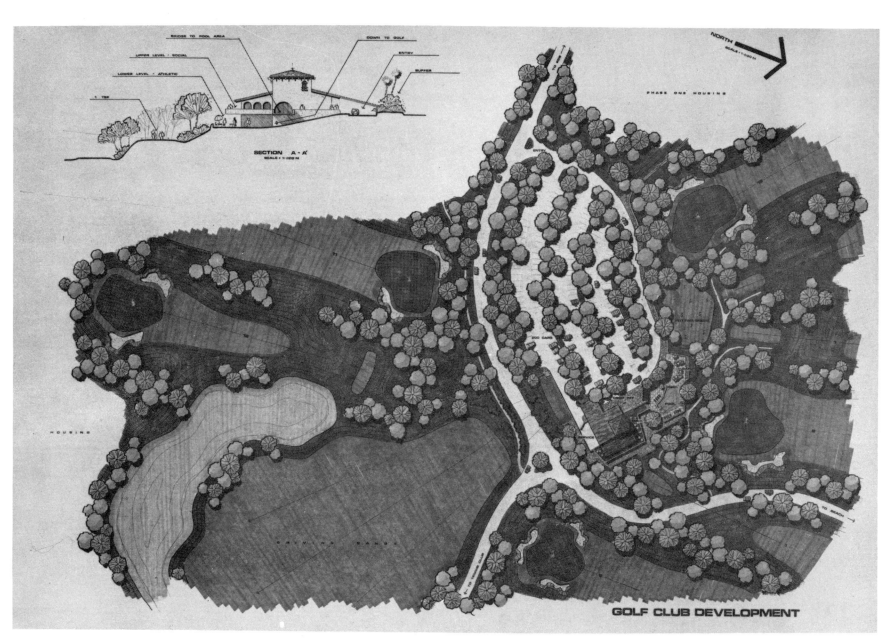

SECTION A - A'
SCALE : 1:1,000 M

NORTH

PHASE ONE HOUSING

HOUSING

GOLF CLUB DEVELOPMENT

Palmer Resort. Edward D. Stone, Jr. & Associates, P. A.

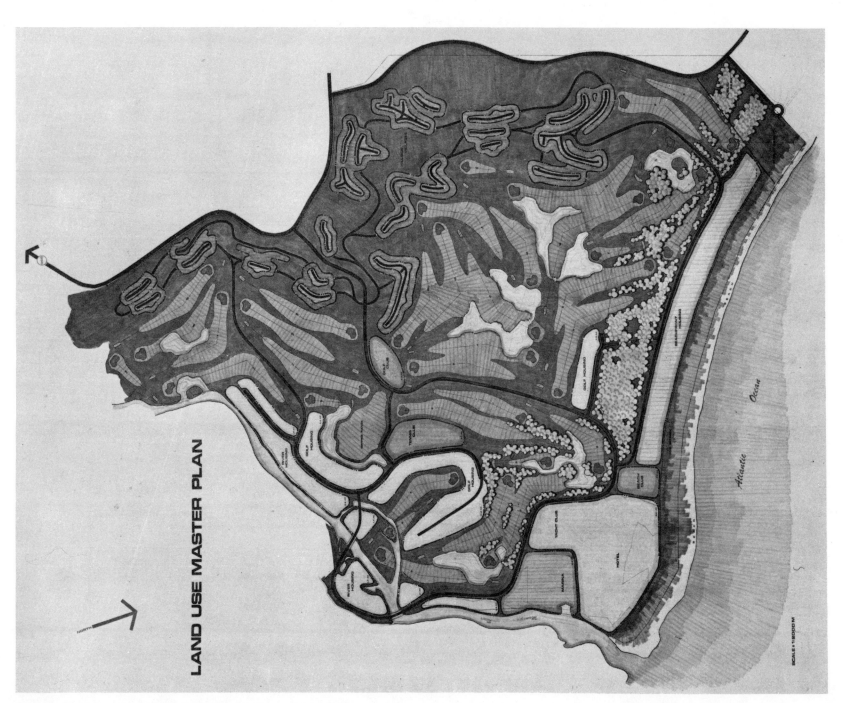

LAND USE MASTER PLAN

Palmer Resort.   Edward D. Stone, Jr. & Associates, P. A.

85

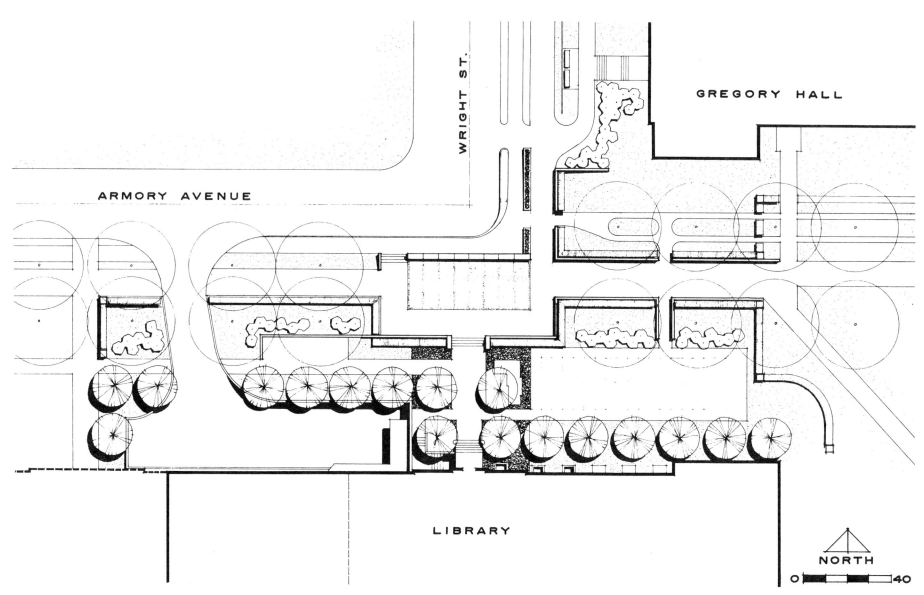

WRIGHT ST.

GREGORY HALL

ARMORY AVENUE

LIBRARY

NORTH

0 ▮▮▮▮▮▮▮▮ 40

University of Illinois Office for Capital Programs.

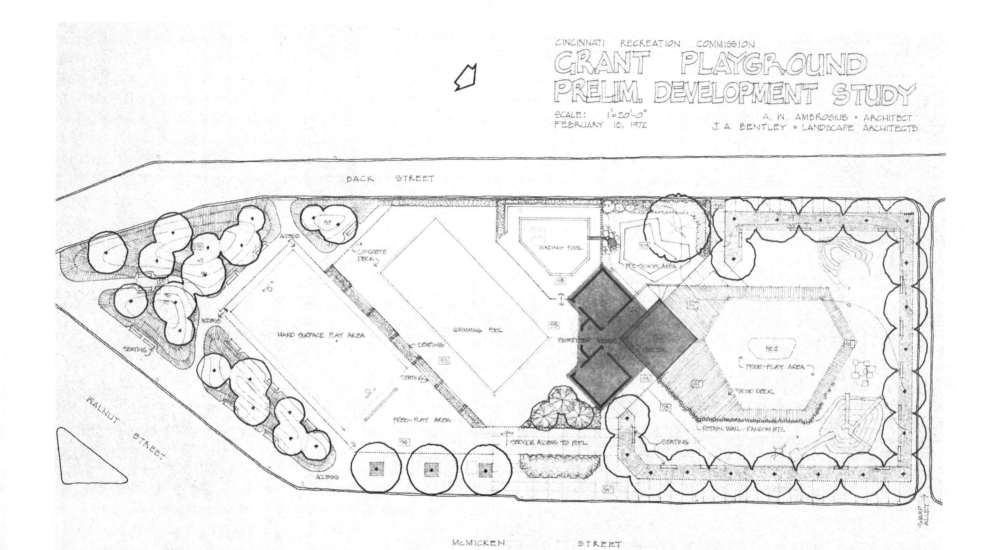

Grant Playground. John A. Bentley. A. W. Ambrosius, Architect.

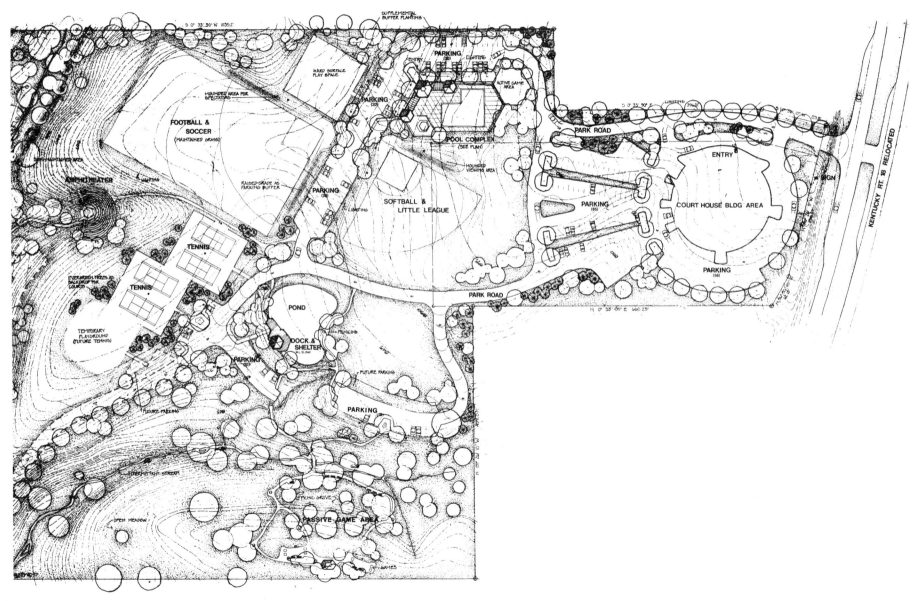

Boone Woods County Park. John A. Bentley.
Robert Ehmet Hayes & Associates, Architects.

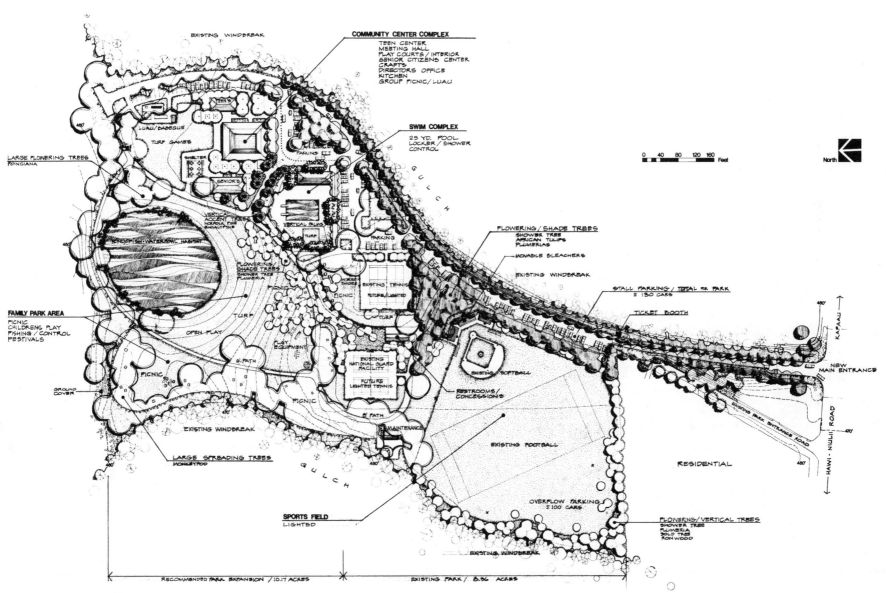

COMMUNITY CENTER COMPLEX
TEEN CENTER
MEETING HALL
PLAY COURTS / INTERIOR
SENIOR CITIZENS CENTER
CRAFTS
DIRECTORS OFFICE
KITCHEN
GROUP PICNIC / LUAU

EXISTING WINDBREAK

SWIM COMPLEX
25 YD. POOL
LOCKER / SHOWER
CONTROL

LUAU / BARBEQUE

TURF GAMES

LARGE FLOWERING TREES
POINCIANA

SHELTER

PARKING

SENIOR'S

VERTICAL ACCENT TREES
NORFOLK PINE
EUCALYPTUS

VERTICAL PALMS

FLOWERING / SHADE TREES
SHOWER TREE
AFRICAN TULIPS
PLUMERIAS

MOVABLE BLEACHERS

EXISTING WINDBREAK

POND / FISH / WATERFALL HABITAT

TURF

FLOWERING / SHADE TREES
SHOWER TREE
PLUMERIA

PARKING

FAMILY PARK AREA
PICNIC
CHILDRENS PLAY
FISHING / CONTROL
FESTIVALS

TURF

OPEN PLAY

PICNIC

HORSE SHOES

EXISTING TENNIS

FUTURE / LIGHTED

TURF

STALL PARKING / TOTAL FOR PARK
± 130 CARS

TICKET BOOTH

PICNIC

PLAY EQUIPMENT

EXISTING SOFTBALL

GROUND COVER

PICNIC

6' PATH

EXISTING NATIONAL GUARD FACILITY

FUTURE LIGHTED TENNIS

RESTROOMS / CONCESSIONS /

NEW MAIN ENTRANCE

EXISTING WINDBREAK

6' PATH

MAINTENANCE

EXISTING FOOTBALL

RESIDENTIAL

LARGE SPREADING TREES
MONKEYPOD

GULCH

OVERFLOW PARKING
± 100 CARS

SPORTS FIELD
LIGHTED

FLOWERING / VERTICAL TREES
SHOWER TREE
PLUMERIA
GOLD TREE
IRONWOOD

EXISTING WINDBREAK

RECOMMENDED PARK EXPANSION / 10.17 ACRES

EXISTING PARK / 8.36 ACRES

0 40 80 120 160 Feet

North

Kamehameha Park, Hawaii. EDAW, Inc., by Ollie K. Davis.

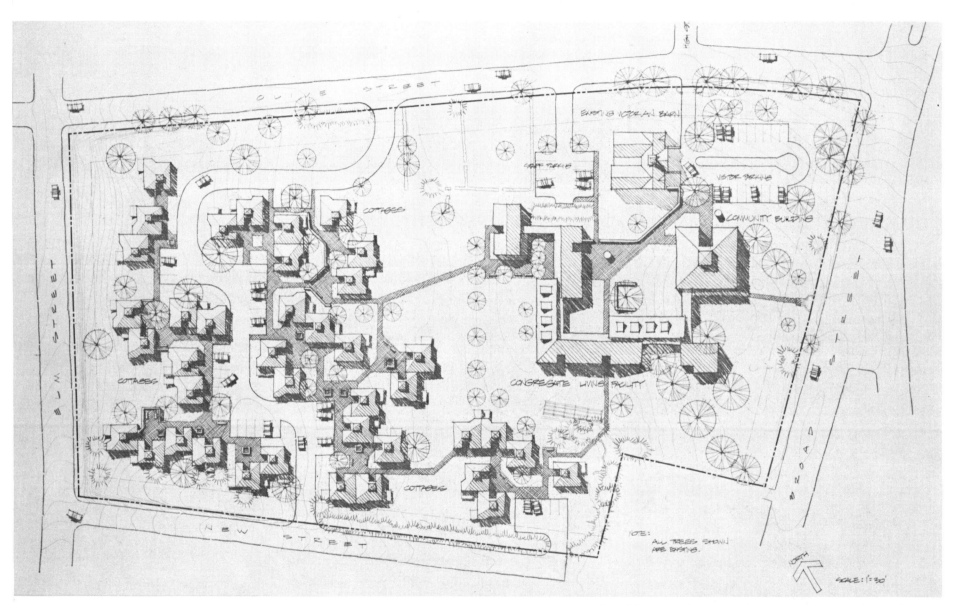

Community for the Elderly. Johnson and Dee. Jeter & Cook, Architects.

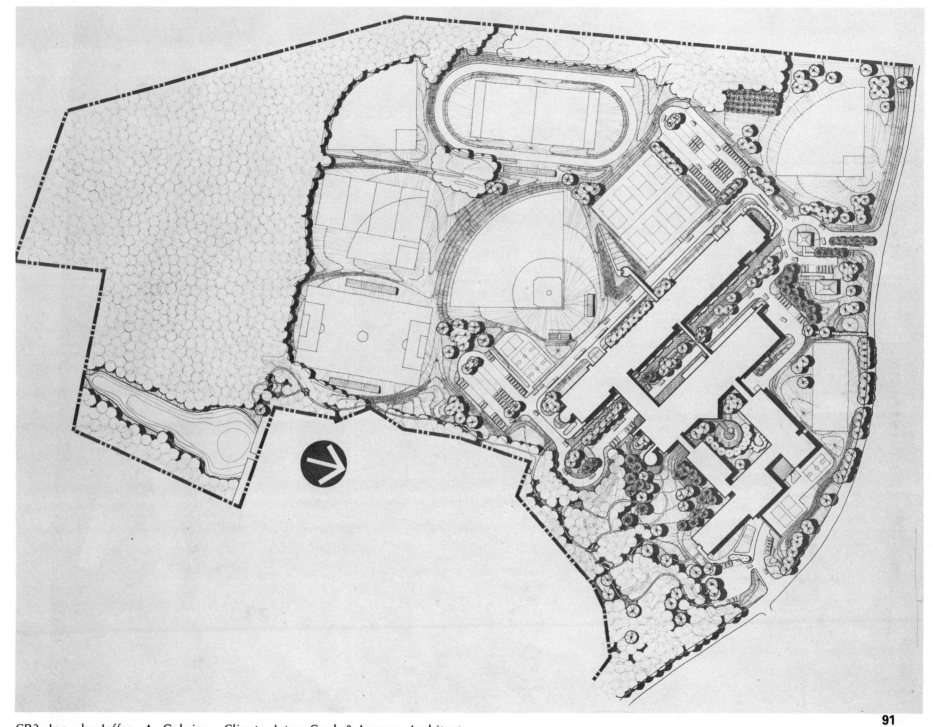

CR3, Inc., by Jeffrey A. Gebrian. Client: Jeter, Cook & Jepson, Architects.

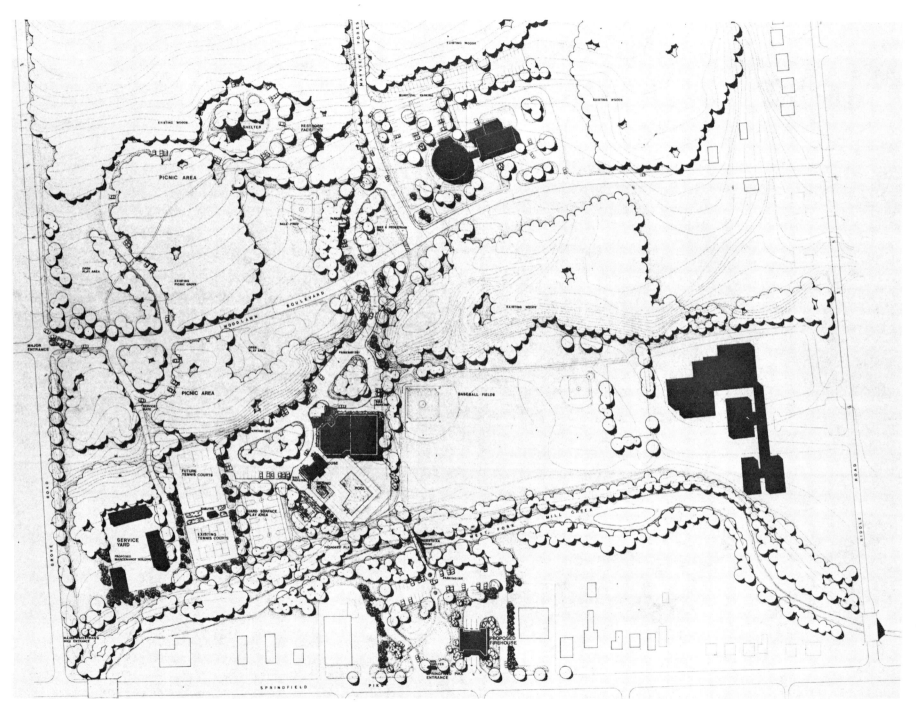

Woodlawn Municipal Park. John A. Bentley.

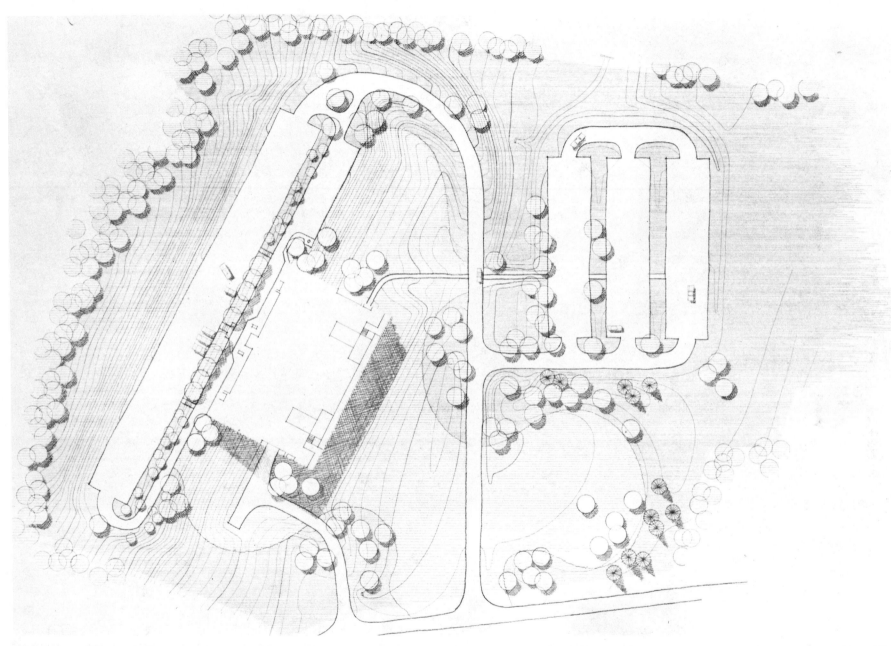

Johnson and Dee.

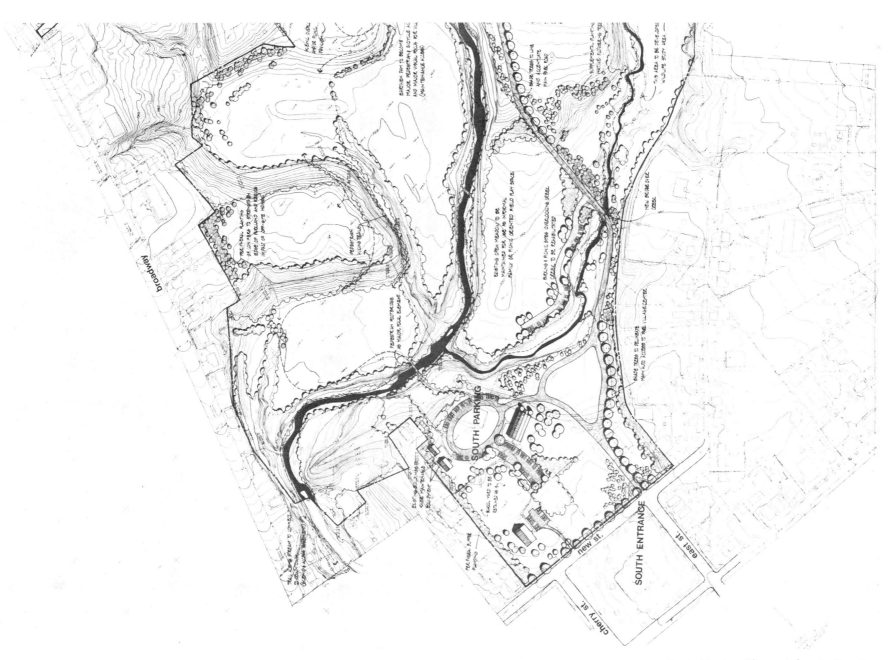

Park Master Plan.   John A. Bentley.

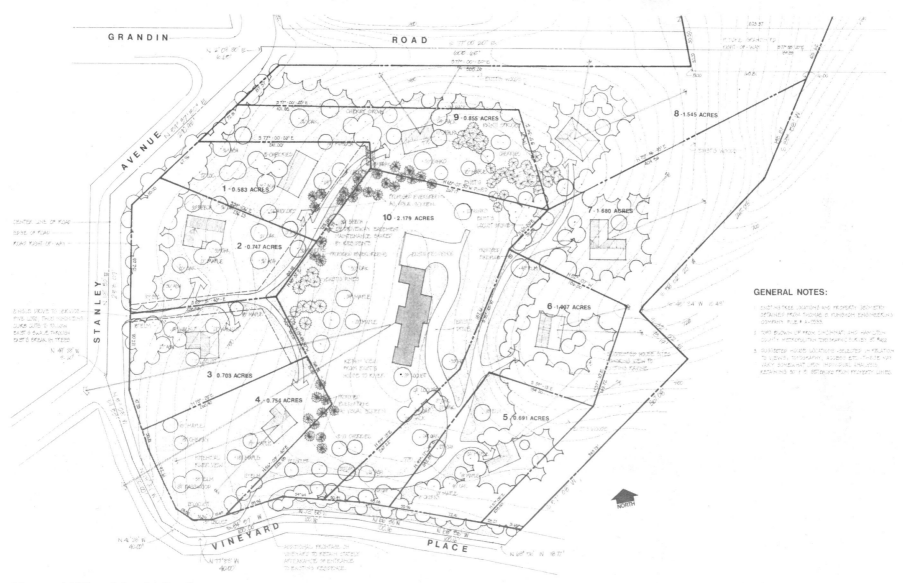

Vineyard Hills. John A. Bentley.

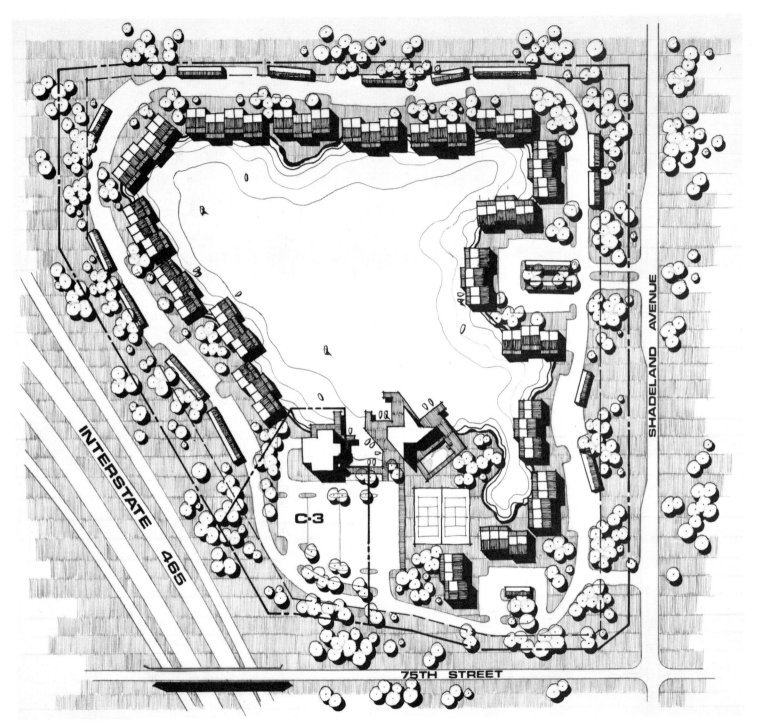

INTERSTATE 465

SHADELAND AVENUE

C-3

75TH STREET

Browning, Day, Pollak Associates, Inc.

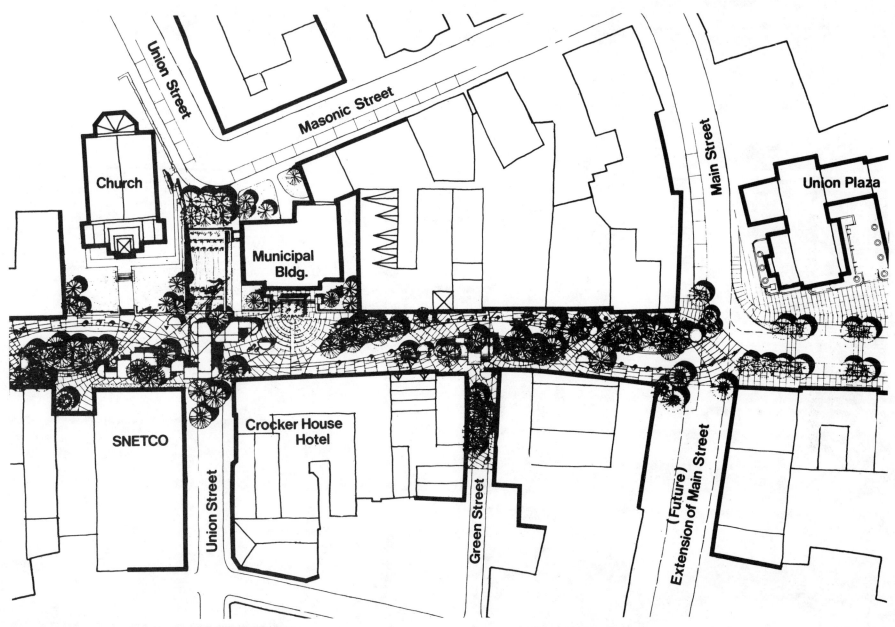

State Street Semi-Mall. Johnson and Dee.

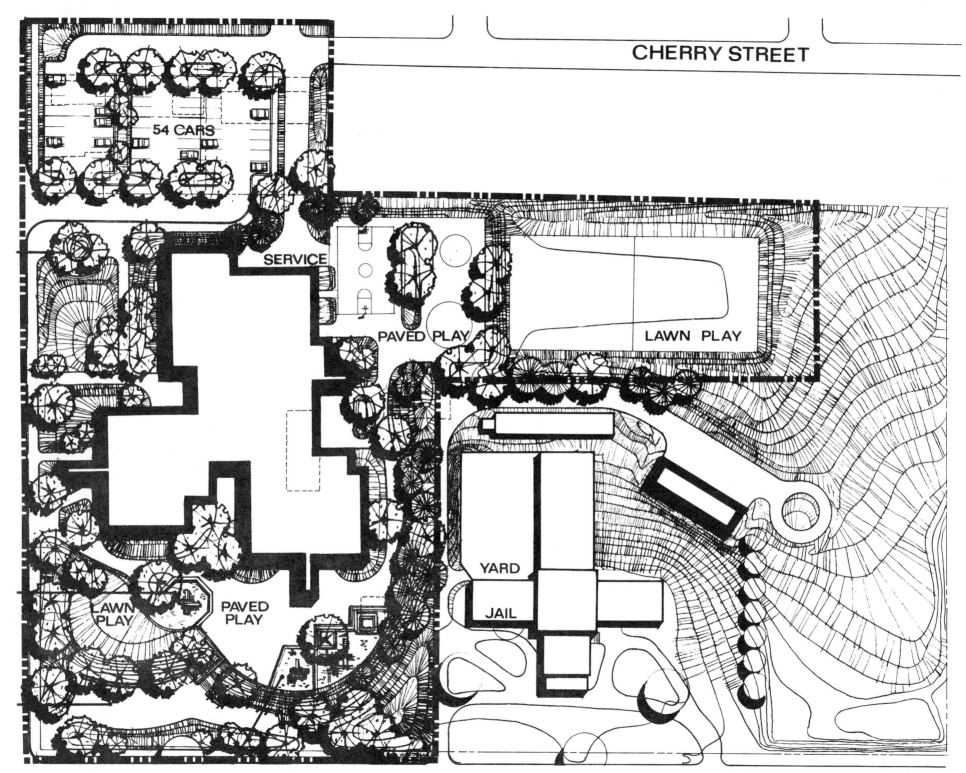

CHERRY STREET

54 CARS

SERVICE

PAVED PLAY

LAWN PLAY

LAWN PLAY

PAVED PLAY

YARD

JAIL

East Side Community School. CR3, Inc., by Robert Wordell.

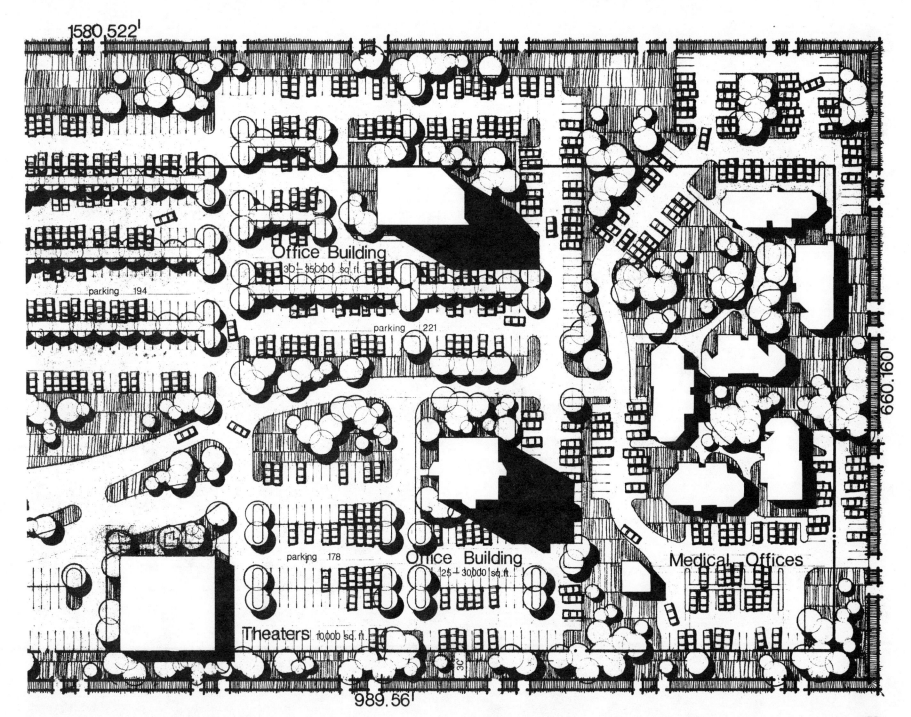

1580,522'

660.160'

parking 194

Office Building
30 - 35000 sq. ft.

parking 221

parking 178

Office Building
25 - 30,000 sq. ft.

Medical Offices

Theaters 10,000 sq. ft.

30'

989.56'

Fidelity Center. Browning, Day, Pollak Associates, Inc.

99

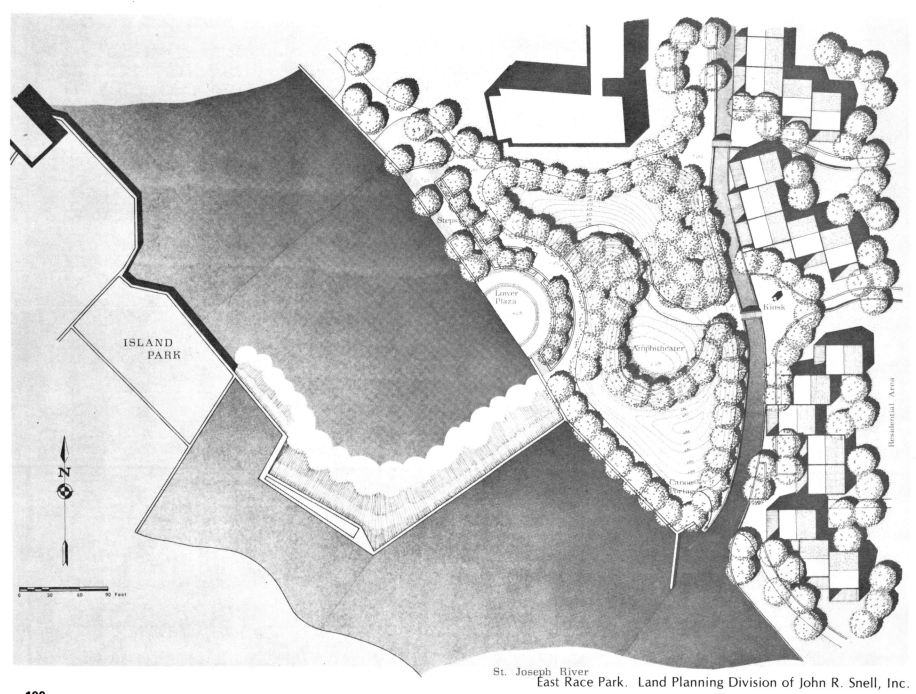

ISLAND PARK

Steps

Lower Plaza

Amphitheater

Kiosk

Canoe Portage

Residential Area

N

0   30   60   90 Feet

St. Joseph River

East Race Park. Land Planning Division of John R. Snell, Inc.

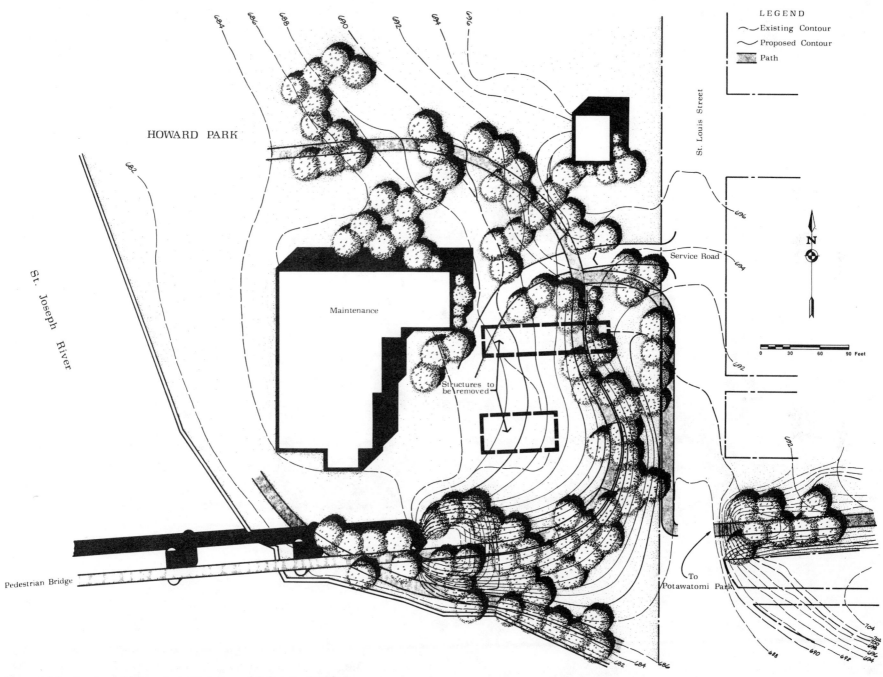

LEGEND
〜 Existing Contour
〜 Proposed Contour
▨ Path

HOWARD PARK

St. Louis Street

St. Joseph River

Service Road

Maintenance

Structures to
be removed

N

0   30   60   90 Feet

Pedestrian Bridge

To
Potawatomi Park

Howard Park. Land Planning Division of John R. Snell, Inc.

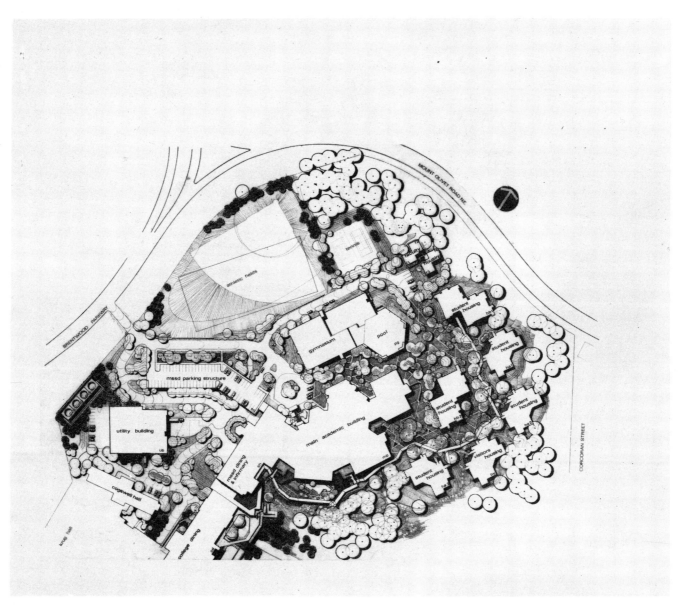

Model Secondary School for the Deaf. CR3, Inc.
Client: Hudgins, Thompson, & Ball, Architects.

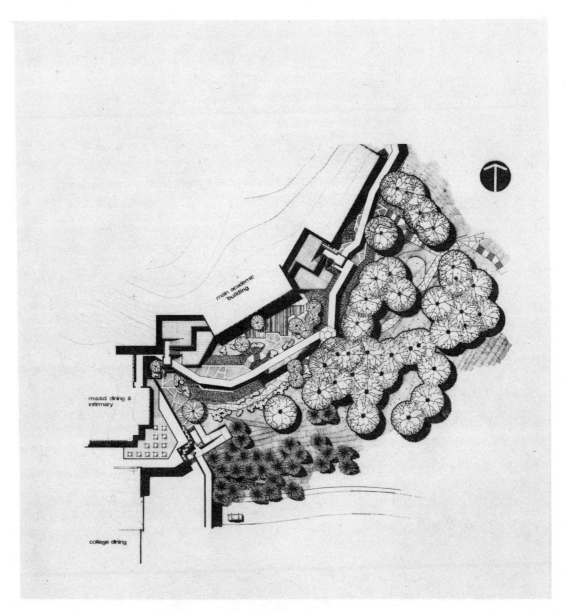

main academic
building

m.s.s.d dining &
infirmary

college dining

Model Secondary School for the Deaf. CR3, Inc.
Client: Hudgins, Thompson, & Ball, Architects.

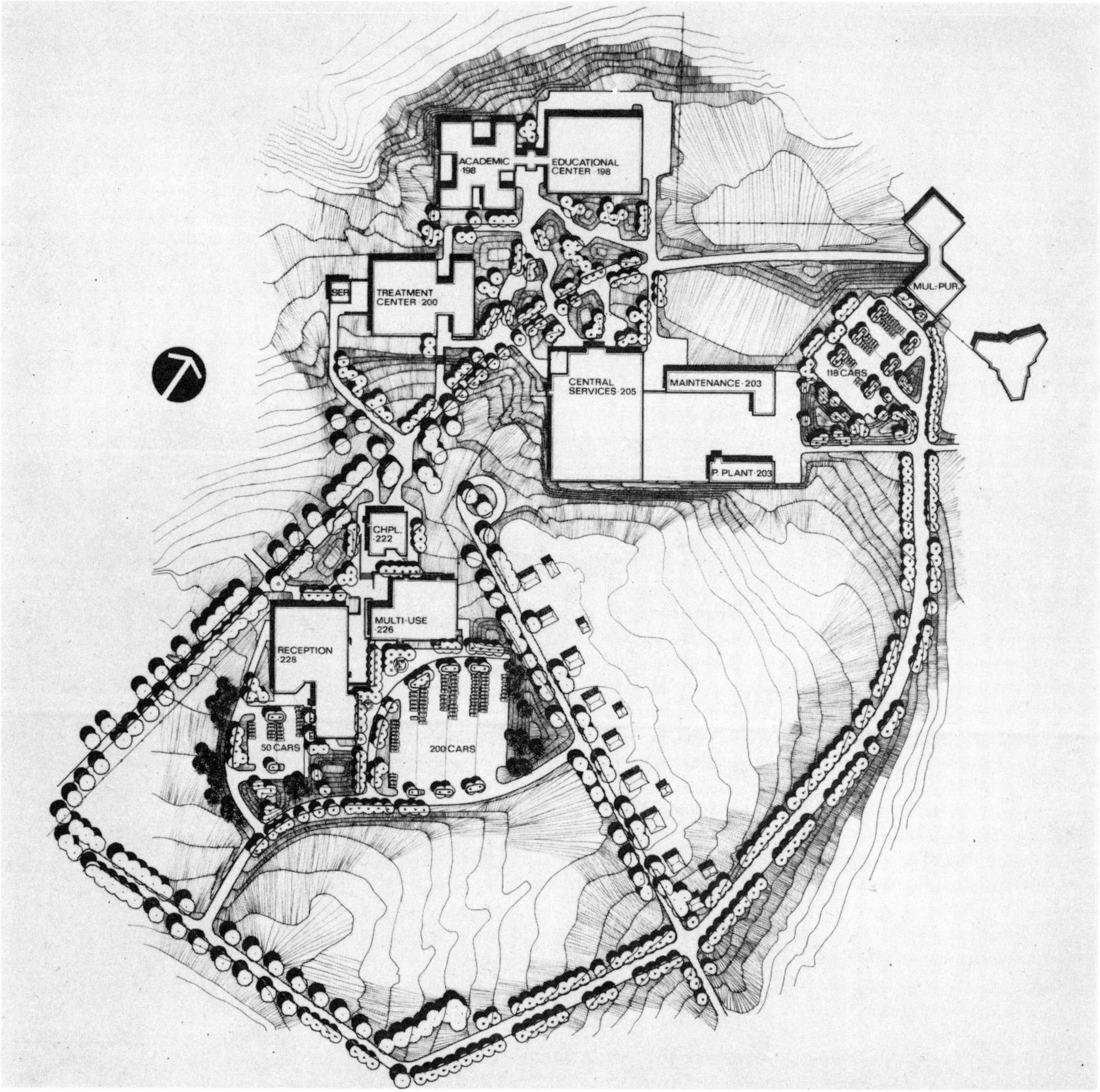
ACADEMIC ·198
EDUCATIONAL CENTER ·198
SER
TREATMENT CENTER ·200
MUL·PUR.
CENTRAL SERVICES·205
MAINTENANCE·203
118 CARS
P. PLANT·203
CHPL. ·222
MULTI·USE ·226
RECEPTION ·228
50 CARS
200 CARS

Cheshire Corrections Community. CR3, Inc., by Jeffrey A. Gebrian. Client: Close, Jensen, Miller.

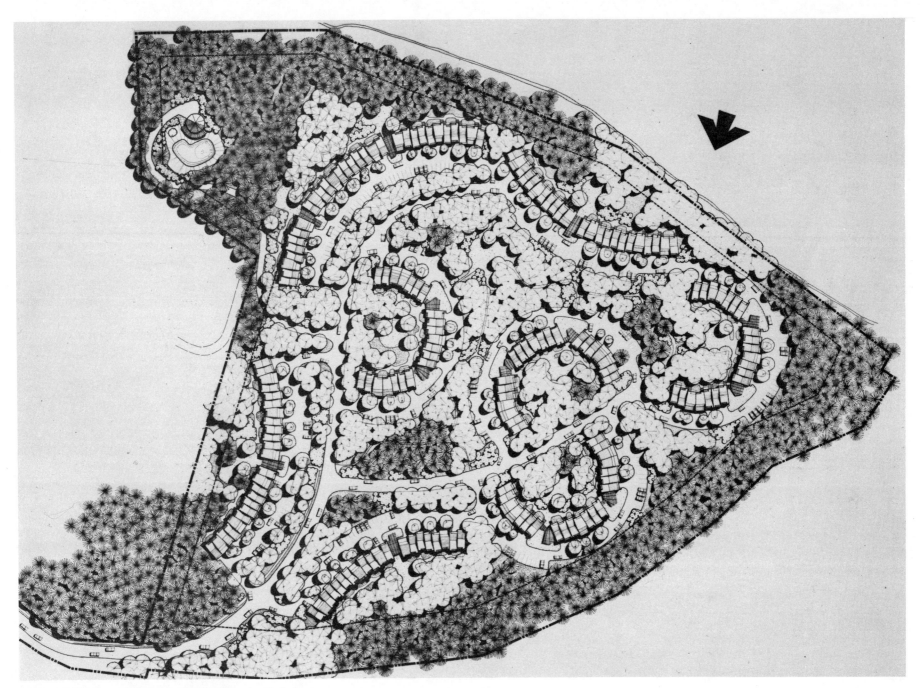

Tunxis Village. CR3, Inc., by Jeffrey A. Gebrian.
Client: Hirsch, Kaestle Boos, Architects.

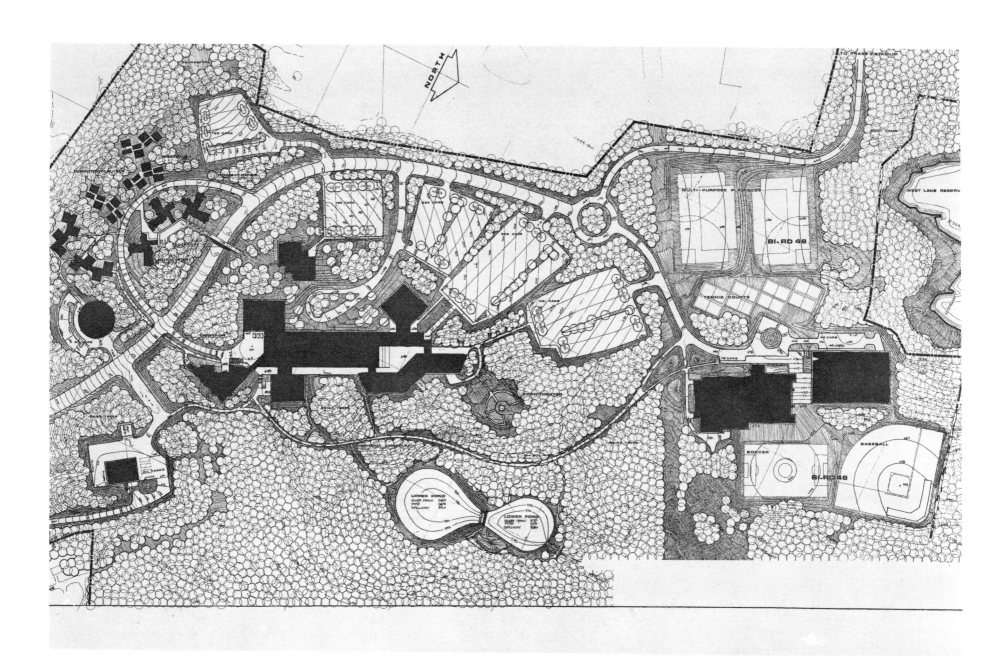

Western Connecticut State College. CR3, Inc., by Jeffrey A. Gebrian.
Coordinating Architect: Russell, Gibson, von Dohlen.

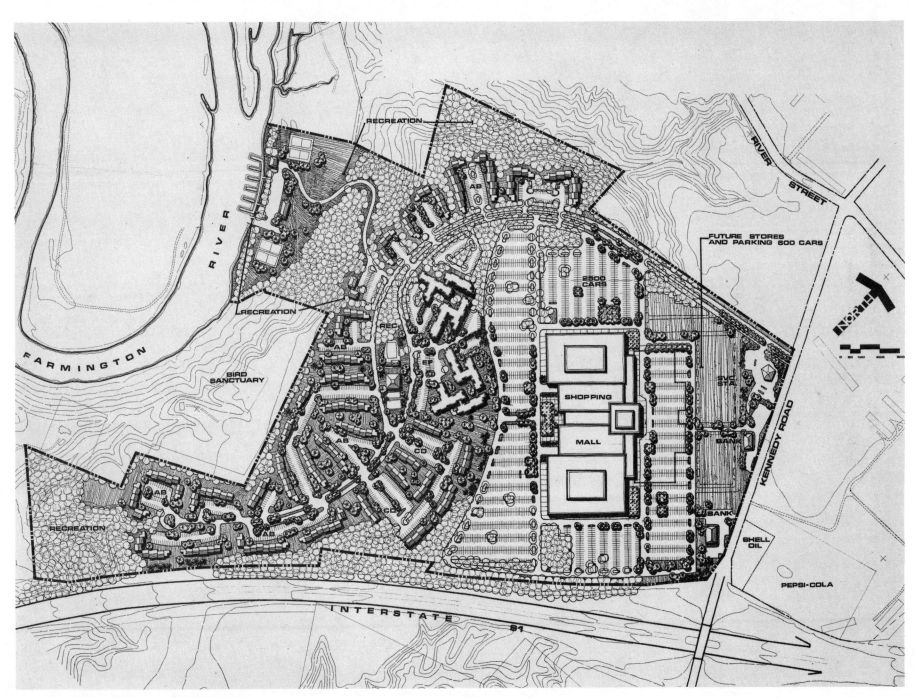

Windsor Plaza. CR3, Inc., by Jeffrey A. Gebrian.
Client: Phillip J. DiCorcia, Architect.

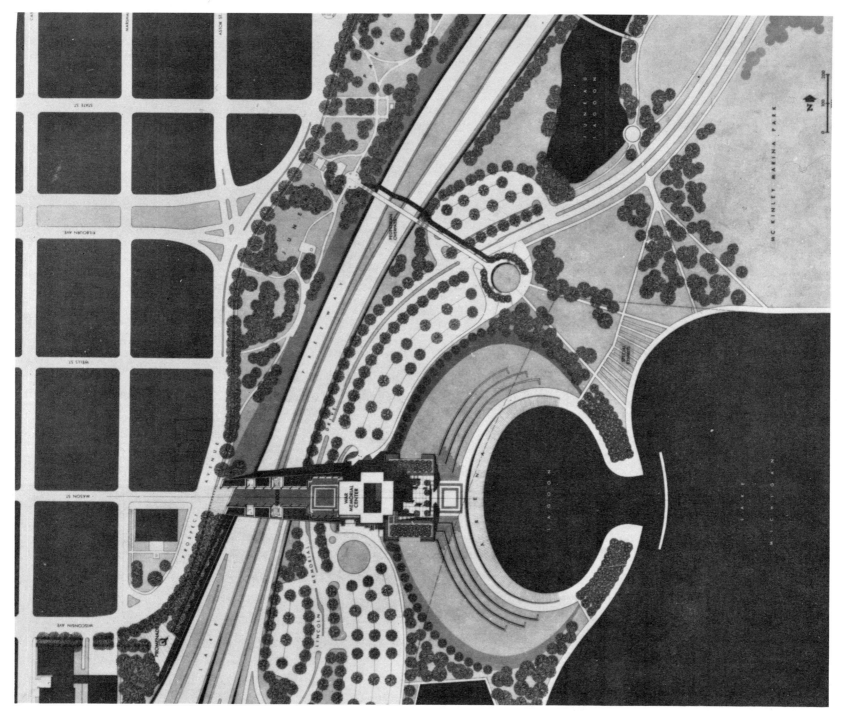

Milwaukee War Memorial. Johnson, Johnson & Roy, Inc.
Pencil, ink, black "zip-a-tone" and "zip-a-tone" screens.

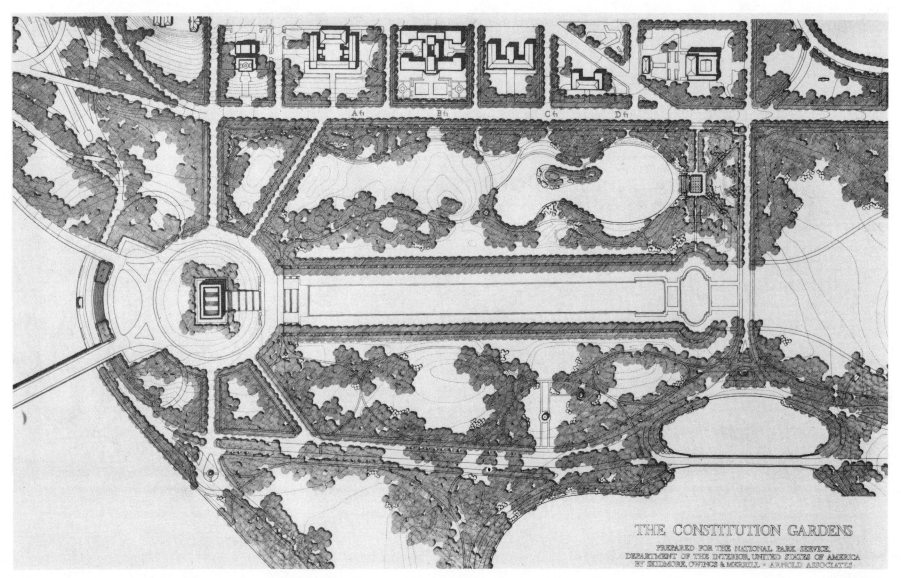

The Constitution Gardens. Skidmore, Owings and Merrill. Arnold Associates.

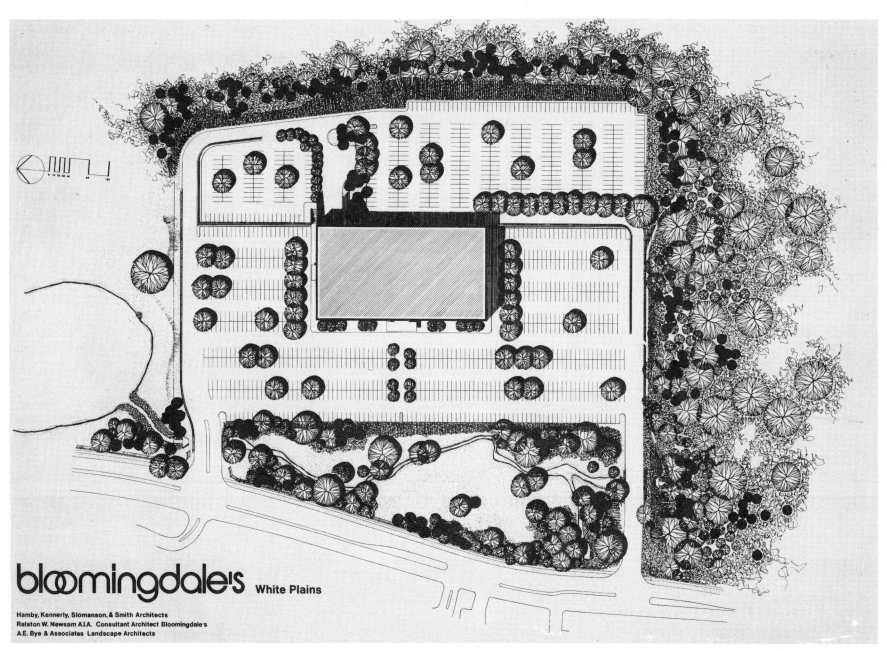

bloomingdale's White Plains

Hamby, Kennerly, Slomanson, & Smith Architects
Ralston W. Newsam A.I.A. Consultant Architect Bloomingdale's
A.E. Bye & Associates Landscape Architects

Bloomingdale's. A. E. Bye & Associates. Kennerly, Slomanson and Smith, Architects. Ralston W. Newsom, A.I.A., Consultant Architect.

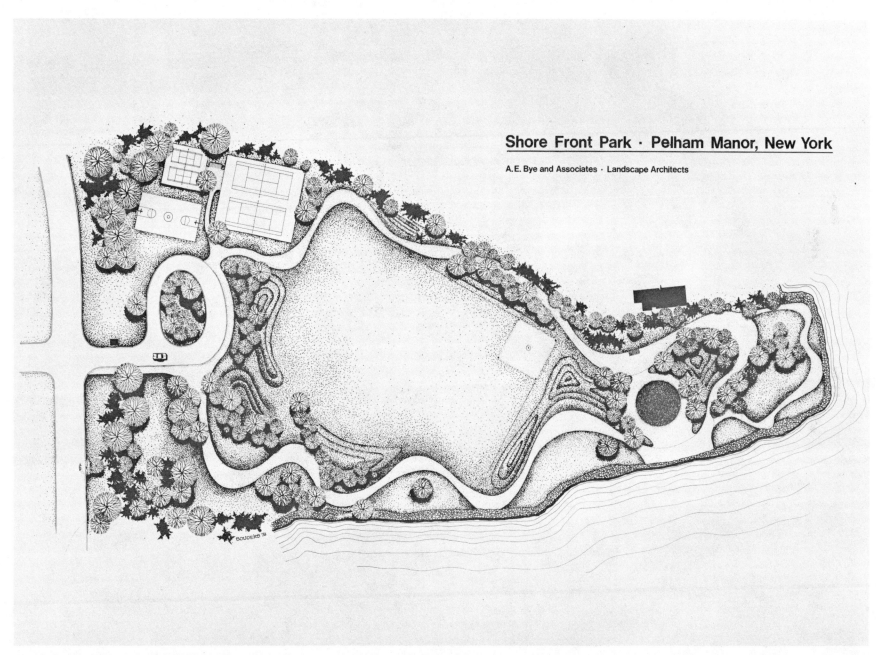

Shore Front Park · Pelham Manor, New York

A. E. Bye and Associates · Landscape Architects

Shore Front Park. A. E. Bye & Associates.

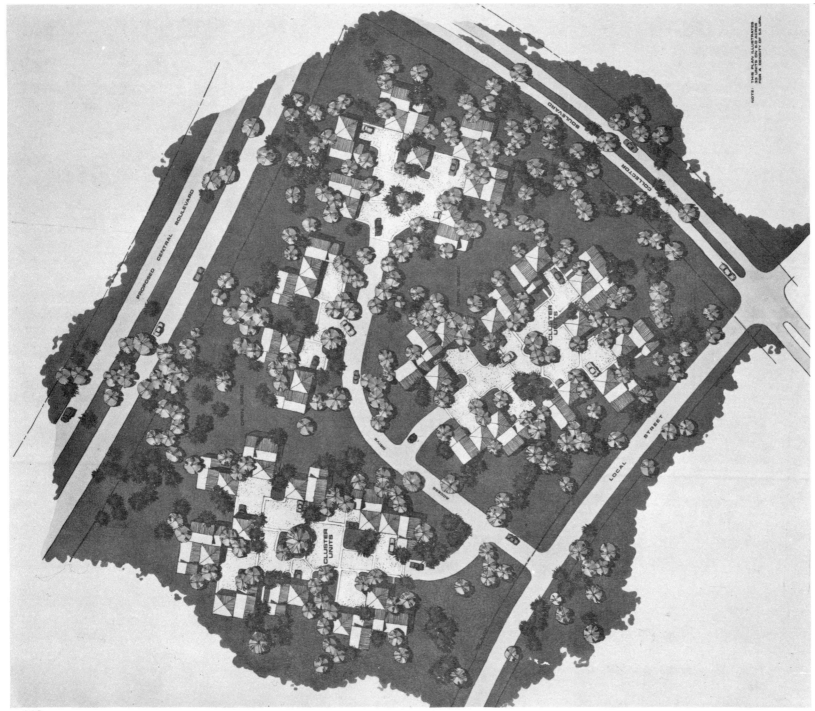

Jupiter Trails. Edward D. Stone, Jr. & Associates, P. A.

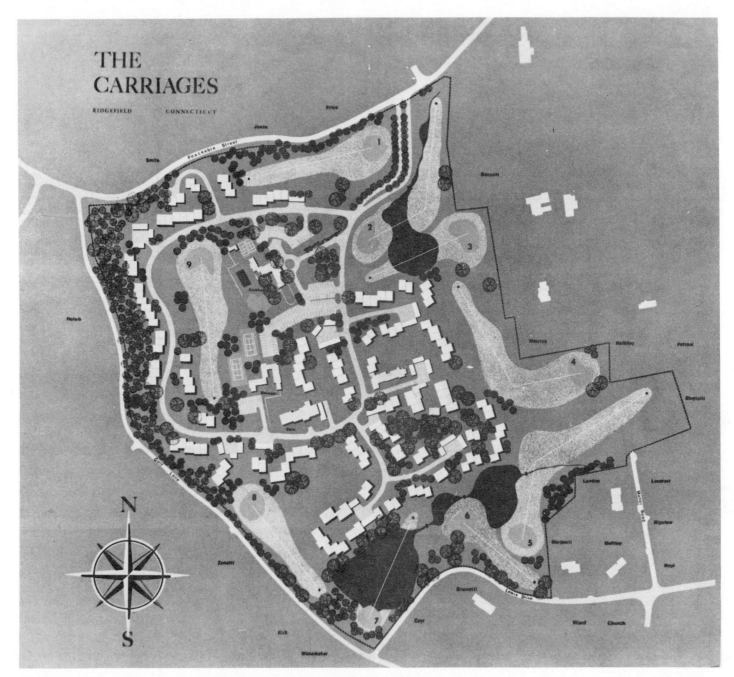

The Carriages. A. E. Bye & Associates. Architect: Fielding L. Bowman.

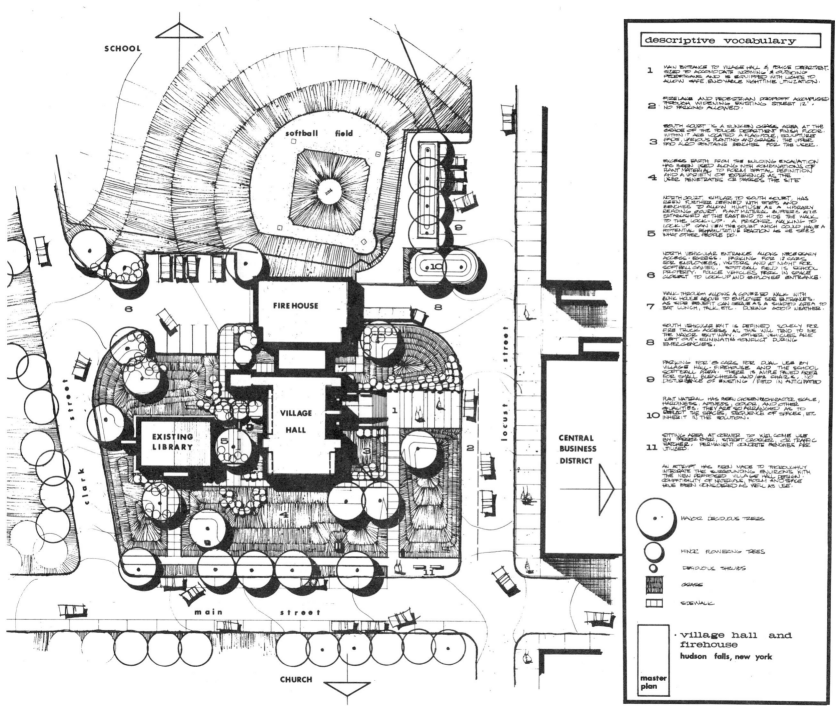

SCHOOL

softball field

FIRE HOUSE

VILLAGE HALL

EXISTING LIBRARY

clark street

locust street

CENTRAL BUSINESS DISTRICT

main street

CHURCH

village hall and firehouse

hudson falls, new york

master plan

114

Village Hall and Firehouse. The Saratoga Associates.

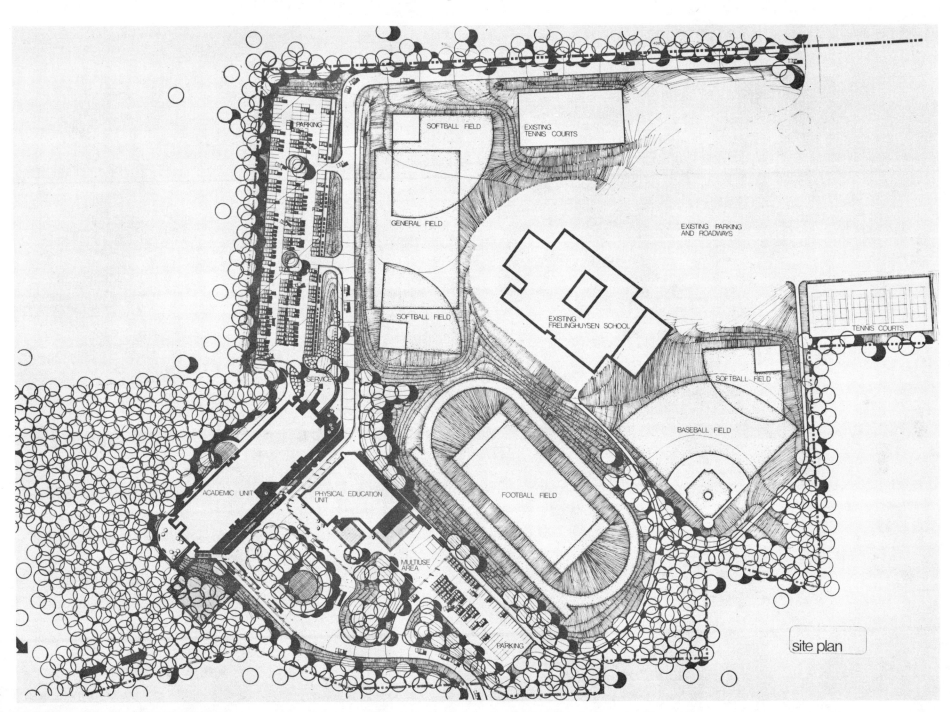

Site Plan. The Saratoga Associates.

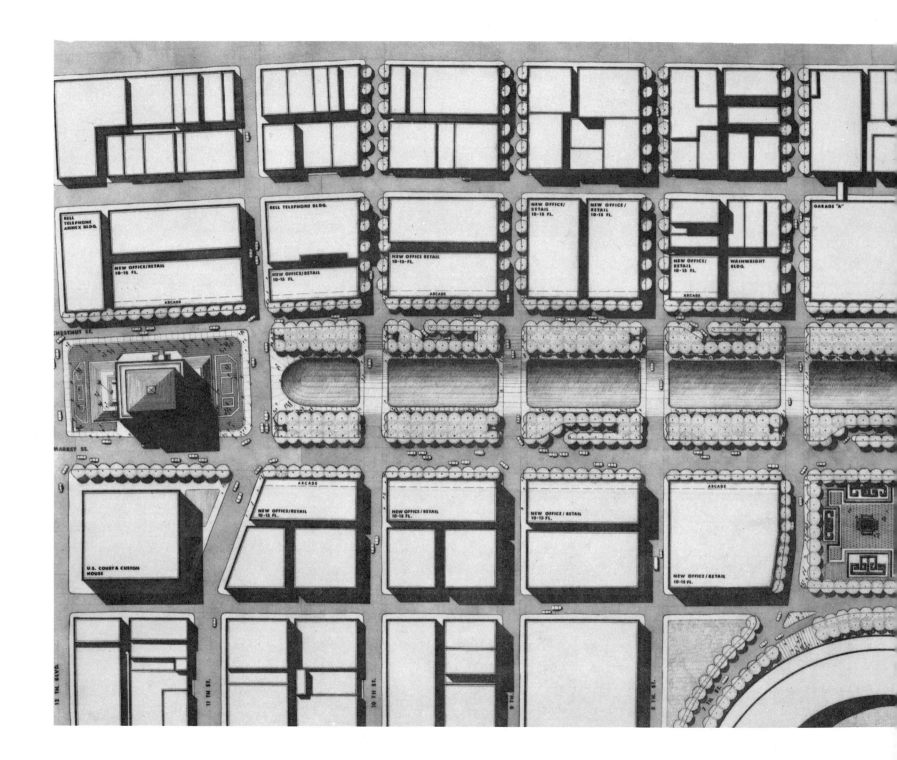

116

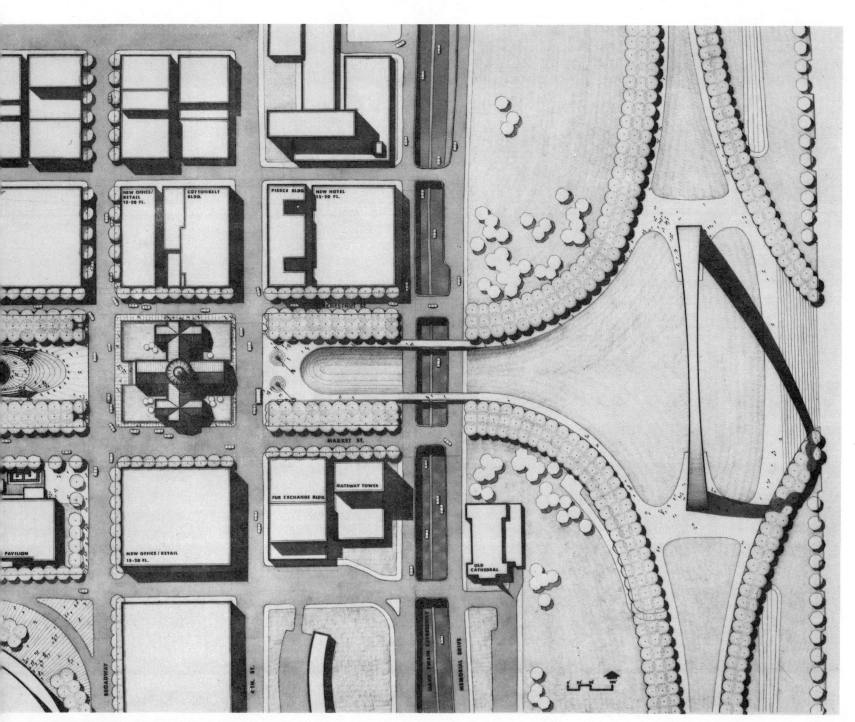

Louis Mall. Sasaki, Dawson, DeMay
sociates, Inc. Hutchins Photography, Inc.

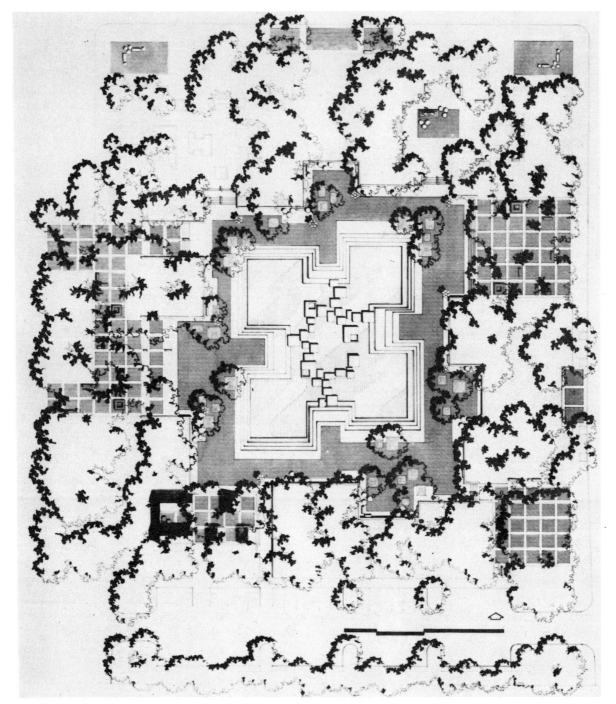

Freimann Square. Browning, Day, Pollak Associates, Inc.

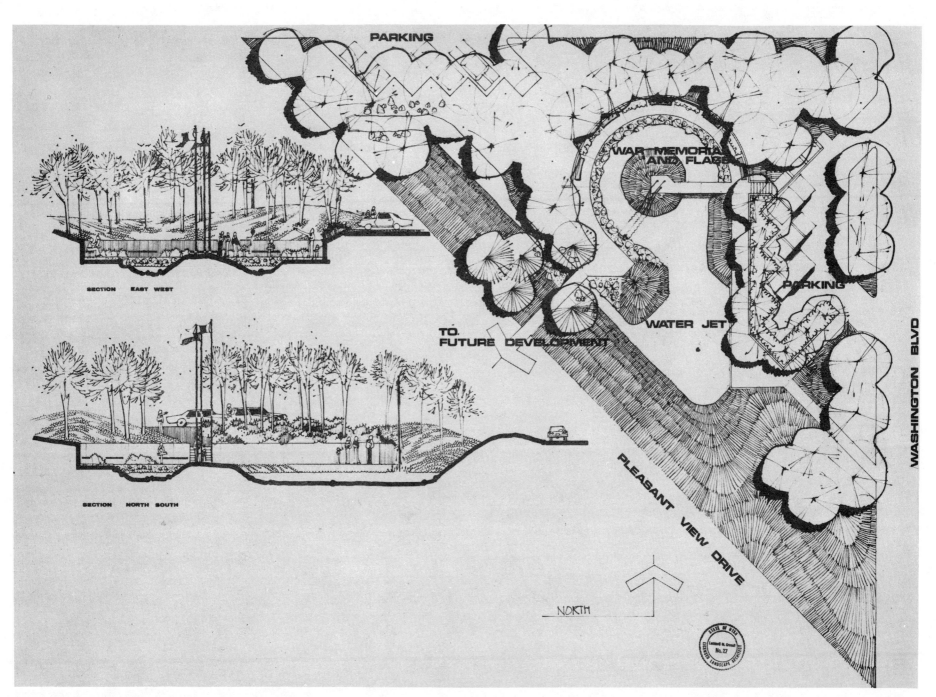

PARKING

WAR MEMORIAL AND FLAGS

PARKING

WATER JET

TO FUTURE DEVELOPMENT

SECTION EAST WEST

SECTION NORTH SOUTH

PLEASANT VIEW DRIVE

WASHINGTON BLVD

NORTH

North Ogden Triangle. Maas and Grassli.

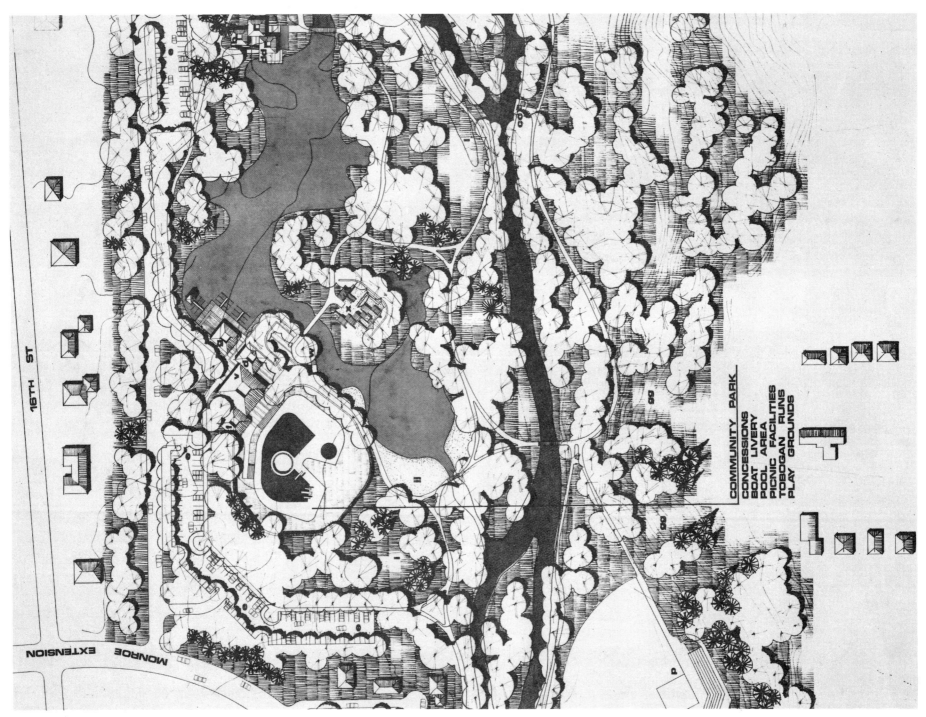

COMMUNITY PARK
CONCESSIONS
BOAT LIVERY
POOL AREA
PICNIC FACILITIES
TOBOGAN RUNS
PLAY GROUNDS

16TH ST

MONROE EXTENSION

Ogden River Parkway. Maas and Grassli.

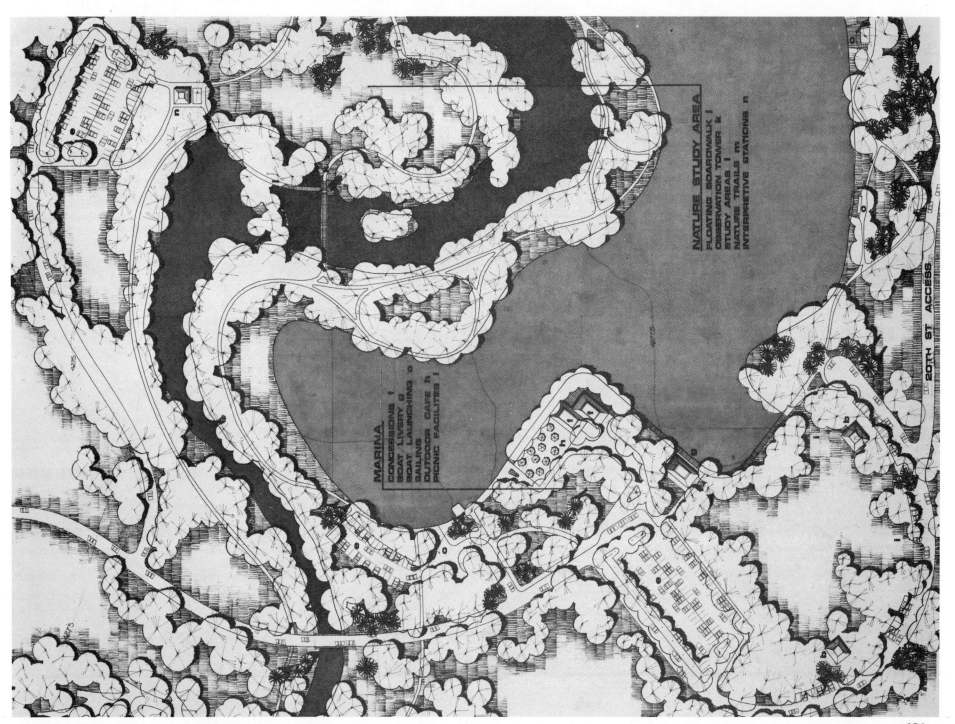

NATURE STUDY AREA
FLOATING BOARDWALK j
OBSERVATION TOWER k
STUDY AREAS l
NATURE TRAILS m
INTERPRETIVE STATIONS n

MARINA
CONCESSIONS f
BOAT LIVERY g
BOAT LAUNCHING o
SAILING
OUTDOOR CAFE h
PICNIC FACILITES i

20TH ST ACCESS

Ogden River Parkway. Maas and Grassli.

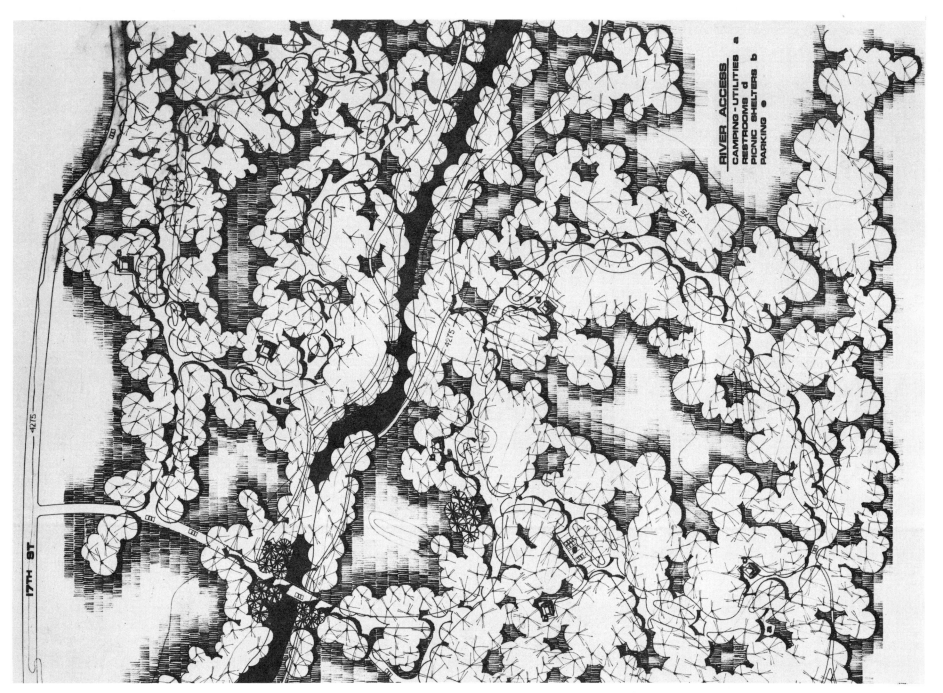

Ogden River Parkway. Maas and Grassli.

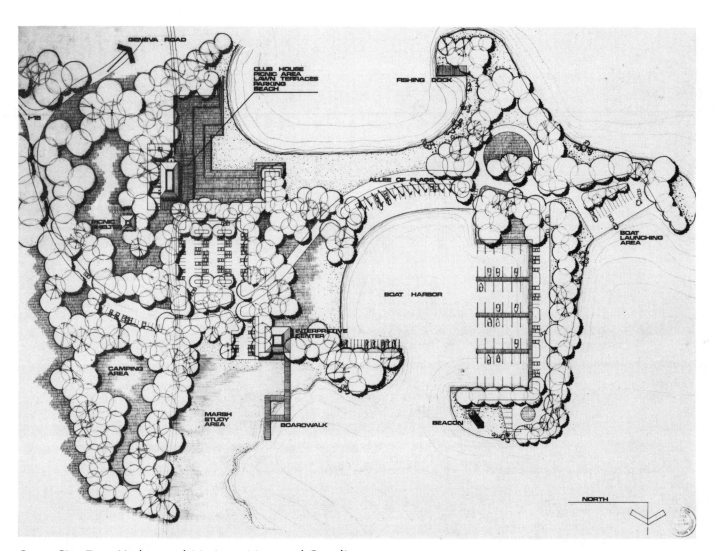

GENEVA ROAD

CLUB HOUSE
PICNIC AREA
LAWN TERRACES
PARKING
BEACH

FISHING DOCK

ALLEE OF FLAGS

PICNIC
SHELTER

BOAT HARBOR

BOAT
LAUNCHING
AREA

INTERPRETIVE
CENTER

CAMPING
AREA

MARSH
STUDY
AREA

BOARDWALK

BEACON

NORTH

Orem City Boat Harbor and Marina. Maas and Grassli.

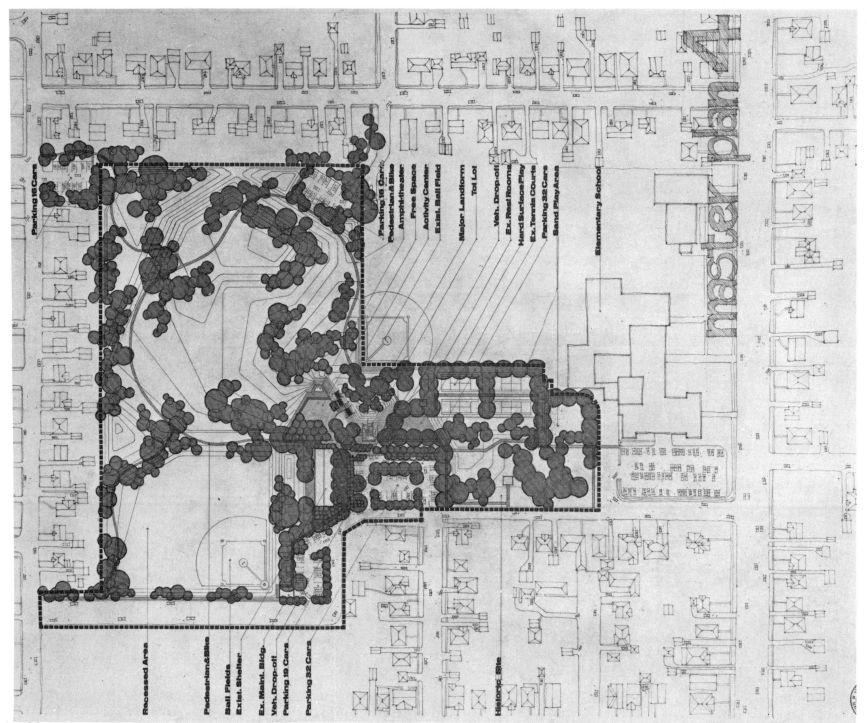

master plan

Parking 16 Cars
Pedestrian & Bike
Amphi-theater
Free Space
Activity Center
Exist. Ball Field
Major Landform
Tot Lot
Veh. Drop-off
Ex. Rest Room
Hard Surface Play
Ex. Tennis Courts
Parking 32 Cars
Sand Play Area

Elementary School

Recessed Area
Pedestrian & Bike
Ball Fields
Exist. Shelter
Ex. Maint. Bldg.
Veh. Drop-off
Parking 19 Cars
Parking 32 Cars

Historic Site

124

Maas and Grassli.

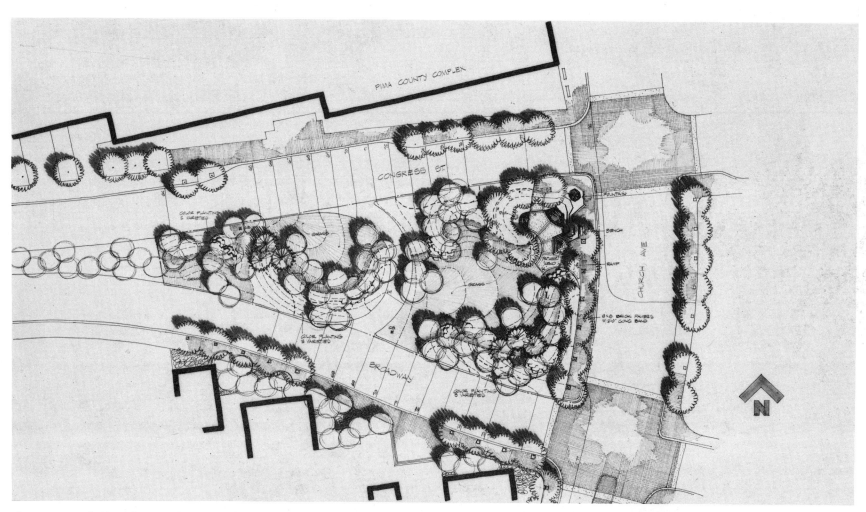

Congress and Church Street Park. EDAW, Inc., by John L. Stevenson.

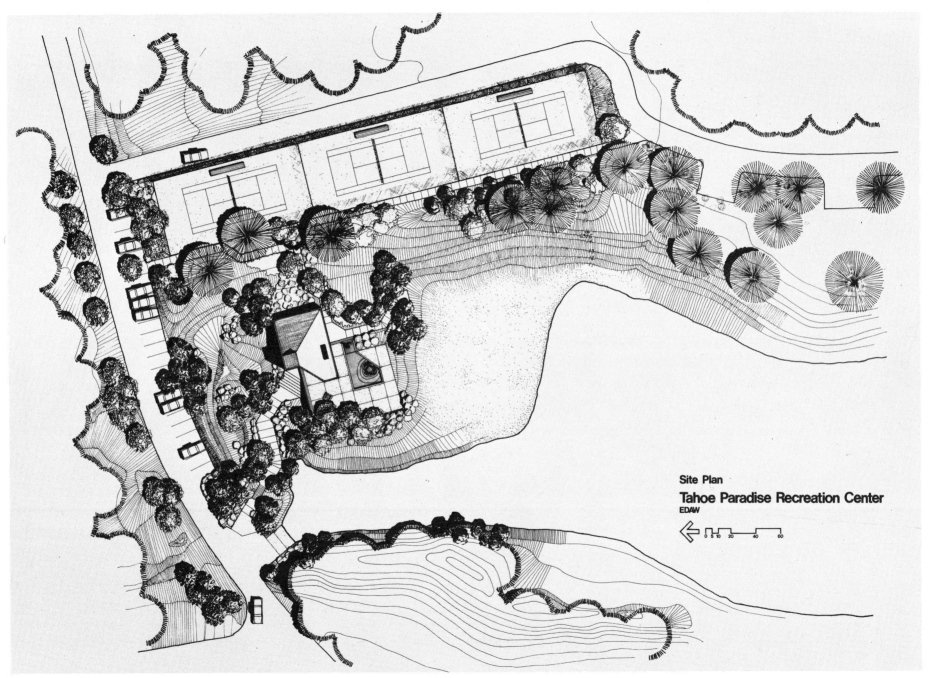

Site Plan
Tahoe Paradise Recreation Center
EDAW

0 5 10   20   40   60

Landscape Design Guide for the Citizens of Pueblo.
EDAW, Inc., by Daniel A. Sudquist.

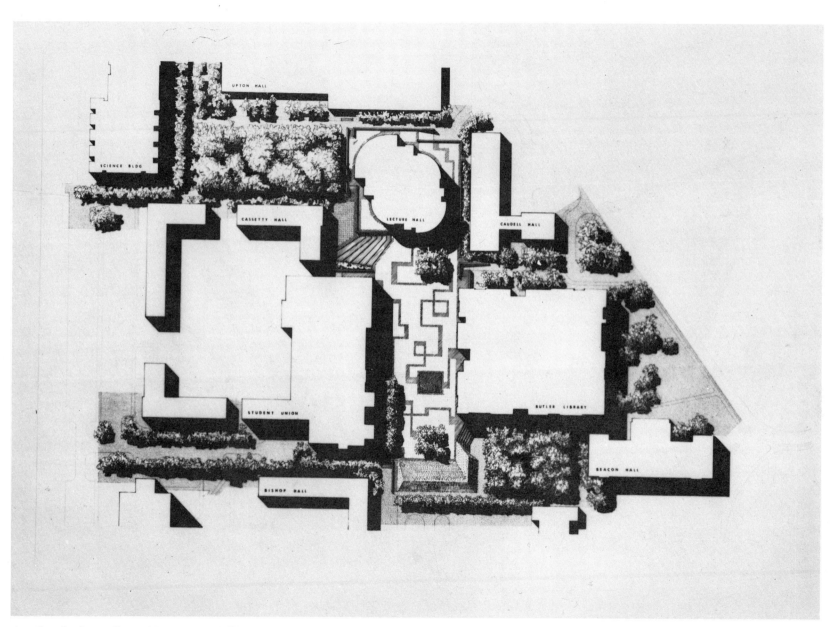

Academic Core, State University College.
A. E. Bye & Associates. Ink on vellum.

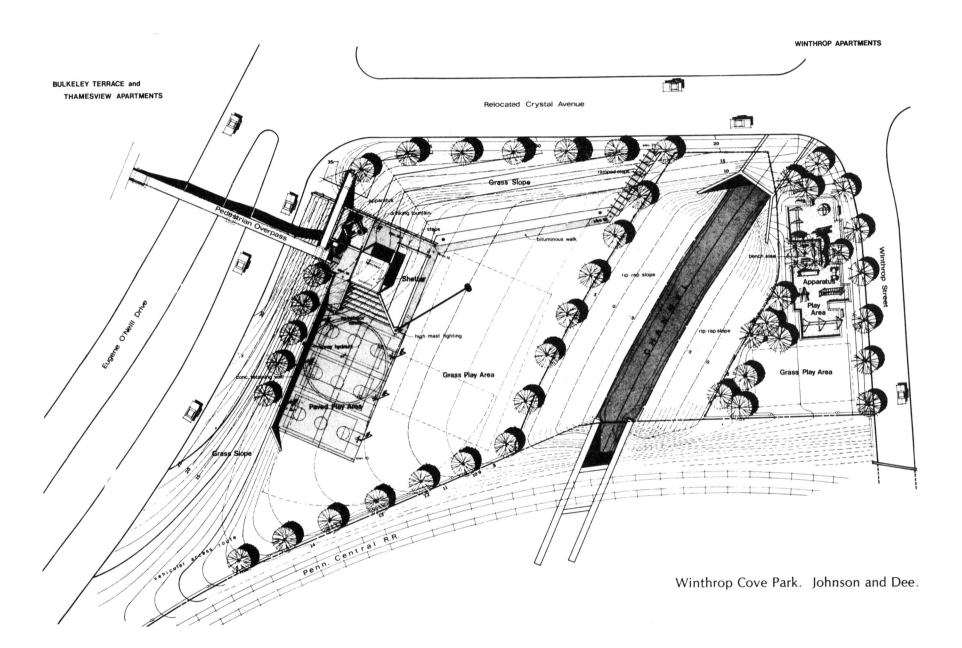

WINTHROP APARTMENTS

BULKELEY TERRACE and
THAMESVIEW APARTMENTS

Relocated Crystal Avenue

Pedestrian Overpass

Eugene O'Neill Drive

Winthrop Street

Grass Slope

ramped steps

apparatus

drinking fountain

bituminous walk

rip-rap slope

bench area

Shelter

high-mast lighting

Apparatus

Play Area

Grass Play Area

Grass Play Area

rip-rap slope

C H A N N E L

Paved Play Area

Grass Slope

Penn Central R.R.

vehicular access route

Winthrop Cove Park.   Johnson and Dee.

128

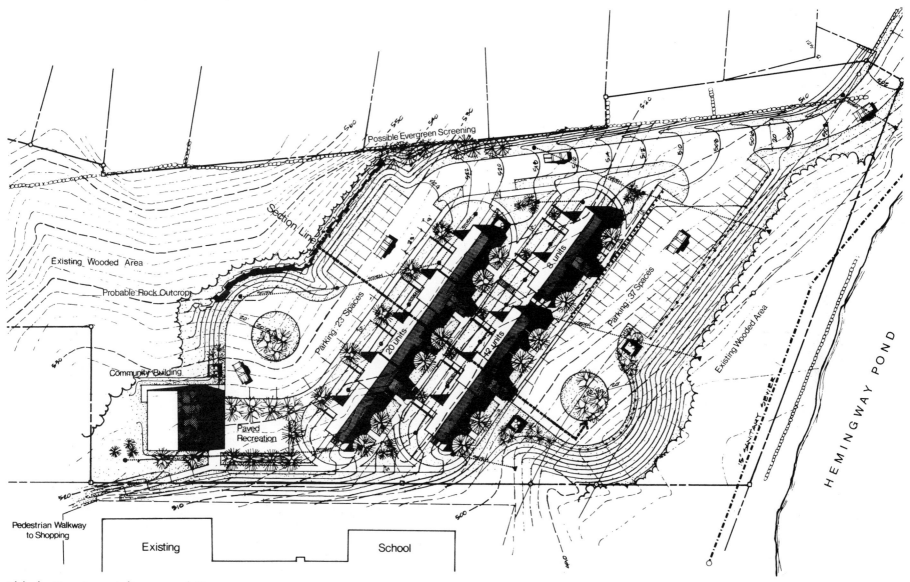

Possible Evergreen Screening

Existing Wooded Area

Probable Rock Outcrop

Section Line

Parking · 23 Spaces

8 units

20 units

12 units

Parking · 37 Spaces

Existing Wooded Area

5" SANITARY SEWER

HEMINGWAY POND

Community Building

Paved Recreation

Pedestrian Walkway to Shopping

Existing

School

Elderly Housing. Johnson and Dee.

129

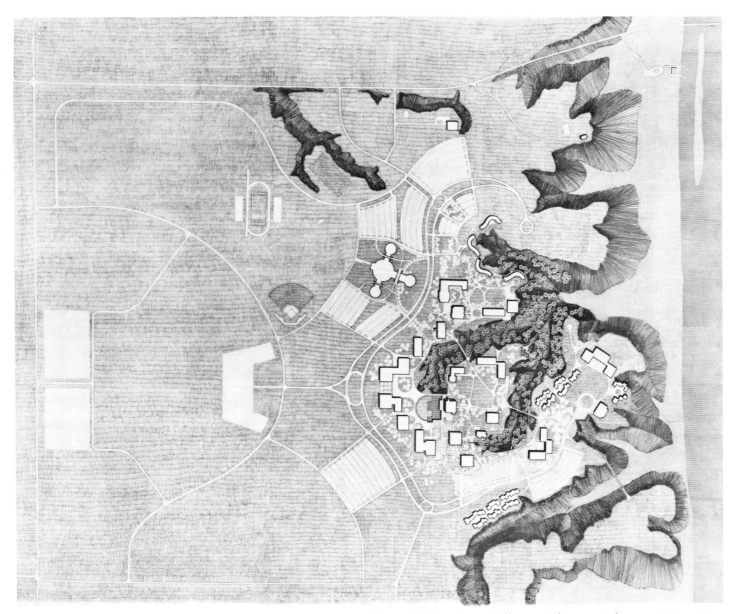

Grand Valley State College. Johnson, Johnson & Roy, Inc.

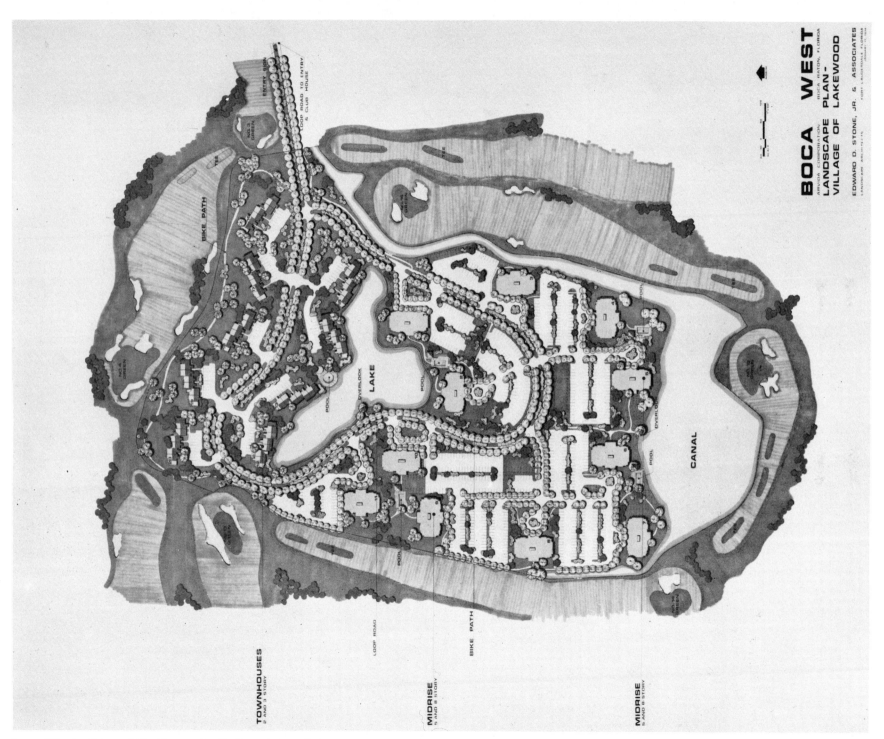

BOCA WEST
ARVIDA CORPORATION
BOCA RATON, FLORIDA
LANDSCAPE PLAN-
VILLAGE OF LAKEWOOD
EDWARD D. STONE, JR. & ASSOCIATES
LANDSCAPE ARCHITECTS
FORT LAUDERDALE, FLORIDA

Boca West. Edward D. Stone, Jr. & Associates, P.A.

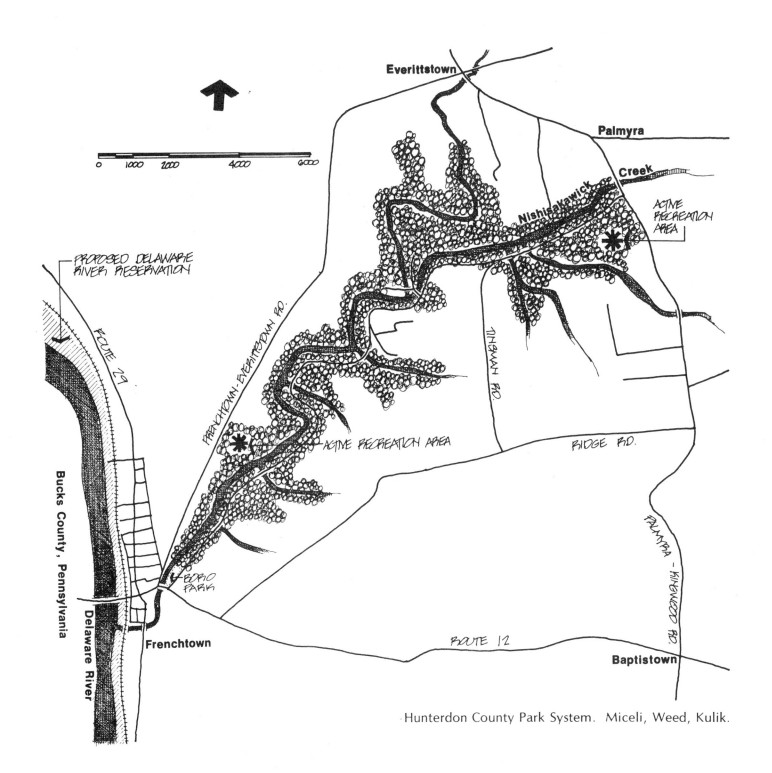

Everittstown

Palmyra

Creek

Nishisakawick

ACTIVE RECREATION AREA

PROPOSED DELAWARE RIVER RESERVATION

FRENCHTOWN-EVERITTSTOWN RD.

ROUTE 29

TINSMAH RD.

ACTIVE RECREATION AREA

RIDGE RD.

PALMYRA-KINGWOOD RD.

Bucks County, Pennsylvania

BORO PARK

Delaware River

ROUTE 12

Frenchtown

Baptistown

0   1000   2000   4000   6000

Hunterdon County Park System.   Miceli, Weed, Kulik.

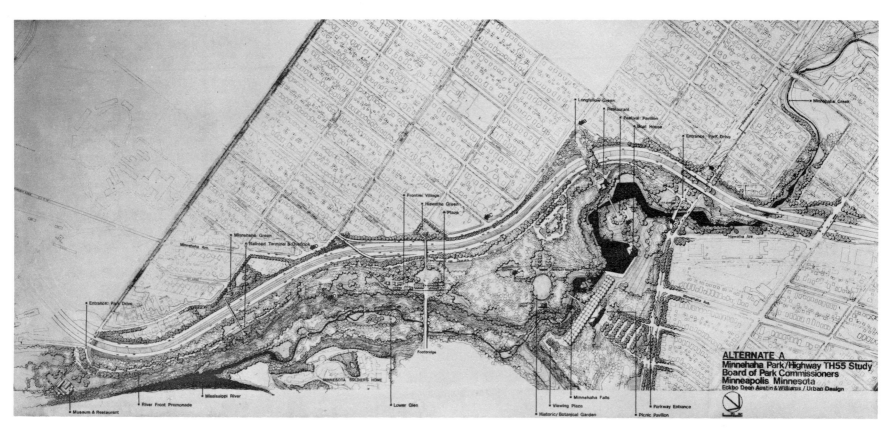

Minnehaha Park. EDAW, Inc., by Charles M. McCulloch.

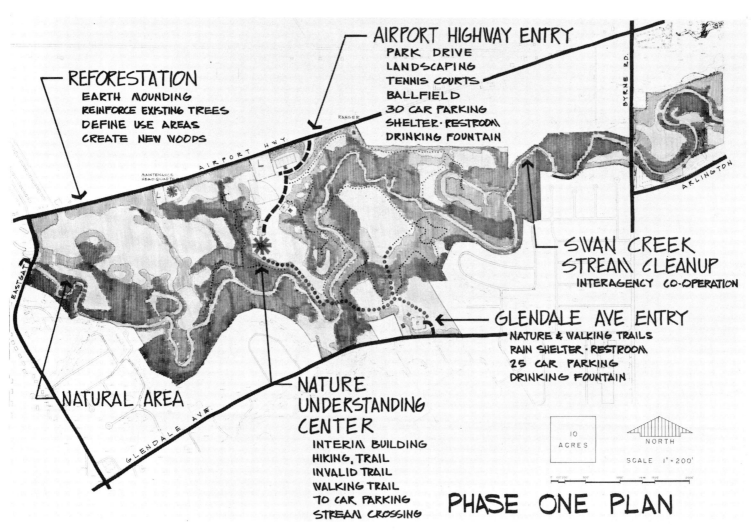

REFORESTATION
EARTH MOUNDING
REINFORCE EXISTING TREES
DEFINE USE AREAS
CREATE NEW WOODS

AIRPORT HIGHWAY ENTRY
PARK DRIVE
LANDSCAPING
TENNIS COURTS
BALLFIELD
30 CAR PARKING
SHELTER · RESTROOM
DRINKING FOUNTAIN

SWAN CREEK STREAM CLEANUP
INTERAGENCY CO-OPERATION

GLENDALE AVE ENTRY
NATURE & WALKING TRAILS
RAIN SHELTER · RESTROOM
25 CAR PARKING
DRINKING FOUNTAIN

NATURAL AREA

NATURE UNDERSTANDING CENTER
INTERIM BUILDING
HIKING TRAIL
INVALID TRAIL
WALKING TRAIL
70 CAR PARKING
STREAM CROSSING

10 ACRES

NORTH

SCALE 1" = 200'

PHASE ONE PLAN

Swan Creek Metro Park. The Collaborative, Inc.

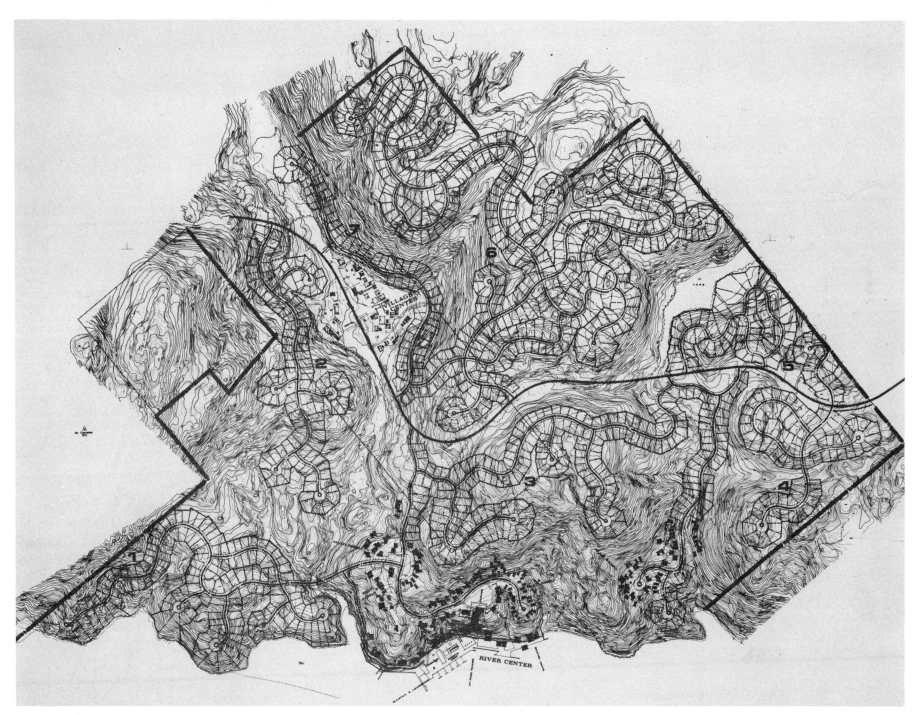

Conner Planned Community. Reimann-Buechner Partnership.

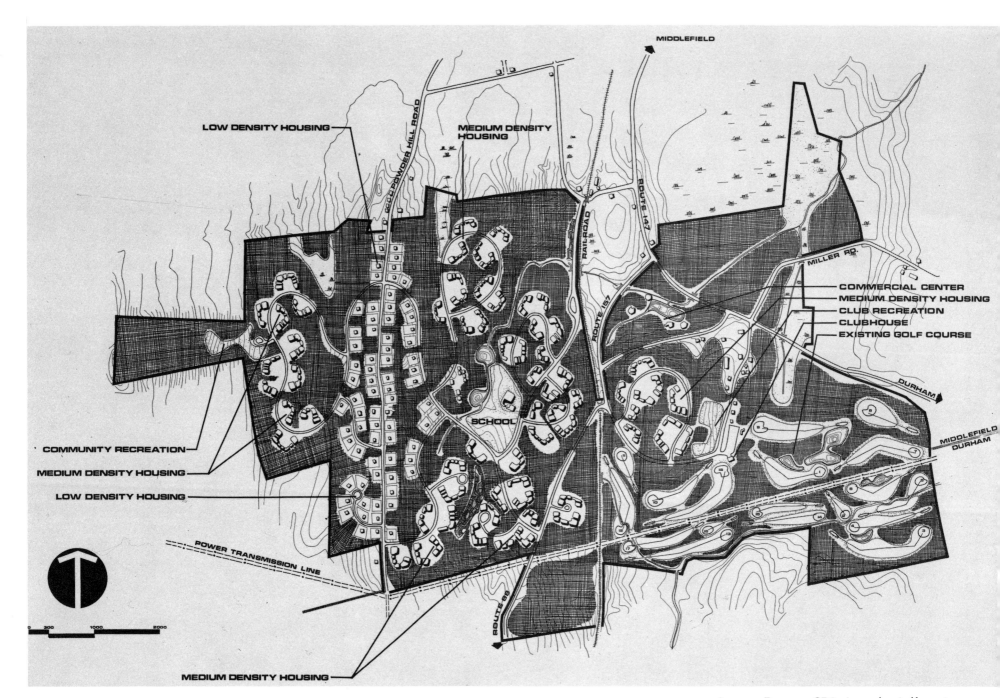

LOW DENSITY HOUSING

MEDIUM DENSITY HOUSING

MIDDLEFIELD

RED POWDER HILL ROAD

RAILROAD

ROUTE 147

ROUTE 157

MILLER RD.

COMMERCIAL CENTER
MEDIUM DENSITY HOUSING
CLUB RECREATION
CLUBHOUSE
EXISTING GOLF COURSE

DURHAM

MIDDLEFIELD
DURHAM

SCHOOL

COMMUNITY RECREATION

MEDIUM DENSITY HOUSING

LOW DENSITY HOUSING

POWER TRANSMISSION LINE

ROUTE 68

MEDIUM DENSITY HOUSING

0 300   1000   2000

136

Lyman Farms. CR3, Inc., by Jeffrey A.
Gebrian. Client: William McHugh, Architect

West Valley Land Plan. Perkins & Will, Inc.

5

FREEHAND PLANS

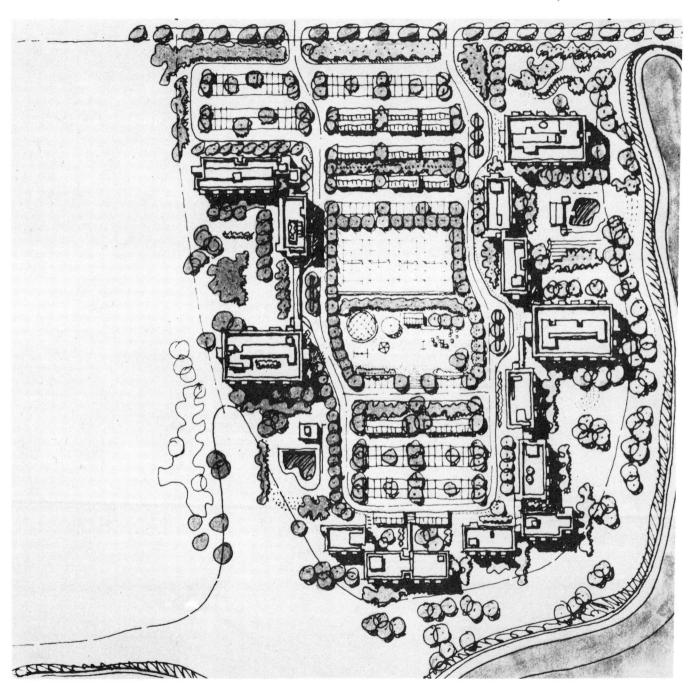

The Hammocks. Sasaki, Dawson, DeMay Associates, Inc., by Frank James.

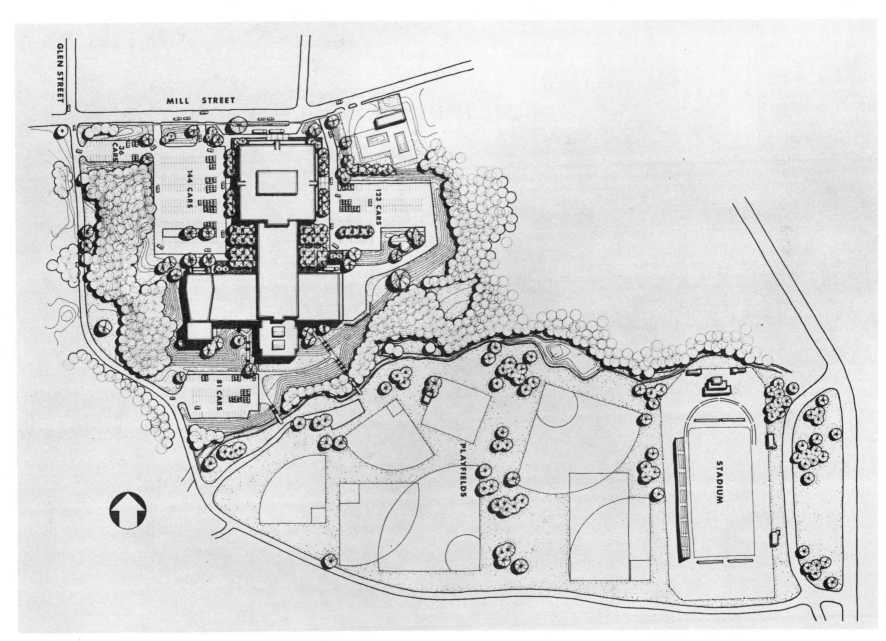

New Britain Senior High School. CR3, Inc., by Jeffrey A.
Gebrian. Client: Hirsch, Kaestle Boos, Architects.

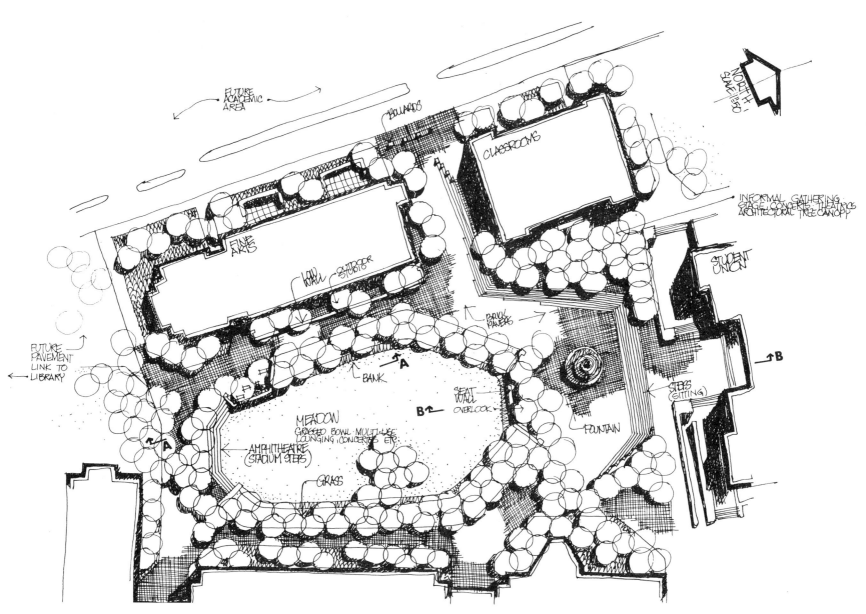

FUTURE ACADEMIC AREA

BOLLARDS

CLASSROOMS

NORTH SCALE 1":50

INFORMAL GATHERING STAGE CONCERTS THEATRICS ARCHITECTURAL TREE CANOPY

FINE ARTS

WALL

OUTDOOR STUDIO

STUDENT UNION

BRICK PAVERS

FUTURE PAVEMENT LINK TO LIBRARY

A

BANK

↑B

SEAT WALL OVERLOOK

B

STEPS (SITTING)

FOUNTAIN

MEADOW GRASSED BOWL MULTI-USE LOUNGING CONCERTS ETC

A

AMPHITHEATRE (STADIUM STEPS)

GRASS

142

Student Center Mall. Miceli, Weed, Kulik.

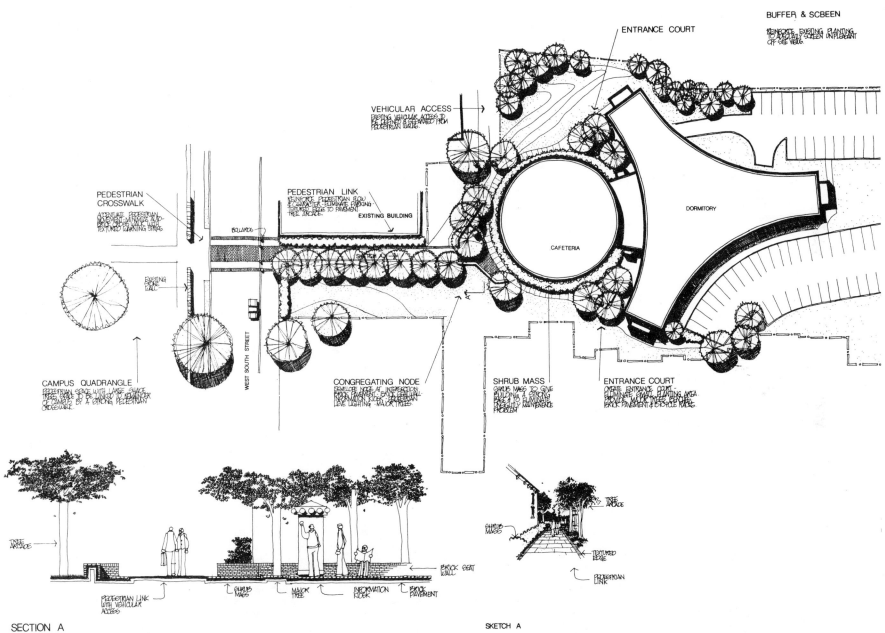

SECTION A
Wilkes College. Miceli, Weed, Kulik.

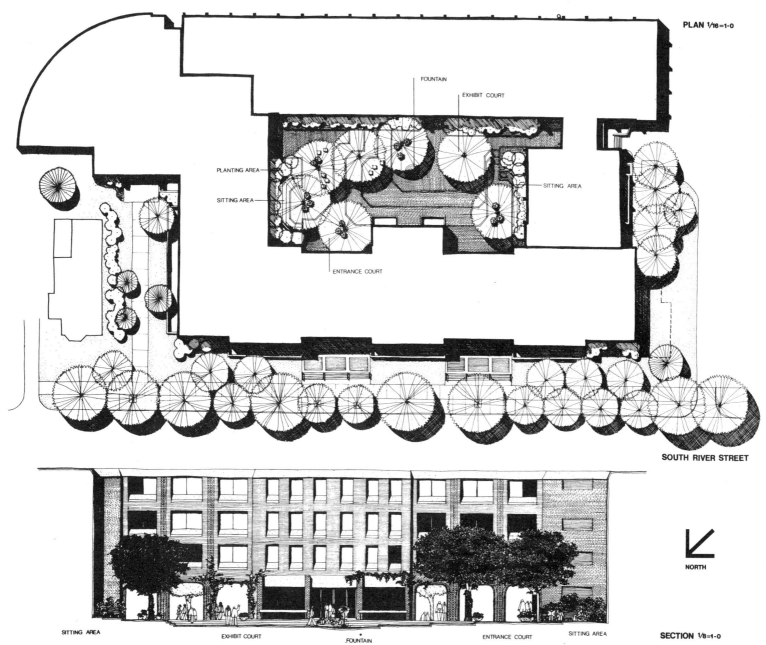

PLAN 1/16=1-0

FOUNTAIN

EXHIBIT COURT

PLANTING AREA

SITTING AREA

SITTING AREA

ENTRANCE COURT

SOUTH RIVER STREET

NORTH

SITTING AREA

EXHIBIT COURT

FOUNTAIN

ENTRANCE COURT

SITTING AREA

SECTION 1/8=1-0

Wilkes College.   Miceli, Weed, Kulik.

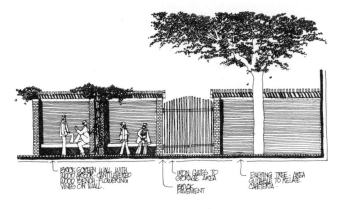

SERVICE ENTRY

SOUTH FRANKLIN STREET

LIBRARY COURT

LIBRARY

EXISTING
BUILDING

ENTRANCE PORTICO
MAJOR ENTRANCE TO LIBRARY.
INCREASE IMPORTANCE BY EXTENDING
ENTRY DEVELOPMENT INTO SPACE.
(USE OF STEPS & SITTING STEPS)

SCREEN & BUFFER
TO CONTAIN SPACE VISUALLY.
PROVIDE AREA FOR OUTDOOR
STORAGE. SITTING, AND SCALE -
SCREEN PLANTING.

SCREEN & BUFFER

STORAGE
AREA BETWEEN PROPOSED
SCREEN WALL & EXISTING
SUITABLE FOR STORAGE

ELEVATION A

RESIDENCE

CHURCH

ROOFTOP
POTENTIAL UTILIZATION FOR
RAISED SITTING TERRACE -
EXTENSION OF CAFETERIA.

CAFETERIA
POTENTIAL EXTENSION
OF FUNCTION TO THE
OUT OF DOORS.

NOTES
REMOVE SPACE CLUTTERING ELEMENTS
PROVIDE SCREEN WALL - FENCES TO
PROVIDE A UNIFIED GATHERING SPACE
FOR USE AS OUTDOOR STUDY ROOM-
THEATRICS.

PEDESTRIAN ENTRANCE
APPROPRIATE ENTRANCE INTO RESERVOIR
SPACE. GOOD SCALE & CHARACTER. POINT
OF ENTRY GOOD IN RELATION TO MOVE-
MENT THRU SPACE.

ELEVATION   A

BRICK SCREEN WALL WITH
WOOD ARBOR CANTILEVERED
BRICK TRENCH. FLOWERING
VINES ON WALL.

IRON GATES TO
STORAGE AREA.
BRICK
PAVEMENT

EXISTING TREE: AREA
SUITABLE TO RELATE
CAFETERIA.

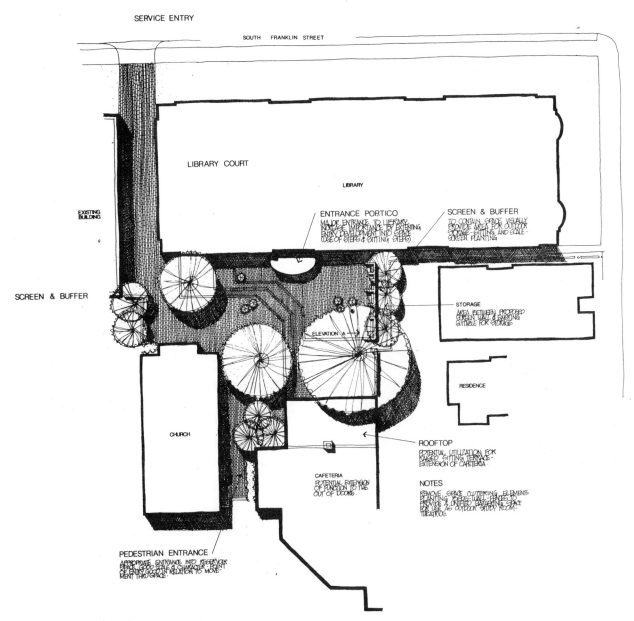

Wilkes College. Miceli, Weed, Kulik.

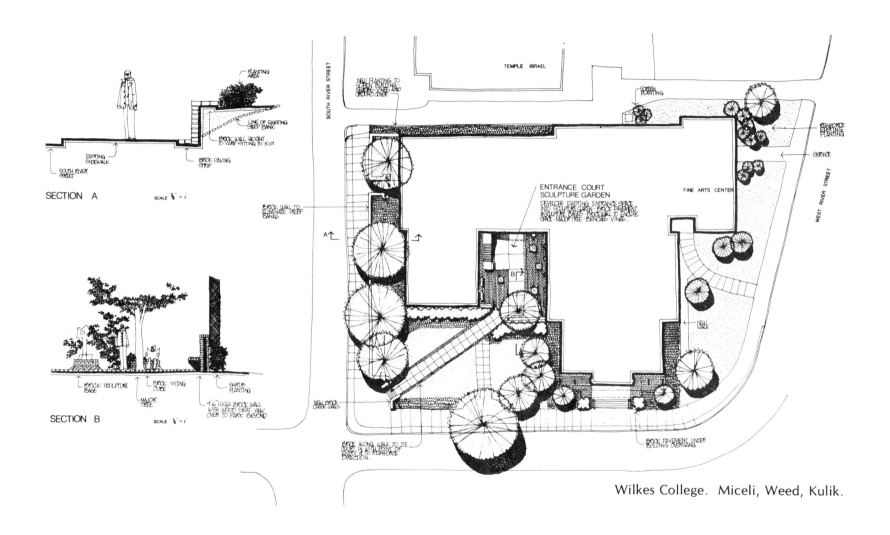

SECTION A   SCALE ⅜" = 1'

PLANTING AREA

LINE OF EXISTING STEEP BANK

BRICK WALL HEIGHT TO VARY SITTING TO 3'0"

BRICK PAVING STRIP

EXISTING SIDEWALK

SOUTH RIVER STREET

SECTION B   SCALE ⅛" = 1'

BRICK SCULPTURE BASE

MAJOR TREE

BRICK SITTING CURB

SHRUB PLANTING

4'6" HIGH BRICK WALL WITH WOOD SEAT. VIEW OVER TO PARK BEYOND.

TEMPLE ISRAEL

SOUTH RIVER STREET

WEST RIVER STREET

NEW PLANTING TO SCREEN BUILDING CLIMBING VINES AND GROUND COVER

SCREEN PLANTING

REINFORCE EXISTING PLANTING

SERVICE

ENTRANCE COURT SCULPTURE GARDEN

DEVELOP EXISTING ENTRANCE SPACE INTO SCULPTURE GARDEN. BRICK PAVEMENT, SCULPTURE BASES PROPORTIONAL TO ENCLOSE SPACE. MAJOR TREE. BENCHES. VINES.

FINE ARTS CENTER

BRICK WALL TO ELIMINATE STEEP BANK

NEW WALK

NEW BRICK GARDEN WALLS

BRICK ALONG WALK TO TIE COURT TO ENTRY. SHIFT PATTERN OF DIRECTION.

BRICK PAVEMENT UNDER BUILDING OVERHANG

Wilkes College. Miceli, Weed, Kulik.

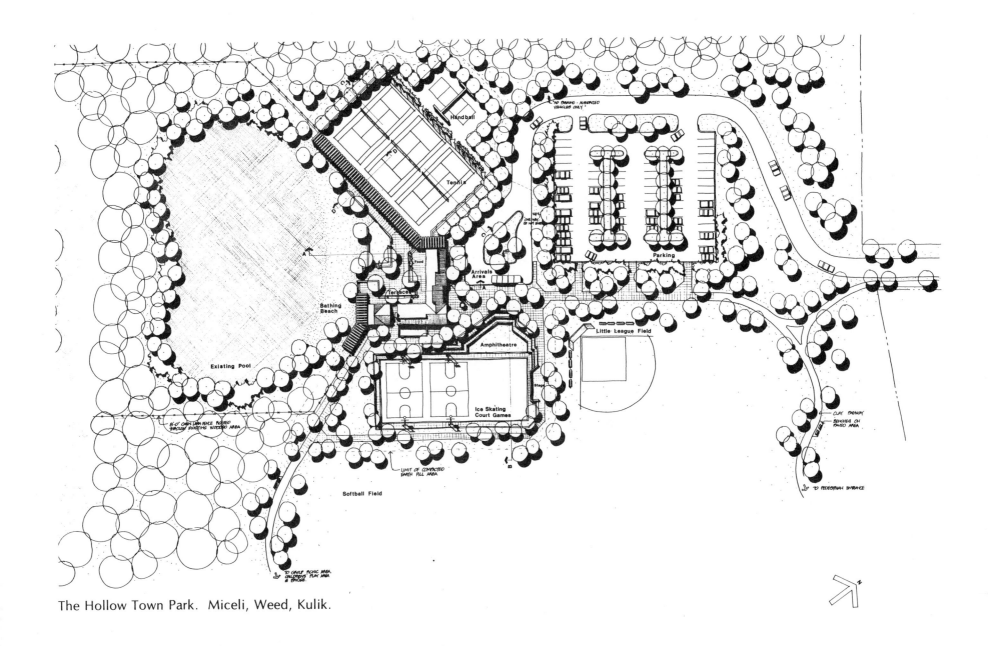

The Hollow Town Park. Miceli, Weed, Kulik.

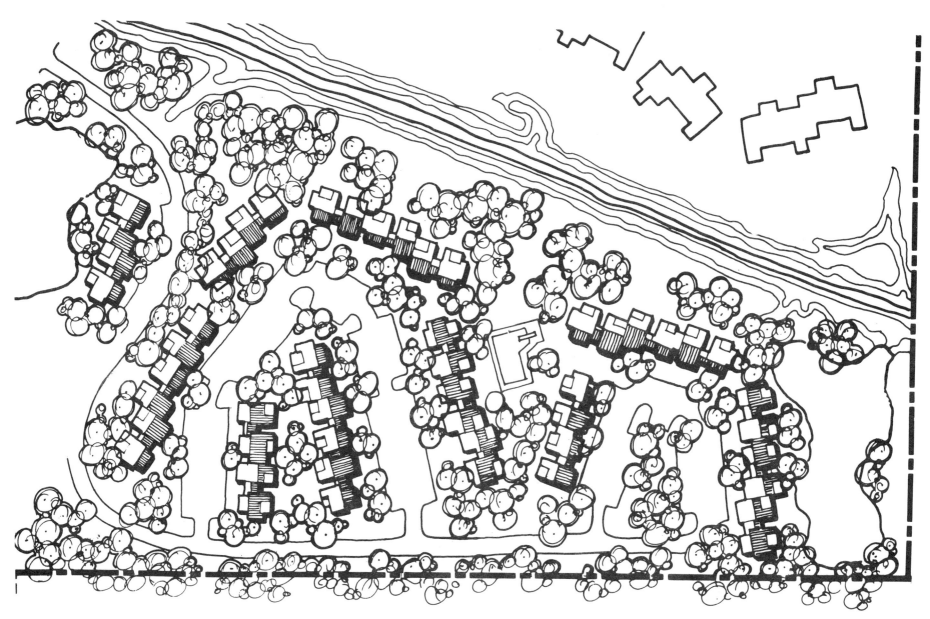

Reynolds, Smith and Hills, by David Linstrum. Ink on mylar.

Reynolds, Smith and Hills, by David Linstrum. Ink on mylar.

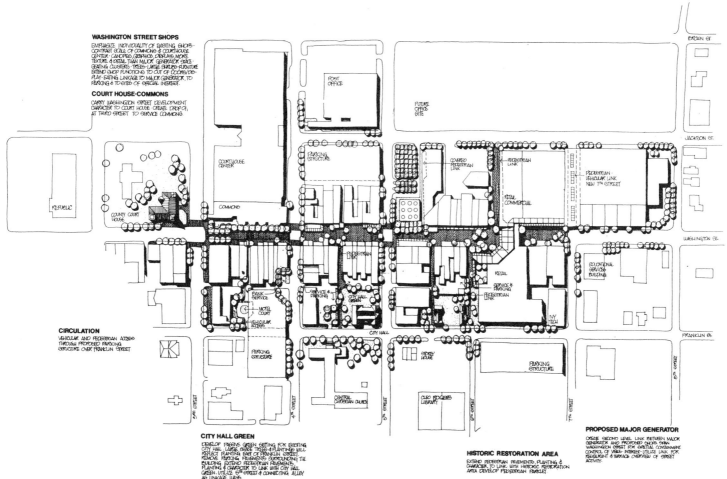

WASHINGTON STREET SHOPS

EMPHASIZE INDIVIDUALITY OF EXISTING SHOPS. CONTRAST SCALE OF COMMONS & COURTHOUSE CENTER. CANOPIES, GRAPHICS, DISPLAYS, MORE TEXTURE & DETAIL THAN MAJOR GENERATOR SPACE. SEATING CLUSTERS. TREES. LARGE BURLAPS. FURNITURE. EXTEND SHOP FUNCTIONS TO OUT OF DOORS, DISPLAY, EATING. LINKAGE TO MAJOR GENERATOR, TO PARKING & TO SITES OF SPECIAL INTEREST.

COURT HOUSE-COMMONS

CARRY WASHINGTON STREET DEVELOPMENT CHARACTER TO COURT HOUSE. CREATE DROP OF AT THIRD STREET TO SERVICE COMMONS.

CIRCULATION

VEHICULAR AND PEDESTRIAN ACCESS THROUGH PROPOSED PARKING STRUCTURE OVER FRANKLIN STREET.

CITY HALL GREEN

DEVELOP PASSIVE GREEN SETTING FOR EXISTING CITY HALL. LARGE SHADE TREES & PLANTING WILL REFLECT PLANTING EAST OF FRANKLIN STREET. REMOVE PARKING PAVEMENTS SURROUNDING THE BUILDING. EXTEND PEDESTRIAN PAVEMENTS, PLANTING & CHARACTER TO LINK WITH CITY HALL GREEN. UTILIZE 5TH STREET & CONNECTING ALLEY AS LINKAGE WAYS.

HISTORIC RESTORATION AREA

EXTEND PEDESTRIAN PAVEMENTS, PLANTING & CHARACTER TO LINK WITH HISTORIC RESTORATION AREA. DEVELOP PEDESTRIAN PASSAGE.

PROPOSED MAJOR GENERATOR

CREATE SECOND LEVEL LINK BETWEEN MAJOR GENERATOR AND PROPOSED SHOPS. SPAN WASHINGTON STREET FOR SPATIAL CONTAINMENT. CONTROL OF VIEWS, INTEREST. UTILIZE LINK FOR RESTAURANT & TERRACE OVERVIEW OF STREET ACTIVITY.

The Washington Street Project. Miceli, Weed, Kulik.

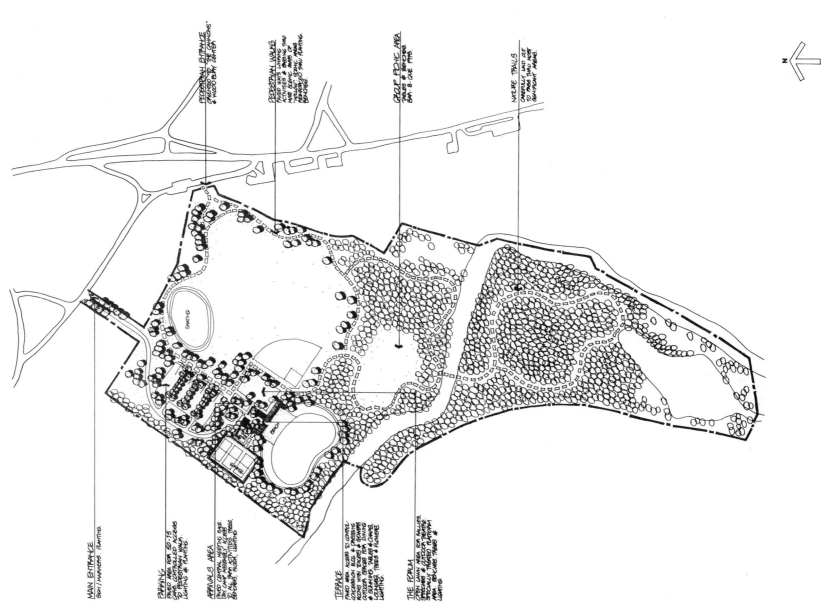

The Hollow Town Park. Miceli, Weed, Kulik.

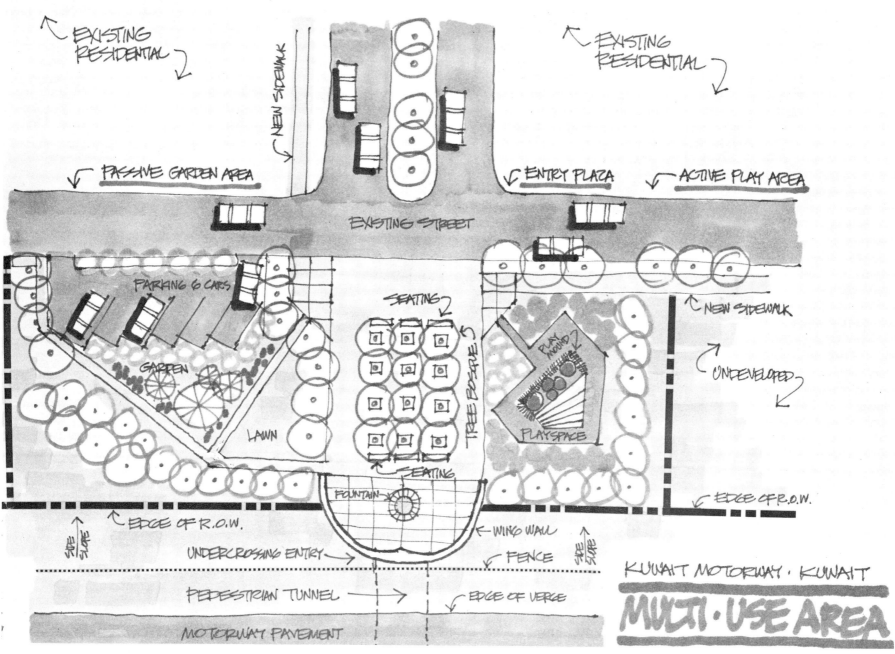

EXISTING RESIDENTIAL

EXISTING RESIDENTIAL

NEW SIDEWALK

PASSIVE GARDEN AREA

ENTRY PLAZA

ACTIVE PLAY AREA

EXISTING STREET

NEW SIDEWALK

PARKING 6 CARS

SEATING

UNDEVELOPED

GARDEN

TREE BOSQUE

PLAY MOUND

LAWN

PLAYSPACE

SEATING

FOUNTAIN

EDGE OF R.O.W.

EDGE OF R.O.W.

WING WALL

SIDE SLOPE

FENCE

SIDE SLOPE

UNDERCROSSING ENTRY

KUWAIT MOTORWAY · KUWAIT

PEDESTRIAN TUNNEL

EDGE OF VERGE

MULTI·USE AREA

MOTORWAY PAVEMENT

DeLeuw, Cather International, by David Linstrum.
Multi-colored, using broad and narrow point markers.

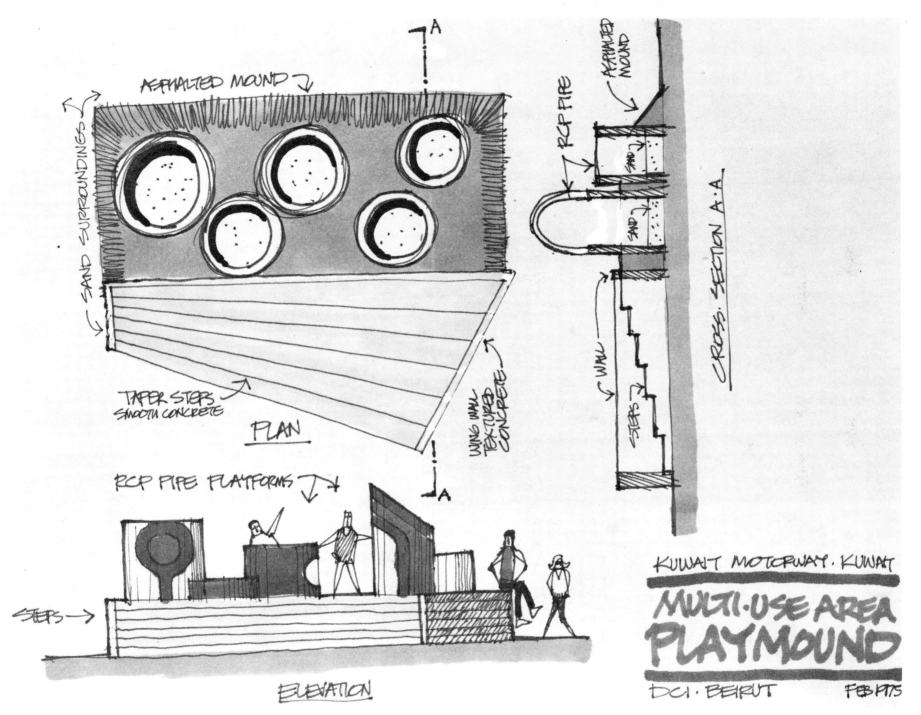

ASPHALTED MOUND

SAND SURROUNDINGS

A

TAPER STEPS
SMOOTH CONCRETE

PLAN

WING WALL
TEXTURED CONCRETE

RCP PIPE PLATFORMS

STEPS →

ELEVATION

A

RCP PIPE

ASPHALTED MOUND

ASPHALTED MOUND

SAND

SAND

WALL

STEPS

CROSS SECTION A·A

KUWAIT MOTORWAY · KUWAIT

MULTI·USE AREA
PLAYMOUND

DCI · BEIRUT   FEB 1975

DeLeuw, Cather International, by David Linstrum.
Multi-colored, using broad and narrow point markers.

153

FULL SIZE PLANS

Lone Cove. Edward D. Stone, Jr. & Associates, P.A.

LOCOS

PLAZA BOLIVAR

TIENDAS

TIOVIVO

LAGO GURI

BARCO PIRATA

CERVECERÍA

CASA EMBRUJADA

ISLA MARGA

LAGO MARACAIBO

VILLA MARACAIBO

TIRO AL BLANCO

PASEO DEL AMAZONAS

MARIONETAS

Theme Park. Edward D. Stone, Jr. & Associates, P.A.

ZOOLOGICO INFANTIL

TIENDAS

Theme Park. Edward D. Stone, Jr. & Associates, P.A.

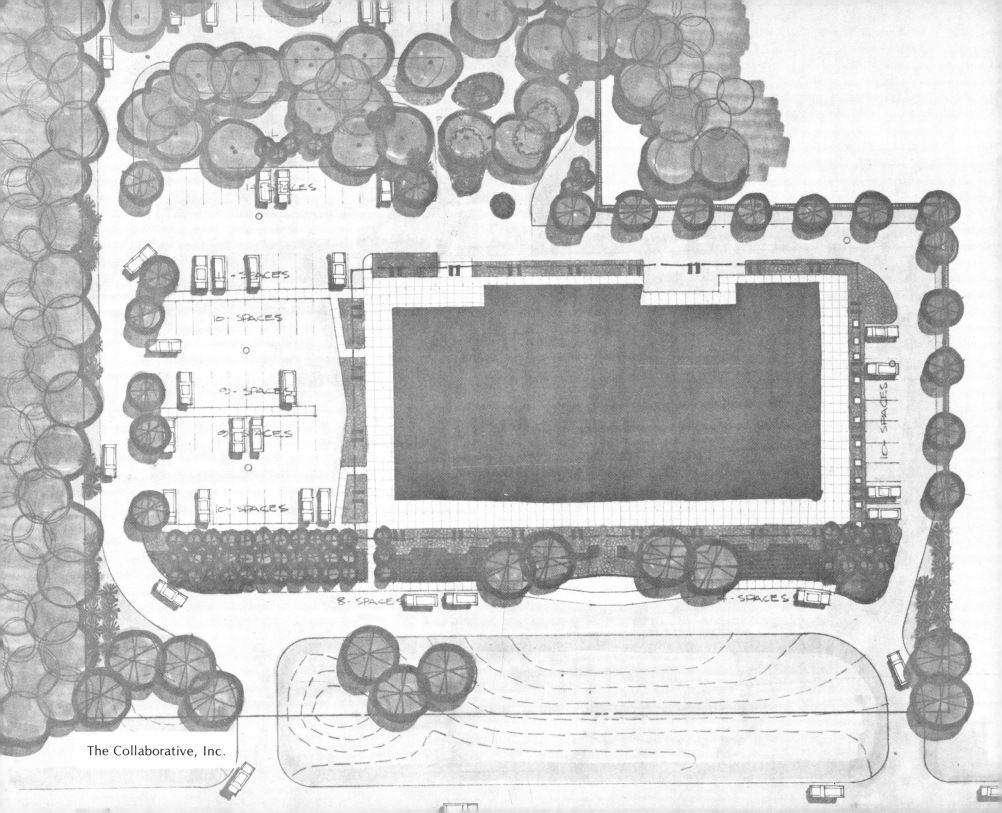

The Collaborative, Inc.

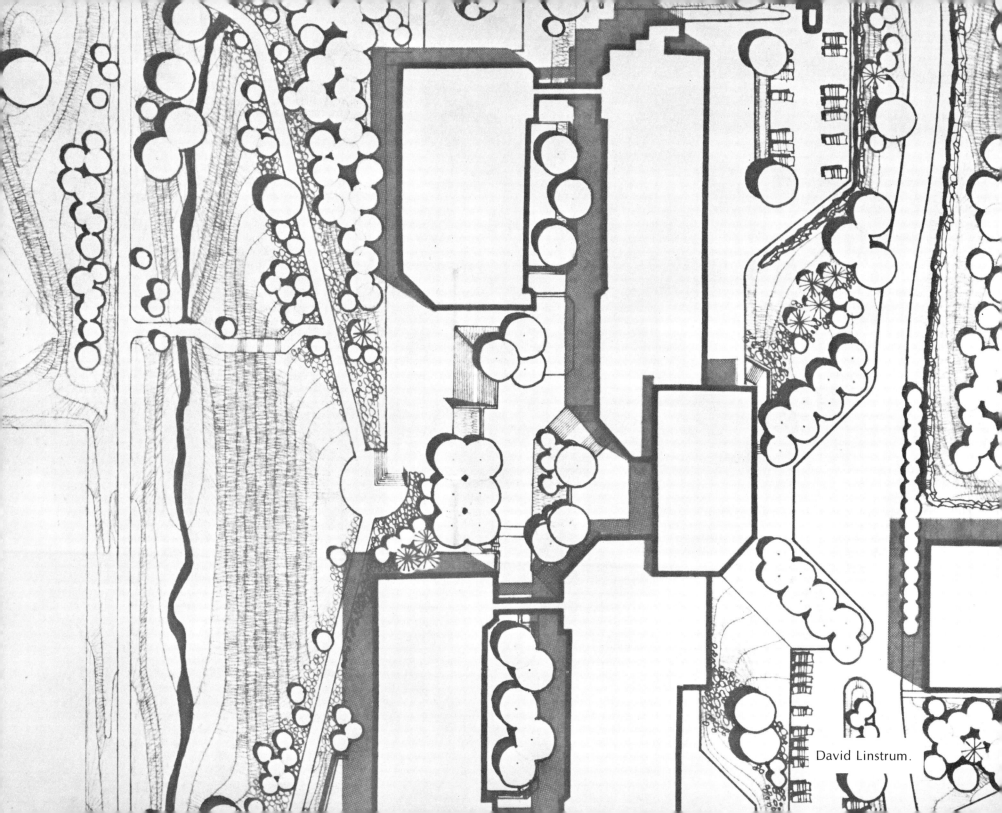

David Linstrum.

David Linstrum.

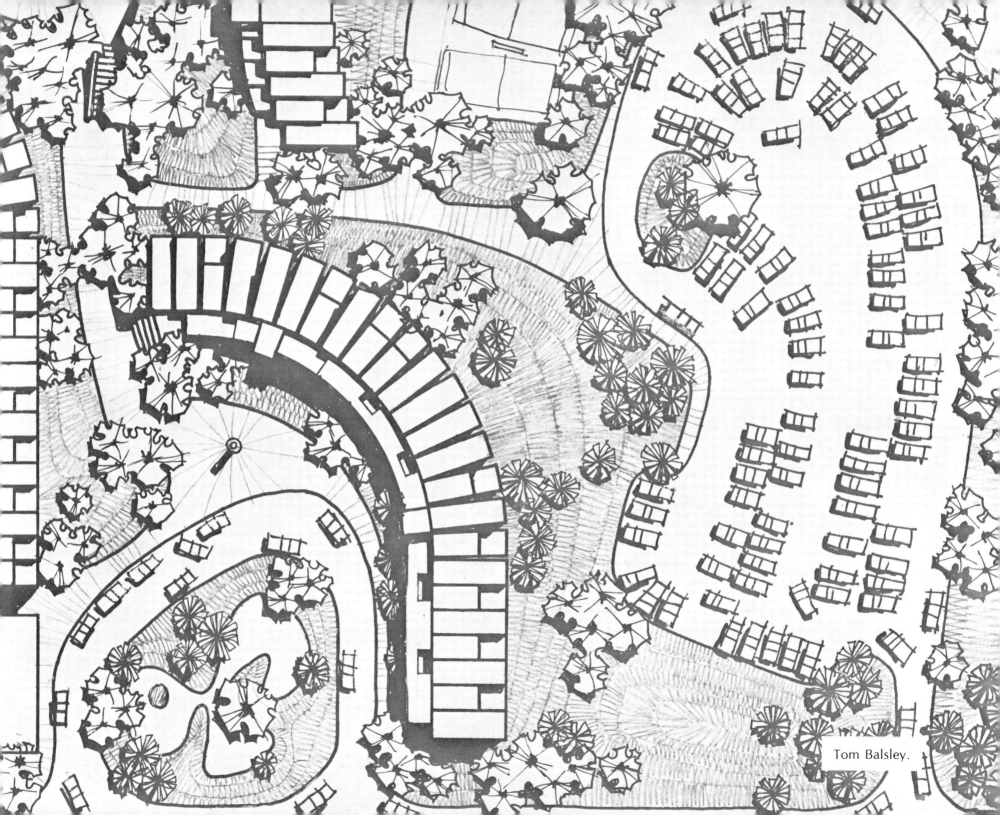

Tom Balsley.

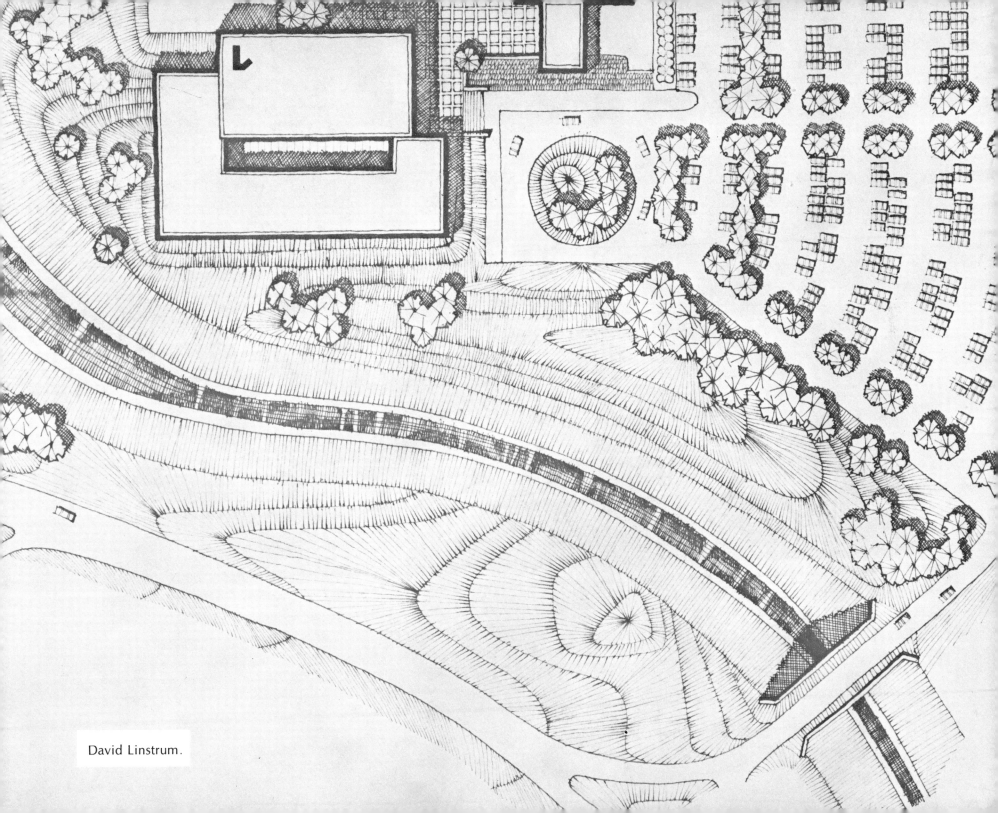

David Linstrum.

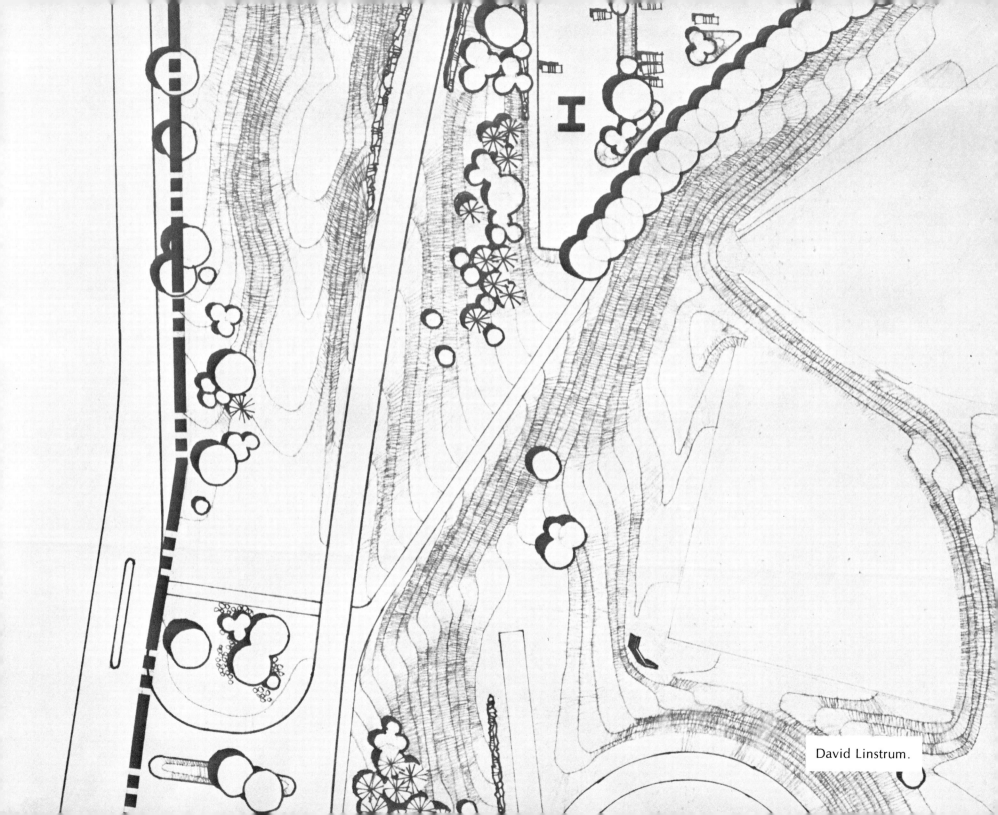

David Linstrum.

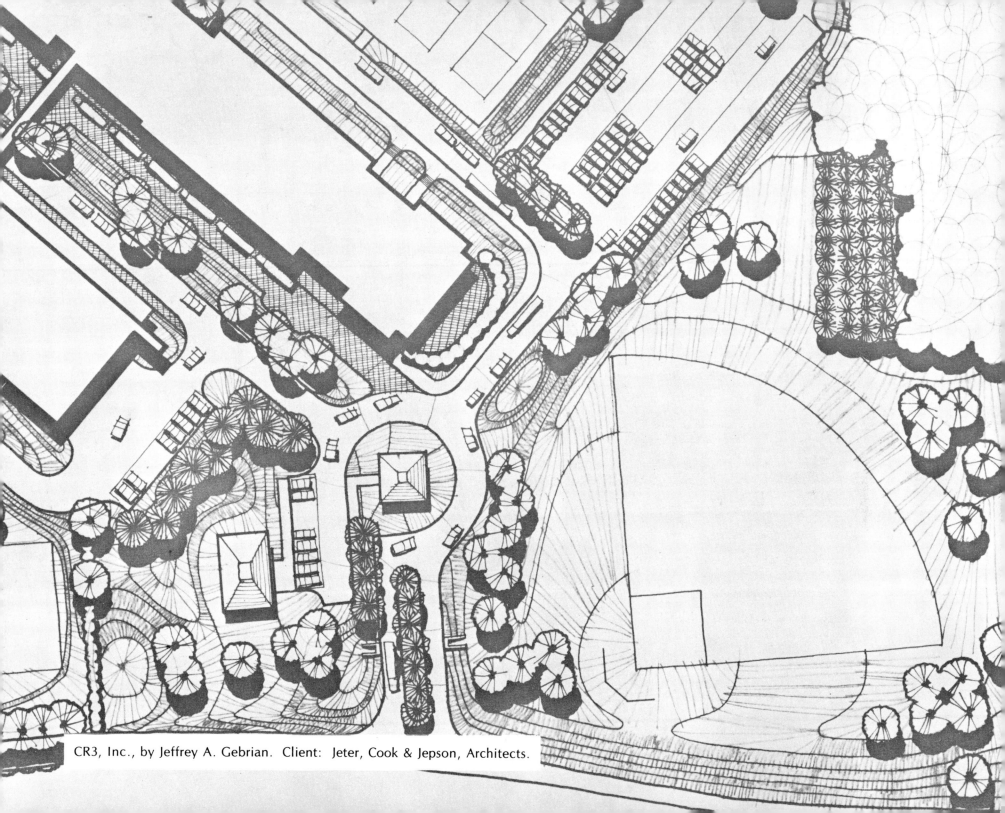

CR3, Inc., by Jeffrey A. Gebrian. Client: Jeter, Cook & Jepson, Architects.

Bristol Harbour. The Reimann-Buechner Partnership, by Cortland Read.

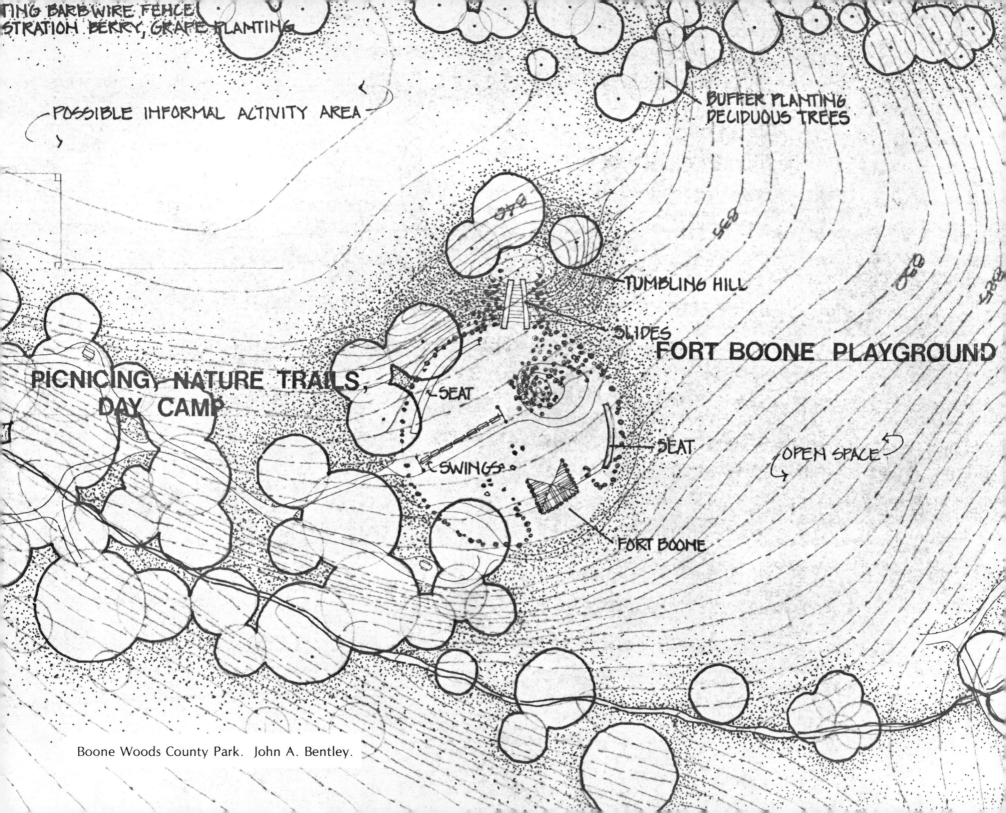

EXISTING BARBWIRE FENCE,
STRATION BERRY, GRAPE PLANTING

POSSIBLE INFORMAL ACTIVITY AREA

BUFFER PLANTING
DECIDUOUS TREES

TUMBLING HILL

SLIDES

FORT BOONE PLAYGROUND

PICNICING, NATURE TRAILS,
DAY CAMP

SEAT

SEAT

OPEN SPACE

SWINGS

FORT BOONE

Boone Woods County Park. John A. Bentley.

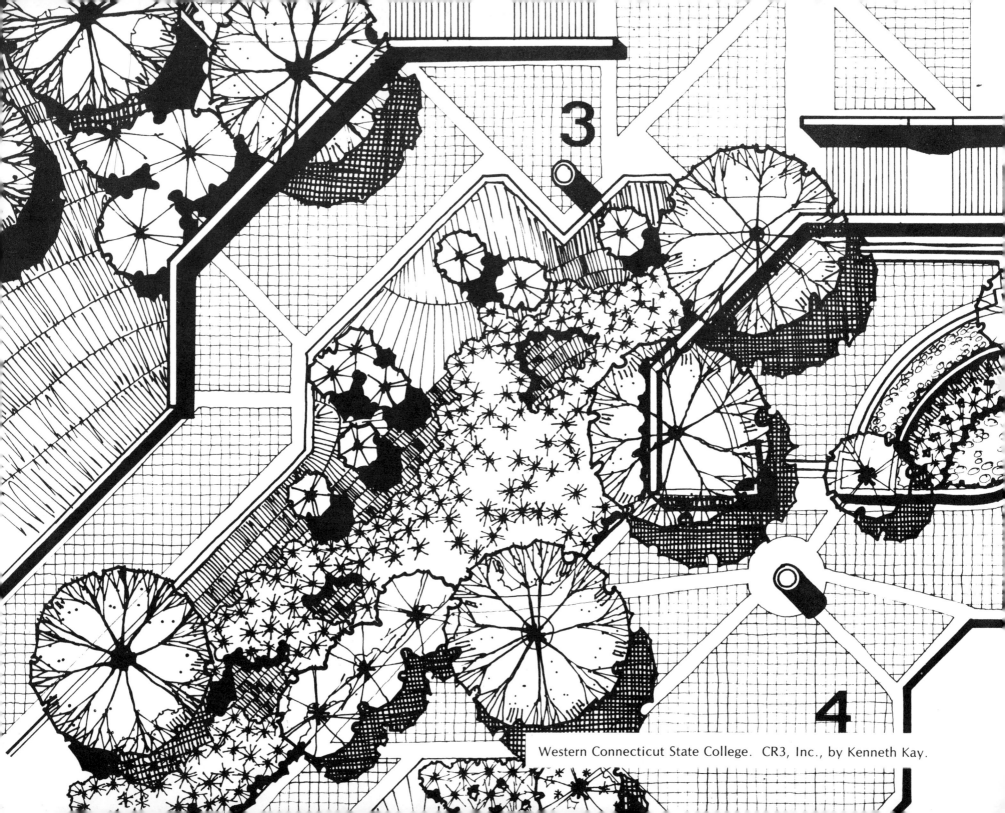

Western Connecticut State College. CR3, Inc., by Kenneth Kay.

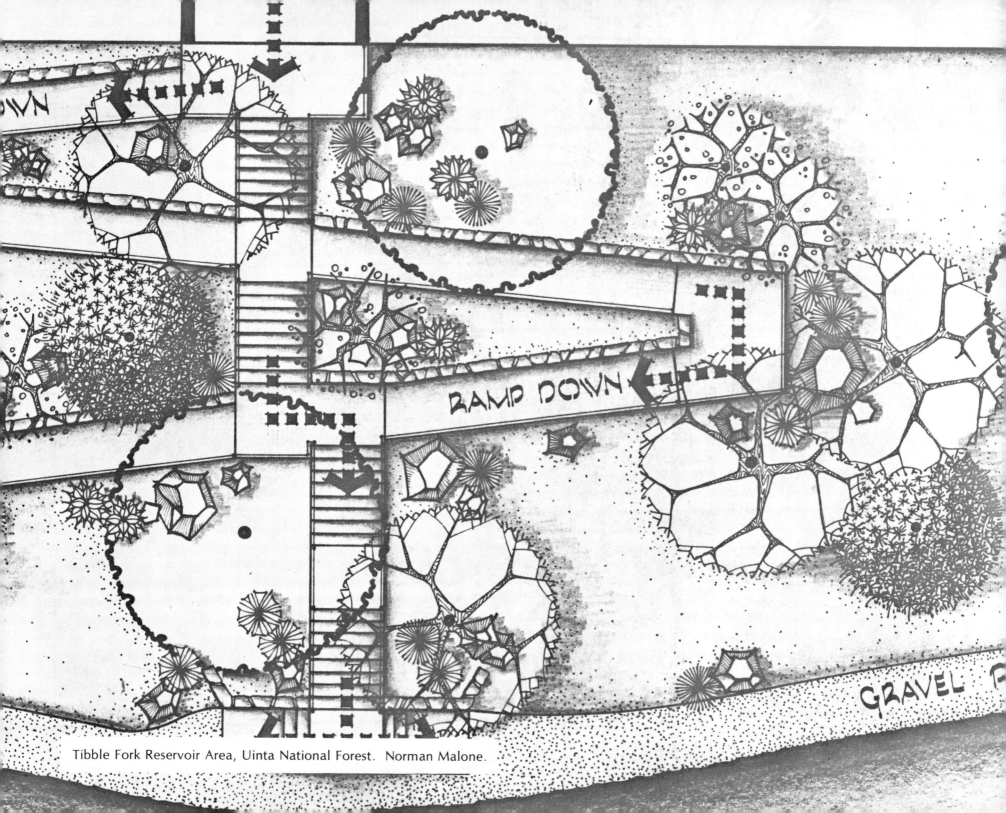

Tibble Fork Reservoir Area, Uinta National Forest. Norman Malone.

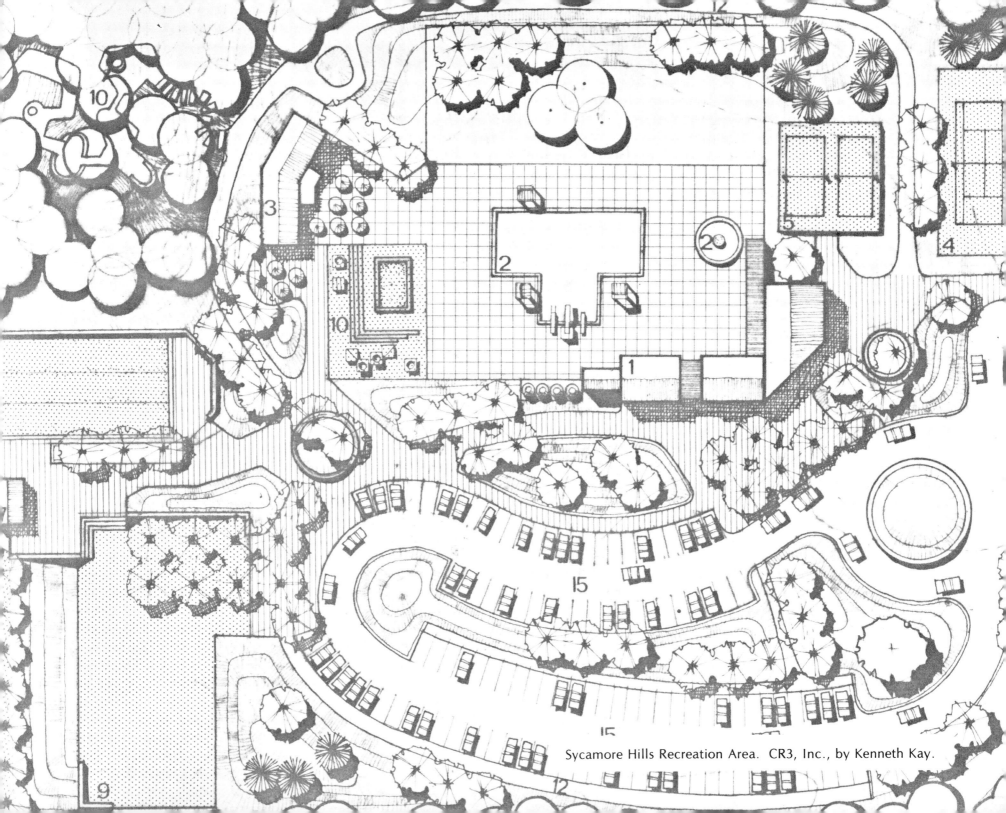

Sycamore Hills Recreation Area. CR3, Inc., by Kenneth Kay.

Chris Macey.

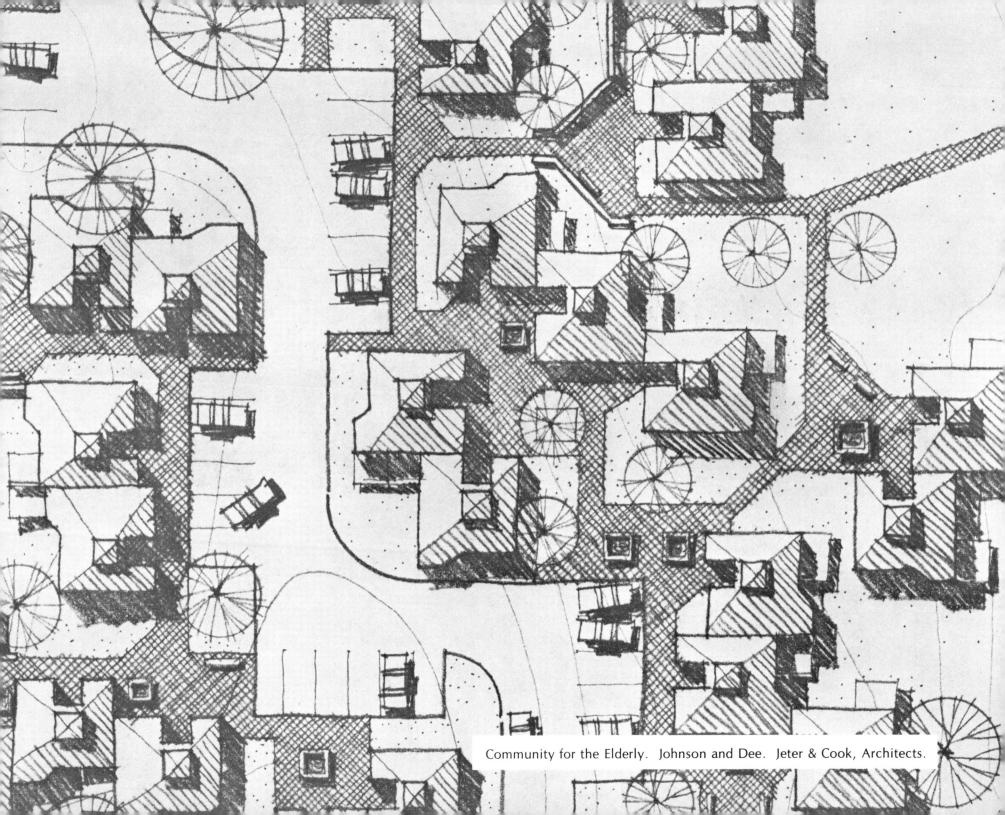

Community for the Elderly. Johnson and Dee. Jeter & Cook, Architects.

Park Master Plan. John A. Bentley.

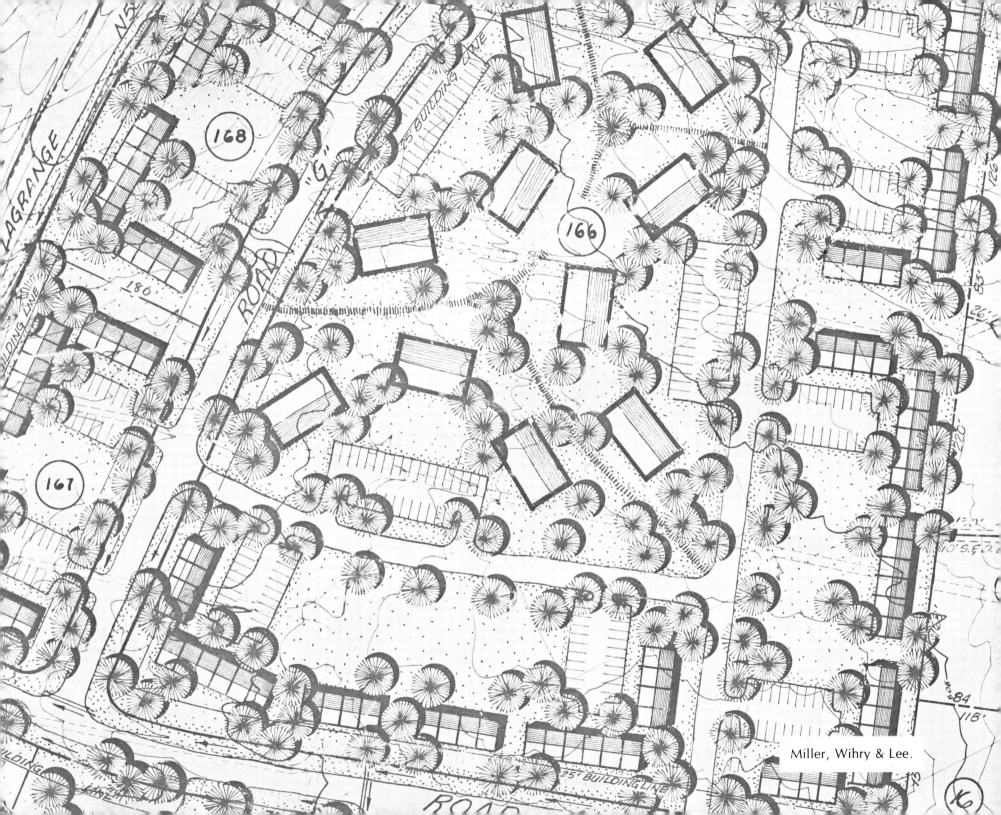

Miller, Wihry & Lee.

Miller, Wihry & Lee.

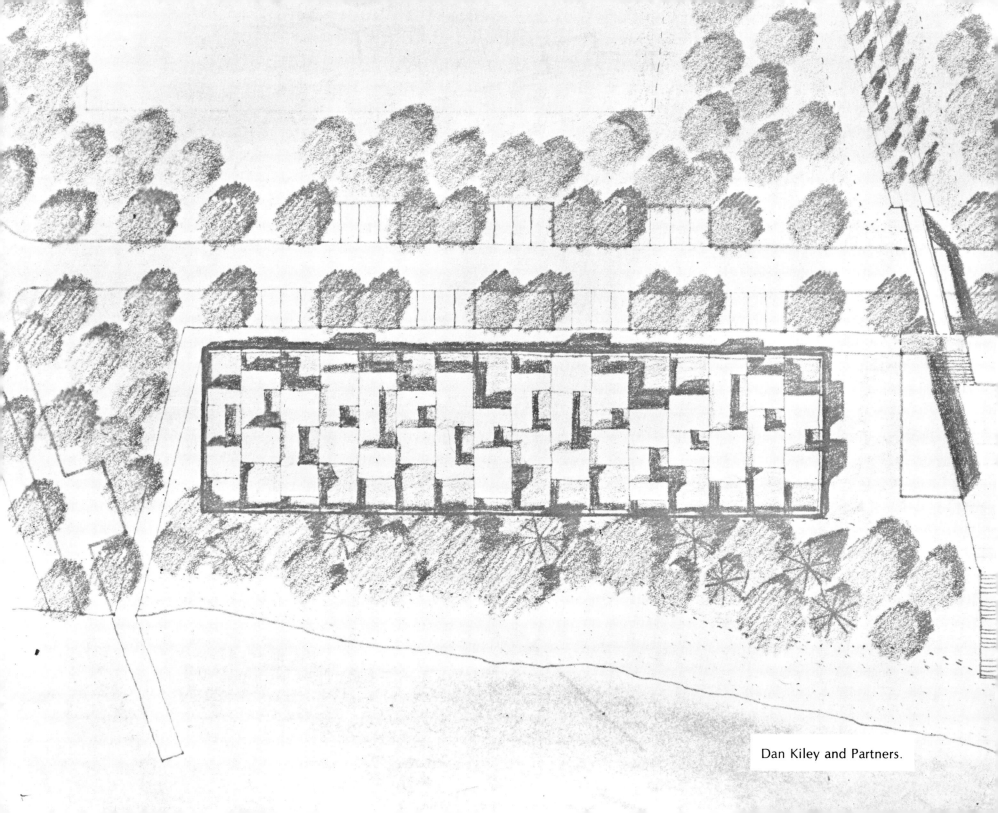

Dan Kiley and Partners.

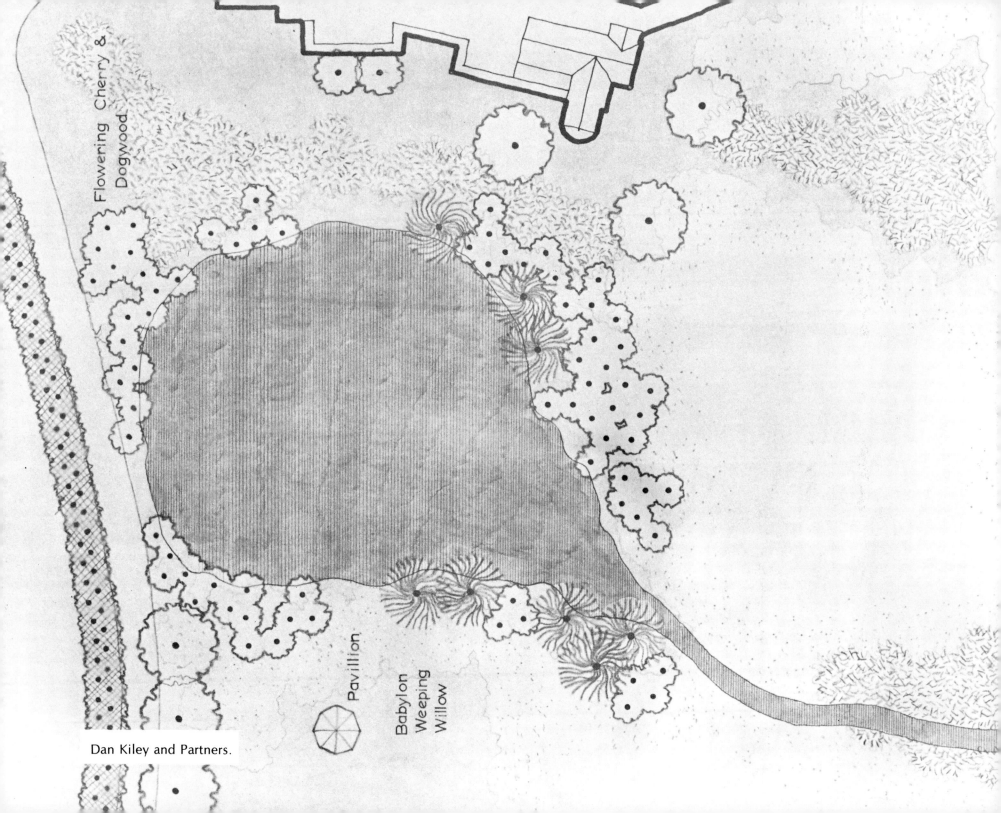

Flowering Cherry & Dogwood

Pavillion

Babylon Weeping Willow

Dan Kiley and Partners.

ELEVATIONS AND SECTIONS

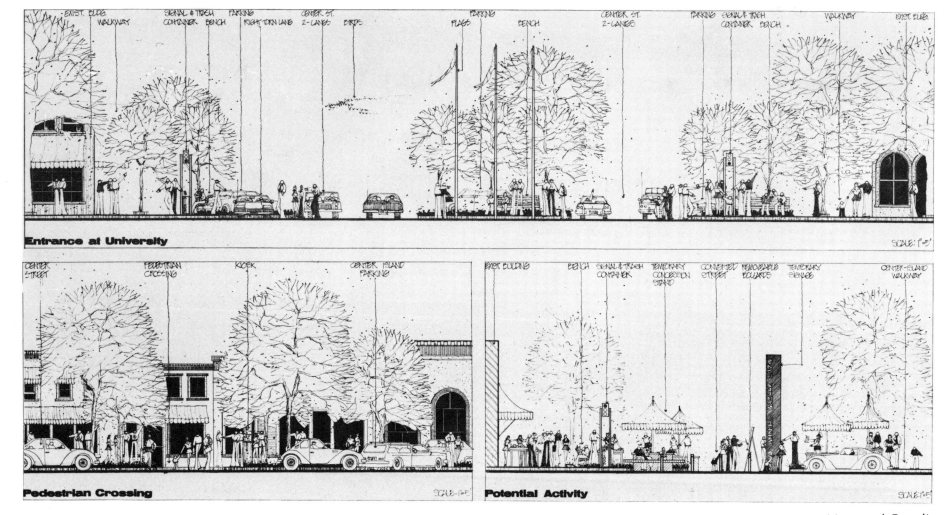

Entrance at University

SCALE: 1"=5'

Pedestrian Crossing

SCALE: 1"=5'

Potential Activity

SCALE: 1"=5'

Maas and Grassli.

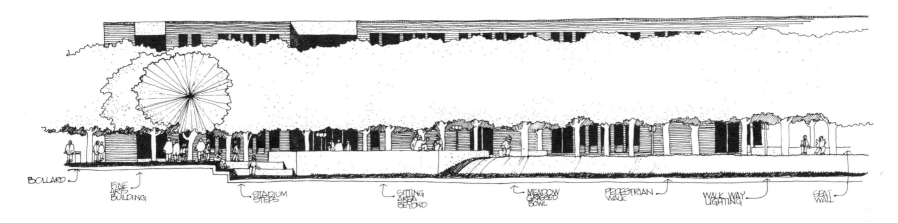

SECTION A·A

BOLLARD · FINE ARTS BUILDING · STADIUM STEPS · SITTING AREA BEYOND · MEADOW GRASSED BOWL · PEDESTRIAN WALK · WALK WAY LIGHTING · SEAT WALL

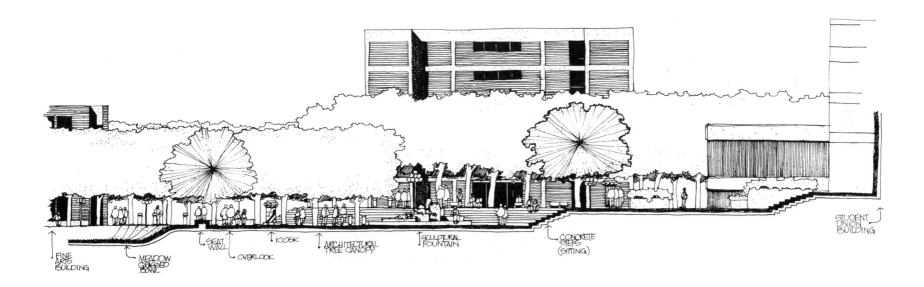

SECTION B·B

Student Center Mall. Miceli, Weed, Kulik.

FINE ARTS BUILDING · MEADOW GRASSED BOWL · SEAT WALL · OVERLOOK · KIOSK · ARCHITECTURAL TREE CANOPY · SCULPTURAL FOUNTAIN · CONCRETE STEPS (SITTING) · STUDENT UNION BUILDING

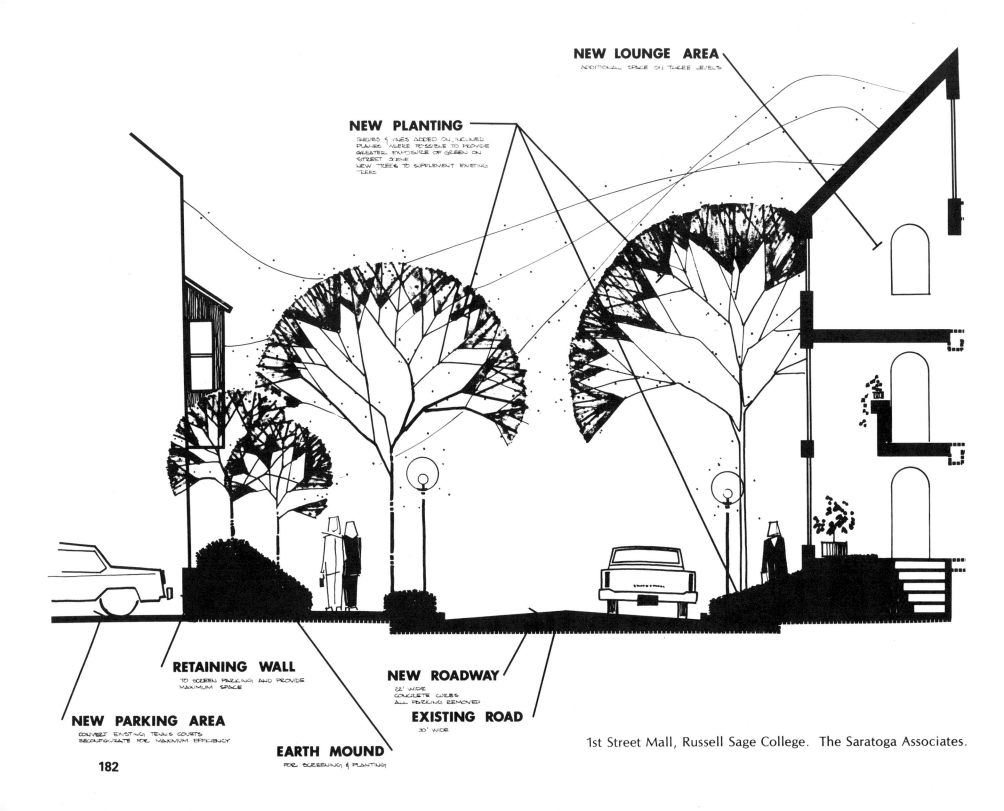

NEW LOUNGE AREA
ADDITIONAL SPACE ON THREE LEVELS

NEW PLANTING
SHRUBS & VINES ADDED ON INCLINED
PLANES WHERE POSSIBLE TO PROVIDE
GREATER EXPOSURE OF GREEN ON
STREET SCENE
NEW TREES TO SUPPLEMENT EXISTING
TREES

RETAINING WALL
TO SCREEN PARKING AND PROVIDE
MAXIMUM SPACE

NEW ROADWAY
22' WIDE
CONCRETE CURBS
ALL PARKING REMOVED

EXISTING ROAD
30' WIDE

NEW PARKING AREA
CONVERT EXISTING TENNIS COURTS
RECONFIGURATE FOR MAXIMUM EFFICIENCY

EARTH MOUND
FOR SCREENING & PLANTING

1st Street Mall, Russell Sage College. The Saratoga Associates.

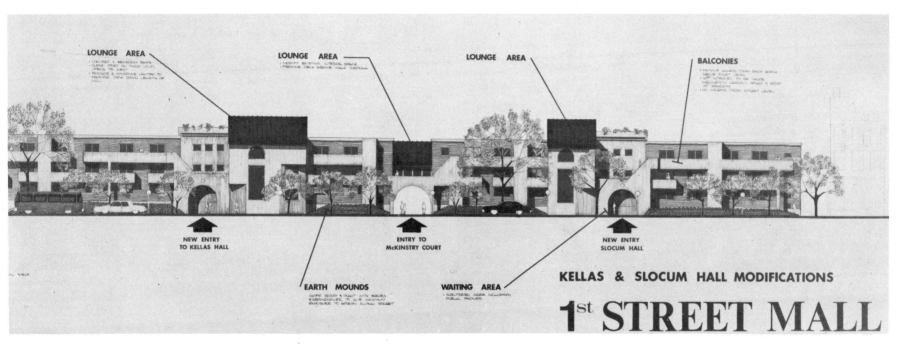

LOUNGE AREA

LOUNGE AREA

LOUNGE AREA

BALCONIES

NEW ENTRY
TO KELLAS HALL

ENTRY TO
McKINSTRY COURT

NEW ENTRY
SLOCUM HALL

EARTH MOUNDS

WAITING AREA

KELLAS & SLOCUM HALL MODIFICATIONS

1st STREET MALL

1st Street Mall, Russell Sage College. The Saratoga Associates.

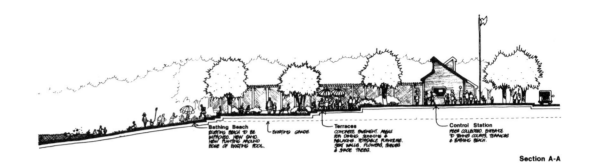

Bathing Beach
EXISTING BEACH TO BE
IMPROVED. NEW SAND.
NEW PLANTING AROUND
EDGE OF BOATING POOL.

EXISTING GRADE

Terraces
CONCRETE PAVEMENT. AREAS
FOR DINING, SUNNING &
MINGLING. MOVEABLE FURNITURE,
SEAT WALLS, FLOWERS, SHRUBS
& SHADE TREES.

Control Station
FEES COLLECTED. ENTRANCE
TO TENNIS COURTS, TERRACES
& BATHING BEACH.

Section A-A

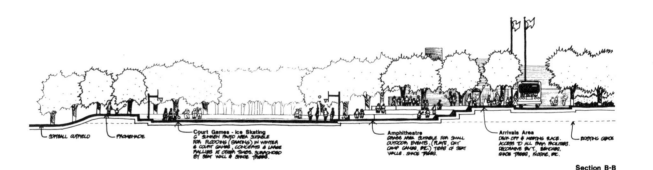

SOFTBALL OUTFIELD

PROMENADE

Court Games - Ice Skating
6" SUNKEN PAVED AREA SUITABLE
FOR FLOODING (SKATING) IN WINTER
& COURT GAMES, CONCERTS & LARGE
RALLIES AT OTHER TIMES. SURROUNDED
BY SEAT WALL & SHADE TREES.

Amphitheatre
GRASS AREA SUITABLE FOR SMALL
OUTDOOR EVENTS (PLAYS, DAY
CAMP GAMES, ETC.) TIERS OF SEAT
WALLS. SHADE TREES.

Arrivals Area
DROP-OFF & MEETING PLACE.
ACCESS TO ALL PARK FACILITIES.
DECORATIVE PAV'T., BENCHES,
SHADE TREES, KIOSK, ETC.

EXISTING GRADE

Section B-B

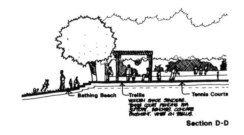

Bathing Beach

Trellis
WOODEN SHADE STRUCTURE.
TENNIS COURT FENCING FOR
SUPPORT. BENCHES. CONCRETE
PAVEMENT. VINES ON TRELLIS.

Tennis Courts

Section D-D

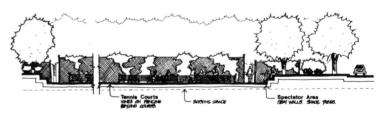

Tennis Courts
VINES ON FENCING
BEYOND COURTS.

EXISTING GRADE

Spectator Area
SEAT WALLS. SHADE TREES.

Section C-C

The Hollow Town Park. Miceli, Weed, Kulik.

184

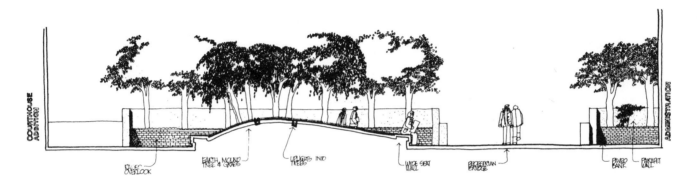

COURTHOUSE ADDITION

ADMINISTRATION

RIVER OVERLOOK

EARTH MOUND TREE & GRASS

UPLIGHTS INTO TREES

WIDE SEAT WALL

PEDESTRIAN BRIDGE

PAVED BANK

PARAPET WALL

SECTION - GARDEN

SECTION - BOSQUE

Detention Center. Miceli, Weed, Kulik.
Kramer, Hirsch, and Carchidi, Architects.

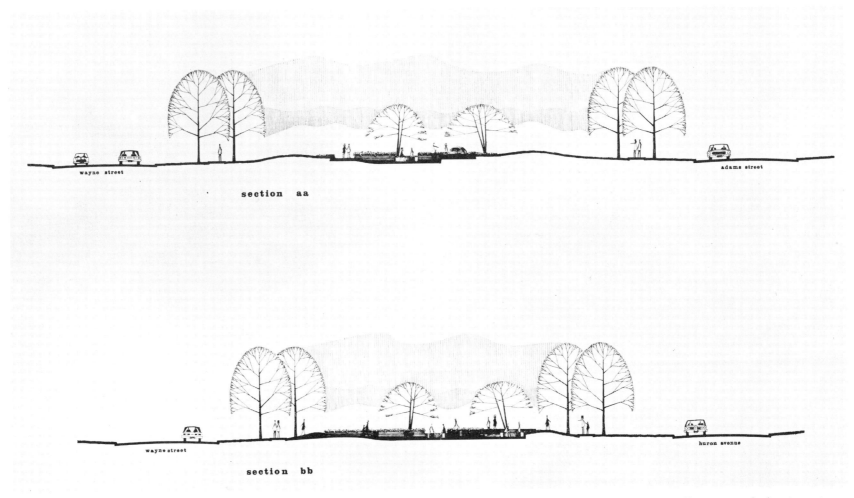

wayne street

section aa

adams street

wayne street

section bb

huron avenue

Dauch Memorial Park. William A. Behnke Associates,
James H. Ness, Associated Landscape Architect.

186

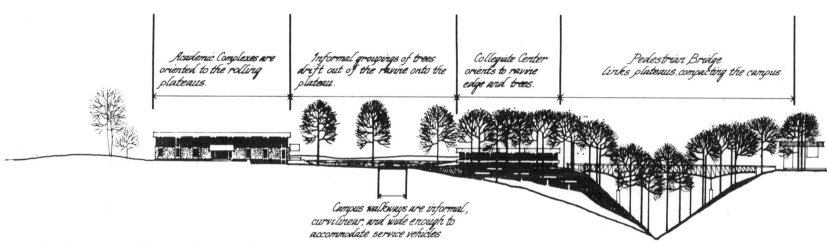

Academic Complexes are oriented to the rolling plateaus.

Informal groupings of trees drift out of the ravine onto the plateau.

Collegiate Center orients to ravine edge and trees.

Pedestrian Bridge links plateaus, compacting the campus.

Campus walkways are informal, curvilinear, and wide enough to accommodate service vehicles.

Grand Valley State College.   Johnson, Johnson & Roy, Inc.

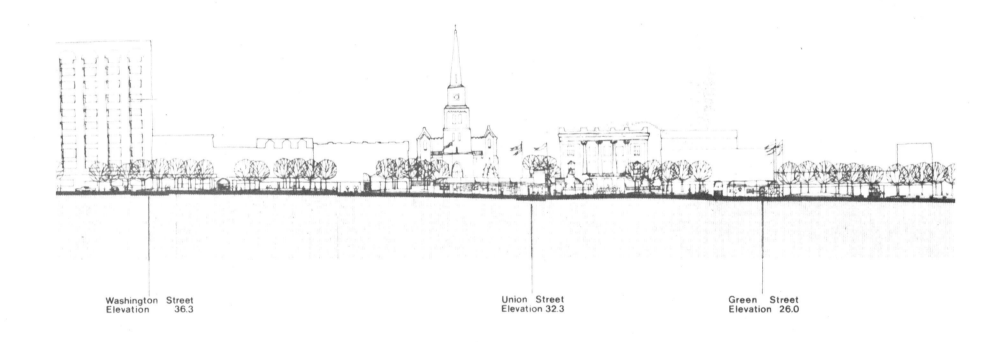

Washington Street
Elevation   36.3

Union Street
Elevation 32.3

Green Street
Elevation 26.0

State Street Semi-Mall. Johnson and Dee.

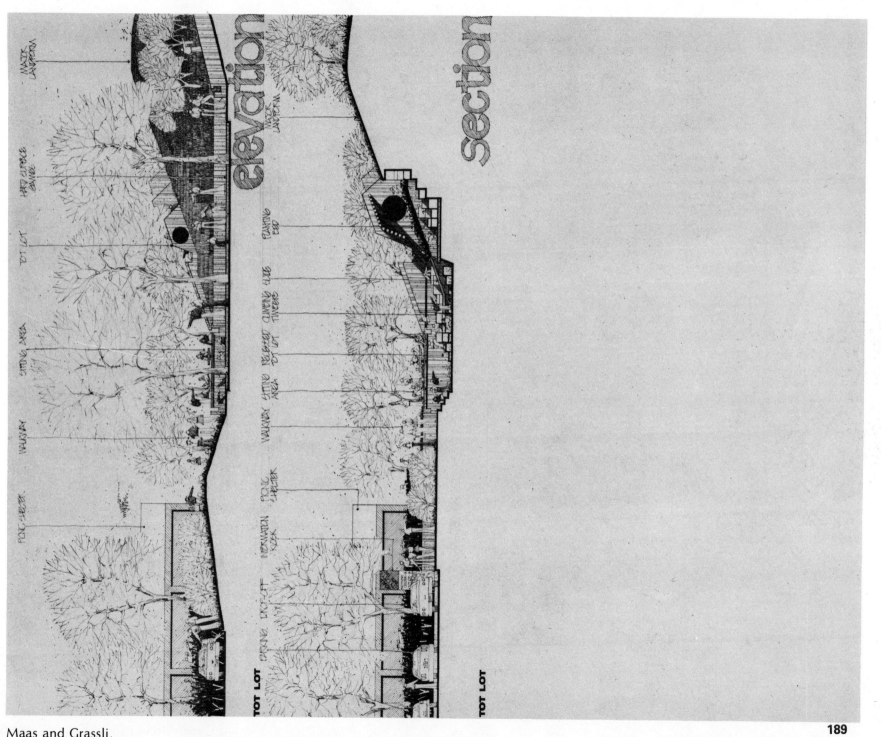

Maas and Grassli.

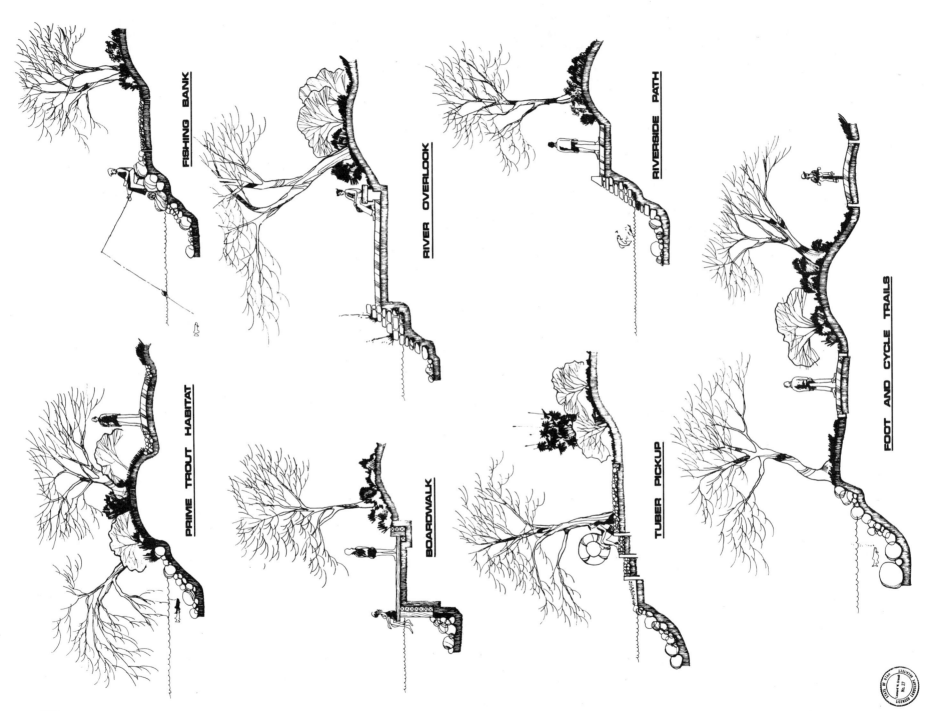

FISHING BANK

RIVER OVERLOOK

RIVERSIDE PATH

PRIME TROUT HABITAT

BOARDWALK

TUBER PICKUP

FOOT AND CYCLE TRAILS

Ogden River Parkway. Maas and Grassli.

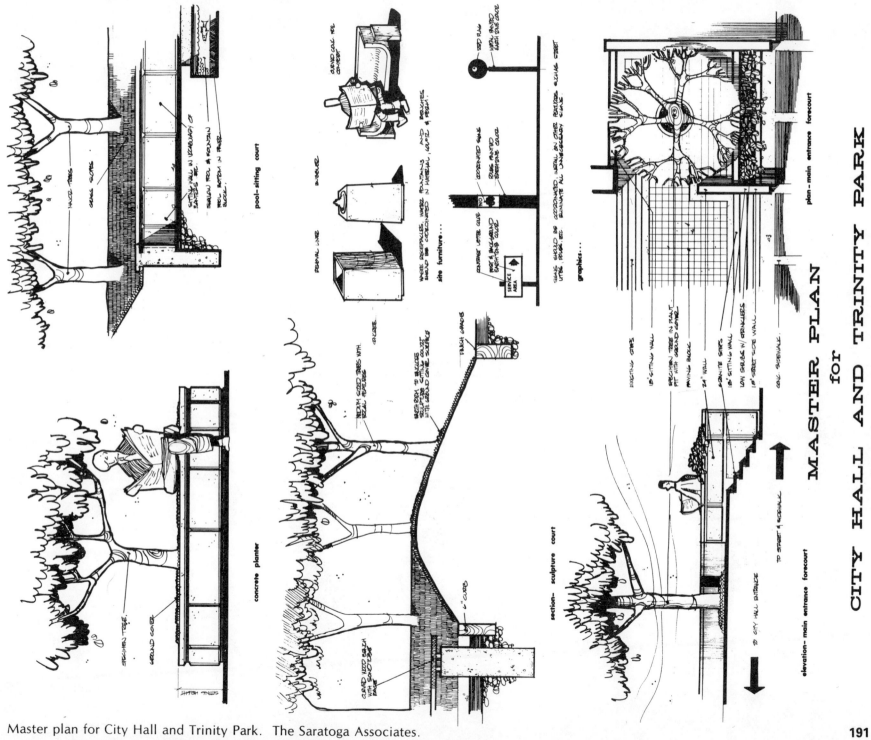

Master plan for City Hall and Trinity Park. The Saratoga Associates.

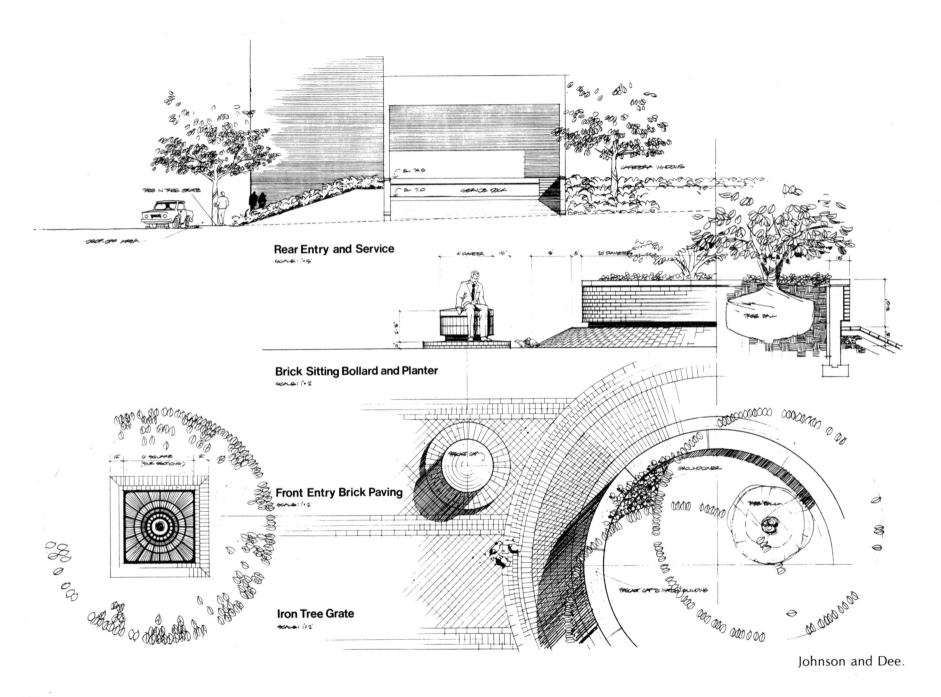

Rear Entry and Service
SCALE: 1'=5'

Brick Sitting Bollard and Planter
SCALE: 1'=2'

Front Entry Brick Paving
SCALE: 1'=2'

Iron Tree Grate
SCALE: 1'=2'

Johnson and Dee.

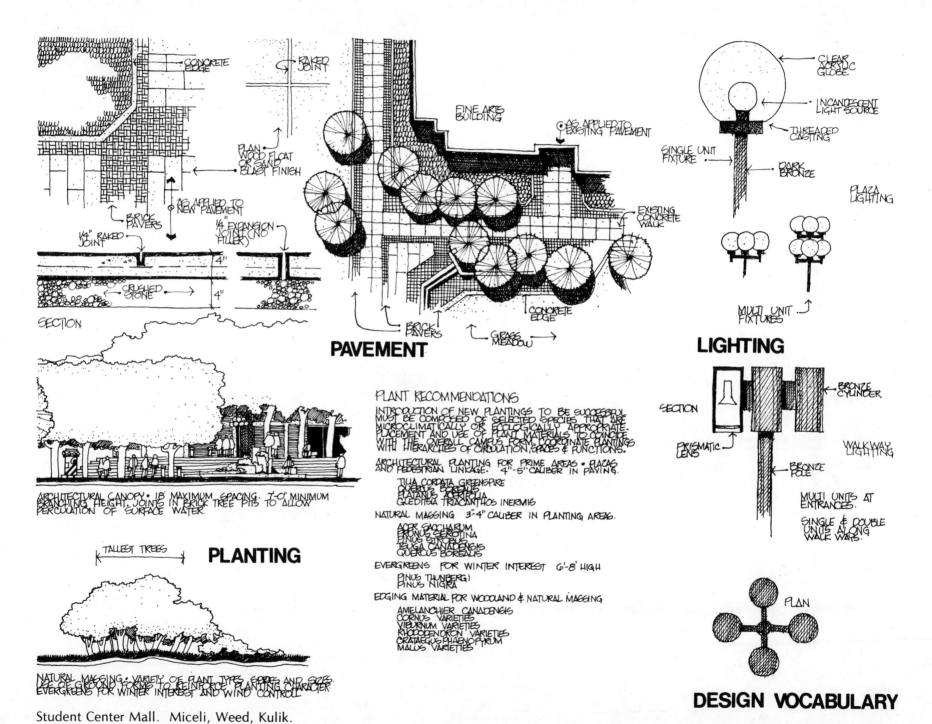

CONCRETE EDGE

RAKED JOINT

FINE ARTS BUILDING

PLAN · WOOD FLOAT OR SAND BLAST FINISH

AS APPLIED TO EXISTING PAVEMENT

AS APPLIED TO NEW PAVEMENT

BRICK PAVERS

¼" EXPANSION JOINT (NO FILLER)

EXISTING CONCRETE WALK

¼" RAKED JOINT

4"

4"

CRUSHED STONE

SECTION

CONCRETE EDGE

BRICK PAVERS

GRASS MEADOW

PAVEMENT

ARCHITECTURAL CANOPY · 18' MAXIMUM SPACING. 7'-0" MINIMUM BRANCHING HEIGHT. JOINTS IN BRICK TREE PITS TO ALLOW PERCOLATION OF SURFACE WATER.

TALLEST TREES

PLANTING

NATURAL MASSING. VARIETY OF PLANT TYPES, SPECIES AND SIZES. EVERGREENS FOR WINTER INTEREST AND WIND CONTROL. VARIETY OF FORMS TO REINFORCE PLANTING CHARACTER

Student Center Mall. Miceli, Weed, Kulik.

PLANT RECOMMENDATIONS

INTRODUCTION OF NEW PLANTINGS TO BE SUCCESSFUL MUST BE COMPOSED OF SELECTED SPECIES THAT ARE MICROCLIMATICALLY OR ECOLOGICALLY APPROPRIATE. PLACEMENT AND USE OF PLANT MATERIALS TO COINCIDE WITH THE OVERALL CAMPUS FORM, COORDINATE PLANTINGS WITH HIERARCHIES OF CIRCULATION, SPACES & FUNCTIONS.

ARCHITECTURAL PLANTING FOR PRIME AREAS · PLAZAS AND PEDESTRIAN LINKAGE. 4"-5" CALIPER IN PAVING.

TILIA CORDATA GREENSPIRE
QUERCUS BOREALIS
PLATANUS ACERFOLIA
GLEDITSIA TRIACANTHOS INERMIS

NATURAL MASSING 3"-4" CALIPER IN PLANTING AREAS.

ACER SACCHARUM
PRUNUS SEROTINA
PINUS STROBUS
TSUGA CANADENSIS
QUERCUS BOREALIS

EVERGREENS FOR WINTER INTEREST 6'-8' HIGH

PINUS THUNBERGI
PINUS NIGRA

EDGING MATERIAL FOR WOODLAND & NATURAL MASSING

AMELANCHIER CANADENSIS
CORNUS VARIETIES
VIBURNUM VARIETIES
RHODODENDRON VARIETIES
CRATAEGUS PHAENOPYRUM
MALUS VARIETIES

CLEAR ACRYLIC GLOBE

INCANDESCENT LIGHT SOURCE

THREADED CASTING

SINGLE UNIT FIXTURE

DARK BRONZE

PLAZA LIGHTING

MULTI UNIT FIXTURES

LIGHTING

SECTION

PRISMATIC LENS

BRONZE CYLINDER

BRONZE POLE

WALKWAY LIGHTING

MULTI UNITS AT ENTRANCES

SINGLE & DOUBLE UNITS ALONG WALK WAYS

PLAN

DESIGN VOCABULARY

193

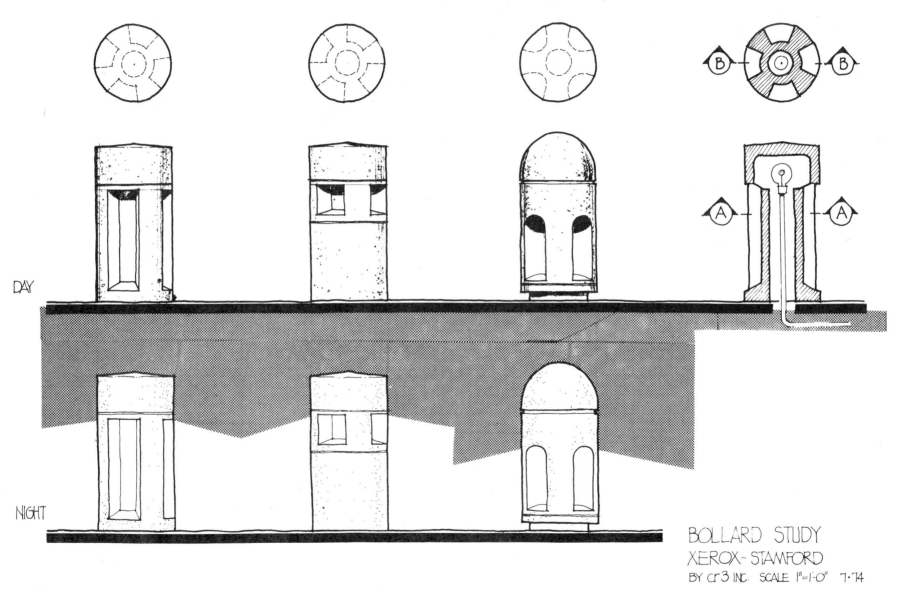

DAY

NIGHT

BOLLARD STUDY
XEROX—STAMFORD
BY Cr3 INC. SCALE 1"=1'-0" 7·74

Bollard Study — Xerox — Stamford. CR3, Inc.,
by Carl Mueller. Client: Charles Luckman Associates.

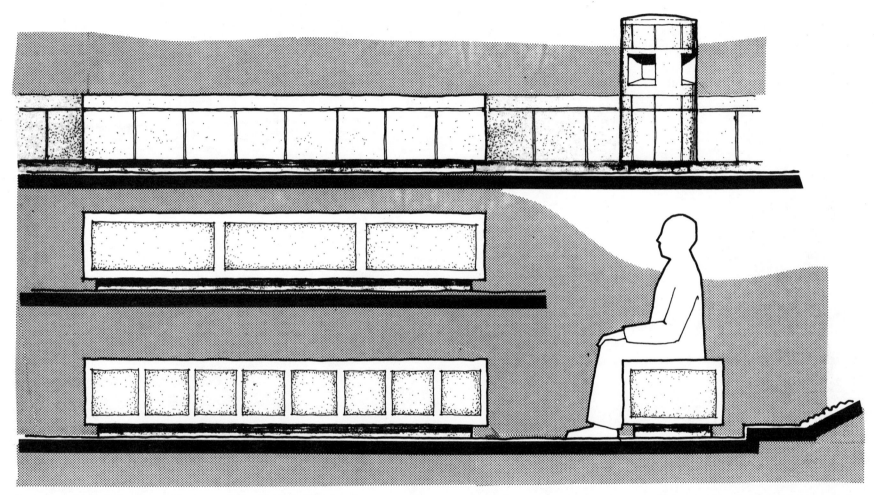

Bench and Wall Study — Xerox — Stamford. CR3, Inc.,
by Carl Mueller. Client: Charles Luckman Associates.

BENCH AND WALL STUDY
XEROX - STAMFORD
BY cr3 INC   SCALE 1"=1'-0"   7·74

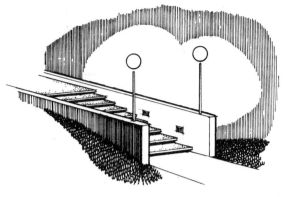

Step lighting

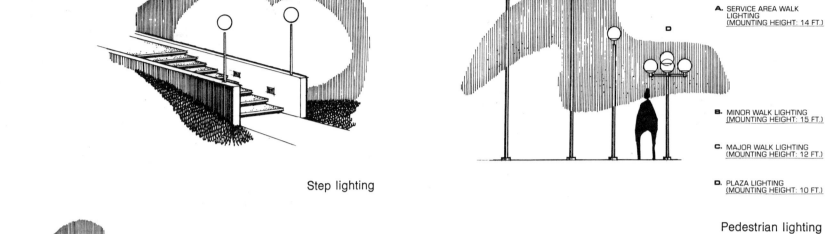

A. SERVICE AREA WALK LIGHTING (MOUNTING HEIGHT: 14 FT.)

B. MINOR WALK LIGHTING (MOUNTING HEIGHT: 15 FT.)

C. MAJOR WALK LIGHTING (MOUNTING HEIGHT: 12 FT.)

D. PLAZA LIGHTING (MOUNTING HEIGHT: 10 FT.)

Pedestrian lighting

Trash receptacle and drinking fountain

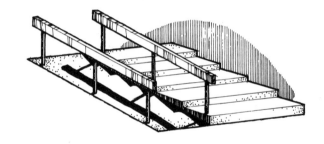

Ramp

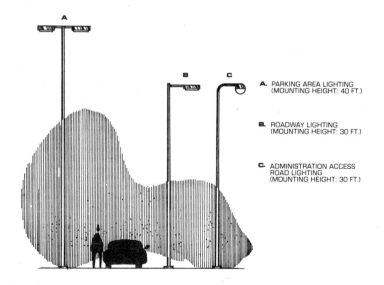

A. PARKING AREA LIGHTING (MOUNTING HEIGHT: 40 FT.)

B. ROADWAY LIGHTING (MOUNTING HEIGHT: 30 FT.)

C. ADMINISTRATION ACCESS ROAD LIGHTING (MOUNTING HEIGHT: 30 FT.)

Parking and road lighting

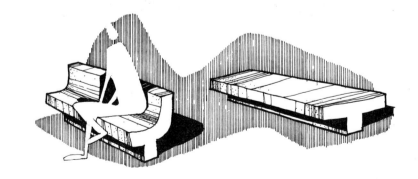

Benches

CR3, Inc., by Cortland Read. Client: Pfohl, Roberts, Biggie, Architects.

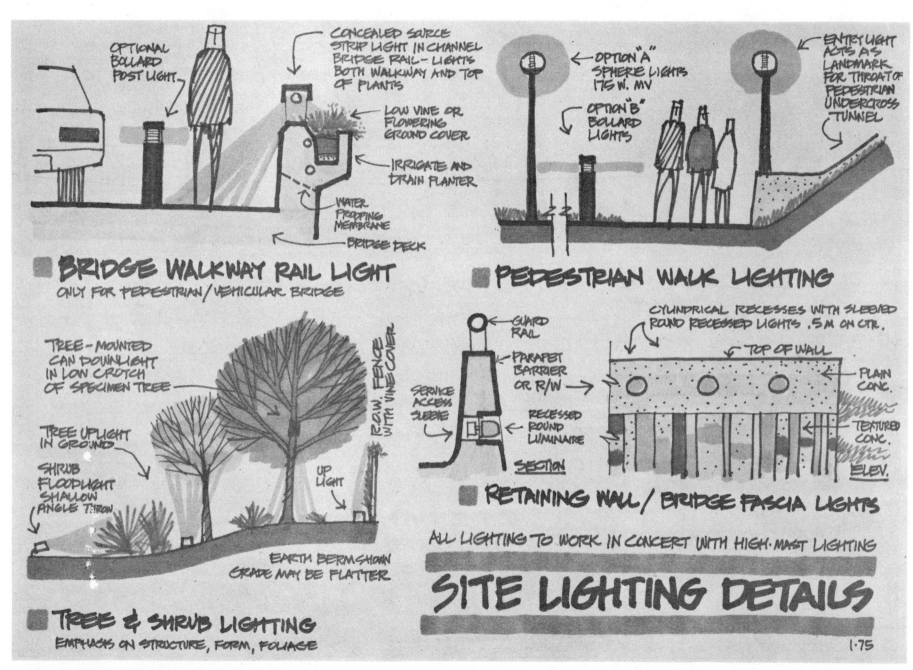

BRIDGE WALKWAY RAIL LIGHT
ONLY FOR PEDESTRIAN/VEHICULAR BRIDGE

OPTIONAL BOLLARD POST LIGHT

CONCEALED SOURCE STRIP LIGHT IN CHANNEL BRIDGE RAIL — LIGHTS BOTH WALKWAY AND TOP OF PLANTS

LOW VINE OR FLOWERING GROUND COVER

IRRIGATE AND DRAIN PLANTER

WATER PROOFING MEMBRANE

BRIDGE DECK

PEDESTRIAN WALK LIGHTING

OPTION "A" SPHERE LIGHTS 175 W. MV

OPTION "B" BOLLARD LIGHTS

ENTRY LIGHT ACTS AS LANDMARK FOR THROAT OF PEDESTRIAN UNDERCROSS TUNNEL

TREE & SHRUB LIGHTING
EMPHASIS ON STRUCTURE, FORM, FOLIAGE

TREE-MOUNTED CAN DOWNLIGHT IN LOW CROTCH OF SPECIMEN TREE

TREE UPLIGHT IN GROUND

SHRUB FLOODLIGHT SHALLOW ANGLE THROW

R.O.W. FENCE WITH VINE COVER

UP LIGHT

EARTH BERM SHOWN GRADE MAY BE FLATTER

RETAINING WALL / BRIDGE FASCIA LIGHTS

GUARD RAIL

PARAPET BARRIER OR R/W

SERVICE ACCESS SLEEVE

RECESSED ROUND LUMINAIRE

SECTION

CYLINDRICAL RECESSES WITH SLEEVED ROUND RECESSED LIGHTS .5M ON CTR.

TOP OF WALL

PLAIN CONC.

TEXTURED CONC.

ELEV.

ALL LIGHTING TO WORK IN CONCERT WITH HIGH-MAST LIGHTING

SITE LIGHTING DETAILS

1·75

DeLeuw, Cather International by David Linstrum.
Multi-colored, using broad and narrow point markers.

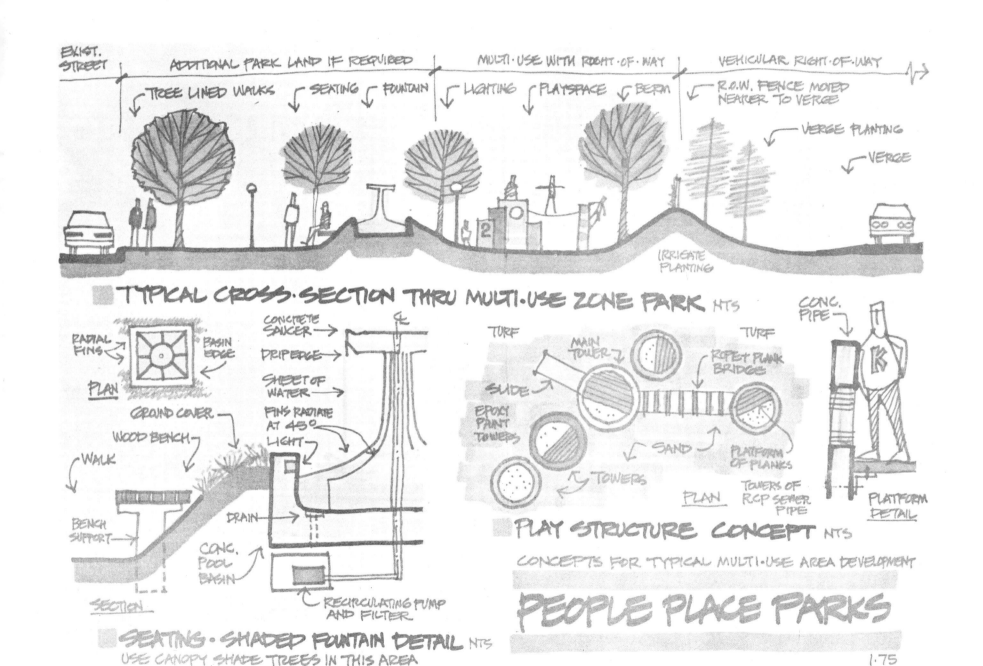

TYPICAL CROSS-SECTION THRU MULTI-USE ZONE PARK NTS

EXIST. STREET | ADDITIONAL PARK LAND IF REQUIRED | MULTI-USE WITH RIGHT-OF-WAY | VEHICULAR RIGHT-OF-WAY

TREE LINED WALKS · SEATING · FOUNTAIN · LIGHTING · PLAYSPACE · BERM · R.O.W. FENCE MOVED NEARER TO VERGE · VERGE PLANTING · VERGE · IRRIGATE PLANTING

SEATING · SHADED FOUNTAIN DETAIL NTS

RADIAL FINS · BASIN EDGE · PLAN · GROUND COVER · WOOD BENCH · WALK · BENCH SUPPORT · SECTION · CONCRETE SAUCER · DRIPEDGE · SHEET OF WATER · FINS RADIATE AT 45° · LIGHT · DRAIN · CONC. POOL BASIN · RECIRCULATING PUMP AND FILTER

USE CANOPY SHADE TREES IN THIS AREA

PLAY STRUCTURE CONCEPT NTS

TURF · MAIN TOWER · TURF · SLIDE · ROPE & PLANK BRIDGE · EPOXY PAINT TOWERS · SAND · PLATFORM OF PLANKS · TOWERS · PLAN · TOWERS OF RCP SEWER PIPE · CONC. PIPE · PLATFORM DETAIL

CONCEPTS FOR TYPICAL MULTI-USE AREA DEVELOPMENT

PEOPLE PLACE PARKS

1·75

DeLeuw, Cather International by David Linstrum.
Multi-colored, using broad and narrow point markers.

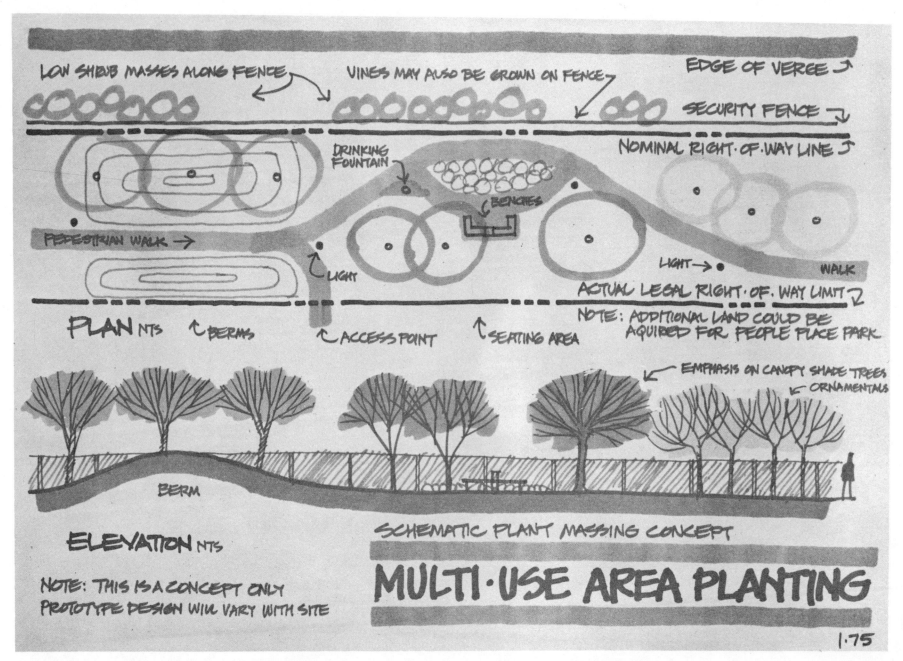

LOW SHRUB MASSES ALONG FENCE

VINES MAY ALSO BE GROWN ON FENCE

EDGE OF VERGE →

SECURITY FENCE →

NOMINAL RIGHT·OF·WAY LINE →

DRINKING FOUNTAIN

BENCHES

PEDESTRIAN WALK →

LIGHT

LIGHT →

WALK

ACTUAL LEGAL RIGHT·OF·WAY LIMIT

PLAN NTS   ↰ BERMS   ↰ ACCESS POINT   ↰ SEATING AREA

NOTE: ADDITIONAL LAND COULD BE AQUIRED FOR PEOPLE PLACE PARK

EMPHASIS ON CANOPY SHADE TREES

↰ ORNAMENTALS

BERM

ELEVATION NTS

NOTE: THIS IS A CONCEPT ONLY PROTOTYPE DESIGN WILL VARY WITH SITE

SCHEMATIC PLANT MASSING CONCEPT

MULTI·USE AREA PLANTING

1·75

DeLeuw, Cather International by David Linstrum.
Multi-colored, using broad and narrow point markers.

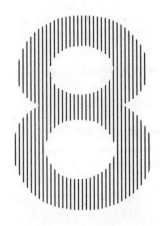

LETTERING

INTRODUCTION

The quality of your work and how it impresses others, especially prospective employers, is largely dependent upon your freehand lettering. The development of a consistent and professional-looking stlye will help you promote your abilities. This section, with its text and illustrations, is intended to provide you with some guidelines and motivation towards that goal.

Please do not be mislead into believing that the press-on style lettering or the use of such mechanical types as the "Leroy" lettering pens will solve your lettering problems. Each has its use in certain situations; none, however, replace freehand lettering. Mechanical lettering is not practical for the amount required on construction drawings and planting plans, whereas freehand lettering is faster and creates an individuality and attractiveness that cannot be achieved with mechanical methods.

Letters and numerals are nothing but symbols which you learn to identify at an early age. When these are grouped together to form words and numbers they acquire meaning which you have also learned and now use freely without much additional thought.

Your freehand lettering will be representative of these common identifiable symbols, which when grouped together will convey important information to your clients and their contractors. Thus, each letter and numeral you form should be a reasonable and readable representation of the original symbol.

ABCDEFGHIJKLMNOPQRSTUVWXYZ 1234567890
AMERICAN SOCIETY OF LANDSCAPE ARCHITECTS

abcdefghijklmnopqrstuvwxyz 1234567890
american society of landscape architects

ABCDEFGHIJKLMNOPQRSTUVWXYZ 1234567890
AMERICAN SOCIETY OF LANDSCAPE ARCHITECTS

abcdefghijklmnopqrstuvwxyz 1234567890
American Society of Landscape Architects

ABCDEFGHIJKLMNOPQRSTUVWXYZ 1234567890910
AMERICAN SOCIETY of LANDSCAPE ARCHITECTS

Johnson, Johnson & Roy, Inc.

RECREATION   COMMISSION

Site Location

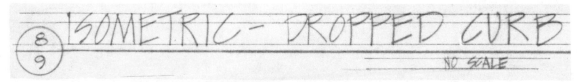

(top) Johnson and Dee, (upper middle) John A. Bentley,
(lower middle) University of Illinois Office for Capital Programs,
(bottom) Browning, Day, Pollak Associates, Inc.

Because a certain attractiveness can be achieved, lettering may also be classified as design. Letters in one style may vary from tall and thin to the wide and broad character of another style. The lines used to form each letter may be narrow and thin, or thick and broad. The spacing between letters may vary, to spread a word out or squeeze it into a small space. Groups of words, and lines of words may be aesthetically placed on the page or drawing.

SUGGESTED TECHNIQUES

1. Always use guidelines when lettering. The spacing of guidelines to each other and between lines of words should always be consistent for the most attractive appearance. A sharp 3H or 4H lead is useful for keeping guidelines light. (Guidelines shown are darker for reproduction purposes only.)

2. Use a soft lead pencil, as it will be easier to control than a hard lead and will glide more easily over the surface of the paper. To start, try an H or HB lead. Later as you become experienced you will select various leads to fit changing situations and different tracing papers. Sharpen your lead frequently to maintain uniform lines in forming your letters and numerals. A sharp lead also provides a cleaner and sharper line, which reproduces better.

3. If you choose to print vertical letters, be sure all vertical lines are consistently vertical. Slanted letters are best when the vertical lines

slant from 15° to 22° right of pure vertical. It will require considerably more practice to keep your letters consistently slanted. (Light guidelines at the desired angle are useful for practicing.)

4. The most popular form of lettering for most situations is all capitals. Lower case letters may be useful, especially for planting plans, if well-done. Script is used occasionally for preliminary plans or freehand style drawings.

5. Because of differences in physical coordination each individual will use a different number of, and direction in the strokes necessary to form each letter or numeral. In your practicing, experiment with a variety of strokes to find those which will fit you best.

6. Be consistent by forming the same letter the same way each time it is used. The height and width of letters should be consistent with each other — each time they are used in the same style. This also applies to the spaces between the letters.

7. As you practice, vary the spacing of your guidelines to give you proficiency in lettering all heights and sizes of letters and numerals.

8. Plan your layout for several lines of lettering on a drawing to create an attractive, balanced and readable arrangement. To achieve this, place an overlay on the final sheet before you start to letter and roughly block out the areas to be lettered. This will also help you to avoid spelling errors.

Juniperus communis	COMMON JUNIPER
Rhus trilobata	SKUNK BUSH
Sambucus canadensis	ELDERBERRY

(top) Browning, Day, Pollak, Associates, Inc., (bottom) Blackhawk Scenic Overlook, Uinta National Forest. Lyle B. Gomm.

9. Begin lettering from the top of the sheet and move downward to avoid smudging. If it is necessary to work on top of previously drafted work lay a sheet of clean paper under your hand to protect the drawing and minimize smudging.

10. Perfection requires considerable practice. Print every chance you get — writing letters home, taking class notes, etc. It will take some time to develop a relaxed, swift, and controlled technique.

11. Refrain from attempting to develop several styles at once. Concentrate on and master one style before trying another.

12. Test the readability of your style by asking a friend, who is not a designer or draftsman, to read it. If he has trouble, revise or start over.

EXAMPLES

On the pages which follow you will find several examples of freehand lettering which may give you some ideas and motivation towards creating your own style.

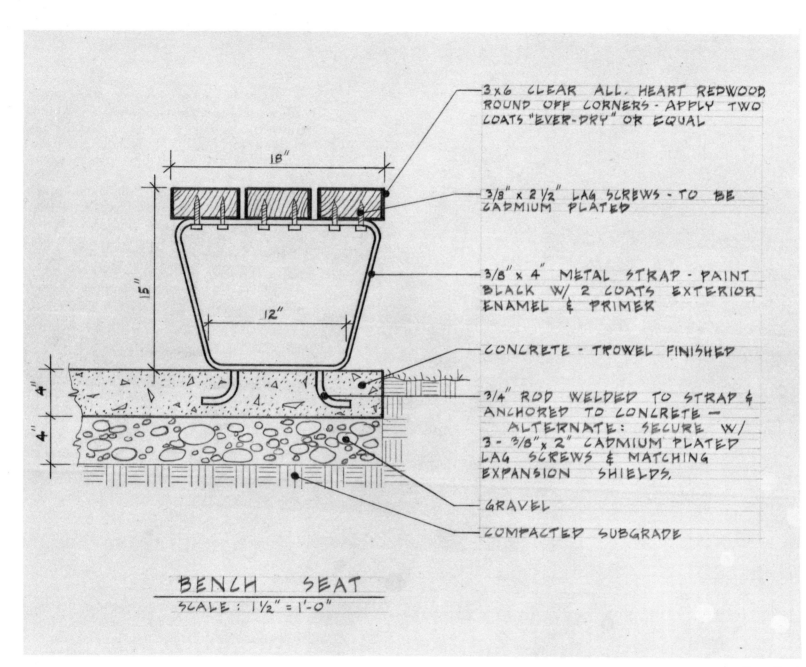

18"

15"

12"

4"

4"

3x6 CLEAR ALL. HEART REDWOOD,
ROUND OFF CORNERS - APPLY TWO
COATS "EVER-DRY" OR EQUAL

3/8" x 2 1/2" LAG SCREWS - TO BE
CADMIUM PLATED

3/8" x 4" METAL STRAP - PAINT
BLACK W/ 2 COATS EXTERIOR
ENAMEL & PRIMER

CONCRETE - TROWEL FINISHED

3/4" ROD WELDED TO STRAP &
ANCHORED TO CONCRETE —
    ALTERNATE: SECURE W/
3 - 3/8" x 2" CADMIUM PLATED
LAG SCREWS & MATCHING
EXPANSION SHIELDS.

GRAVEL

COMPACTED SUBGRADE

BENCH SEAT
SCALE: 1 1/2" = 1'-0"

Don Teal.

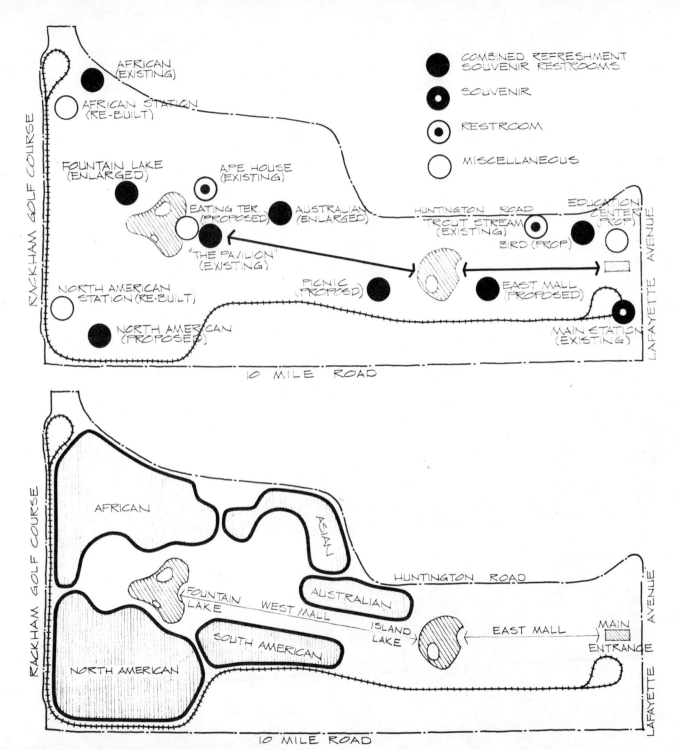

LEGEND

● COMBINED REFRESHMENT SOUVENIR RESTROOMS

◉ SOUVENIR

⦿ RESTROOM

○ MISCELLANEOUS

Top diagram labels:

AFRICAN (EXISTING)

AFRICAN STATION (RE-BUILT)

FOUNTAIN LAKE (ENLARGED)

APE HOUSE (EXISTING)

EATING TER. (PROPOSED)

AUSTRALIAN (ENLARGED)

HUNTINGTON ROAD

TROUT STREAM (EXISTING)

EDUCATION CENTER (PROP)

BIRD (PROP)

"THE PAVILION" (EXISTING)

NORTH AMERICAN STATION (RE-BUILT)

NORTH AMERICAN (PROPOSED)

PICNIC (PROPOSED)

EAST MALL (PROPOSED)

MAIN STATION (EXISTING)

RACKHAM GOLF COURSE

LAFAYETTE AVENUE

10 MILE ROAD

Bottom diagram labels:

RACKHAM GOLF COURSE

AFRICAN

ASIAN

FOUNTAIN LAKE

AUSTRALIAN

HUNTINGTON ROAD

WEST MALL

ISLAND LAKE

EAST MALL

MAIN ENTRANCE

SOUTH AMERICAN

NORTH AMERICAN

LAFAYETTE AVENUE

10 MILE ROAD

Sasaki, Dawson, DeMay Associates, Inc.

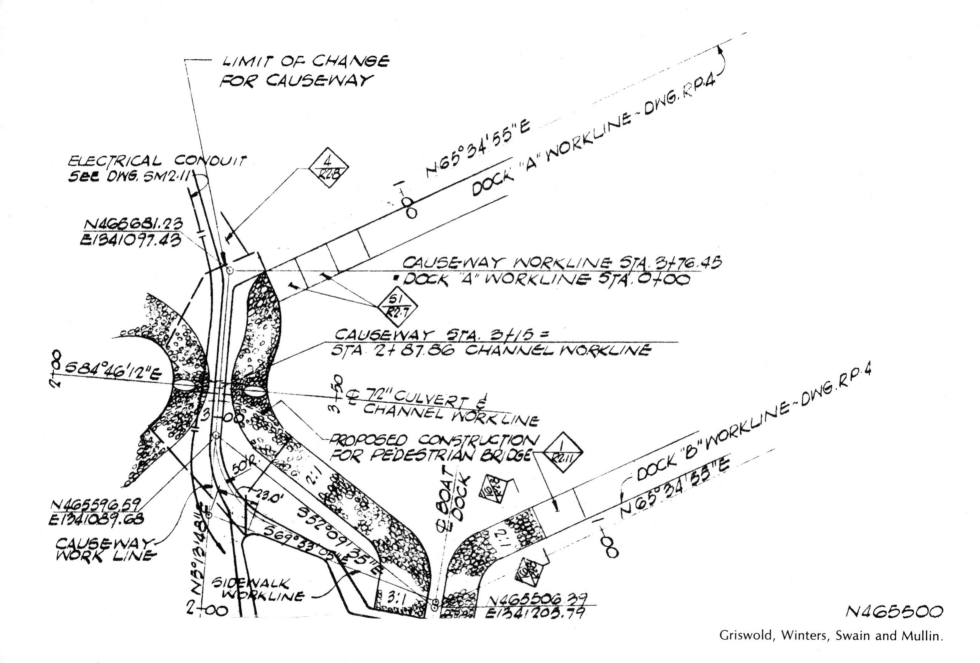

LIMIT OF CHANGE
FOR CAUSEWAY

ELECTRICAL CONDUIT
SEE DWG. SM2-11

N465681.23
E1341097.43

N65°34'55"E

DOCK "A" WORKLINE ~ DWG. R.P.4

4
R2.6

CAUSEWAY WORKLINE STA. 3+76.45
= DOCK "A" WORKLINE STA. 0+00

51
R2.7

CAUSEWAY STA. 3+15 =
STA. 2+87.86 CHANNEL WORKLINE

S84°46'12"E

₵ 72" CULVERT ₵
CHANNEL WORKLINE

PROPOSED CONSTRUCTION
FOR PEDESTRIAN BRIDGE

1
R2.11

DOCK "B" WORKLINE ~ DWG. R.P.4

N65°34'55"E

N465596.59
E1341089.68

CAUSEWAY
WORK LINE

50'R

2:1

23.0'

S57°09'35"E

₵ BOAT DOCK

2:1

N5°13'48"E

S69°33'05"E

SIDEWALK
WORKLINE

2+00

3:1

N465506.39
E1341205.79

N465500

Griswold, Winters, Swain and Mullin.

GRANT PLAYGROUND
PRELIM. DEVELOPMENT STUDY

Canton Public Library

COLLINSVILLE, CONNECTICUT

Community for the Eld

(top) John A. Bentley, (middle and bottom) Johnson and Dee.

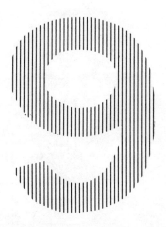

SECOND EDITION SUPPLEMENT

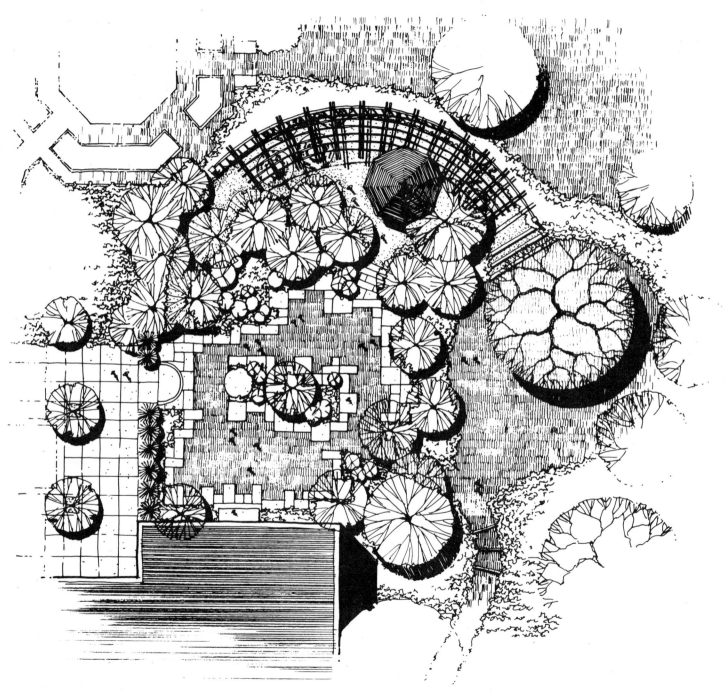

Reading Garden, Cleveland, Ohio. William A. Behnke Associates, by Russell L. Butler II. Ink and pencil on mylar.

Mawardi — Von Baeyer Residences, Cleveland Heights, Ohio.
William A. Behnke Associates, by Russell L.
Butler II. Ink and pencil on yellow tracing paper.

213

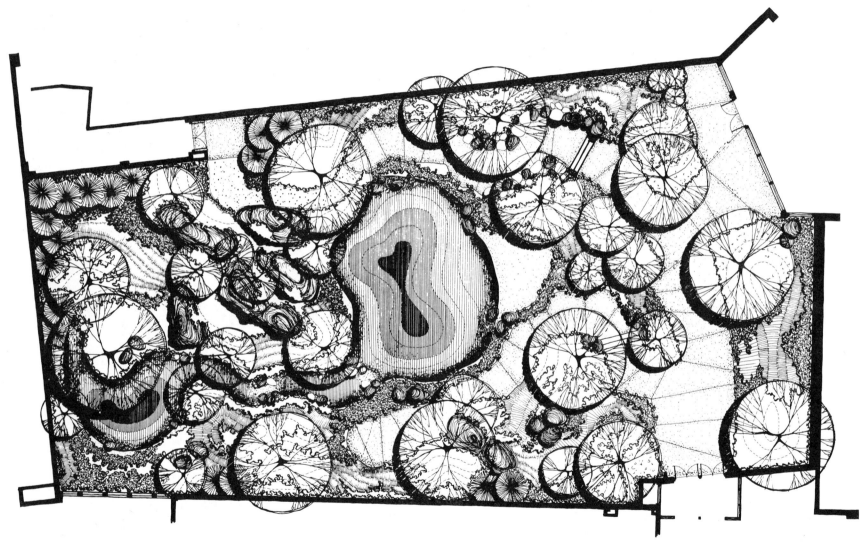

Cleveland Museum of Natural History Courtyard.
William A. Behnke Associates, by Russell L.
Butler II. Ink on yellow tracing paper.

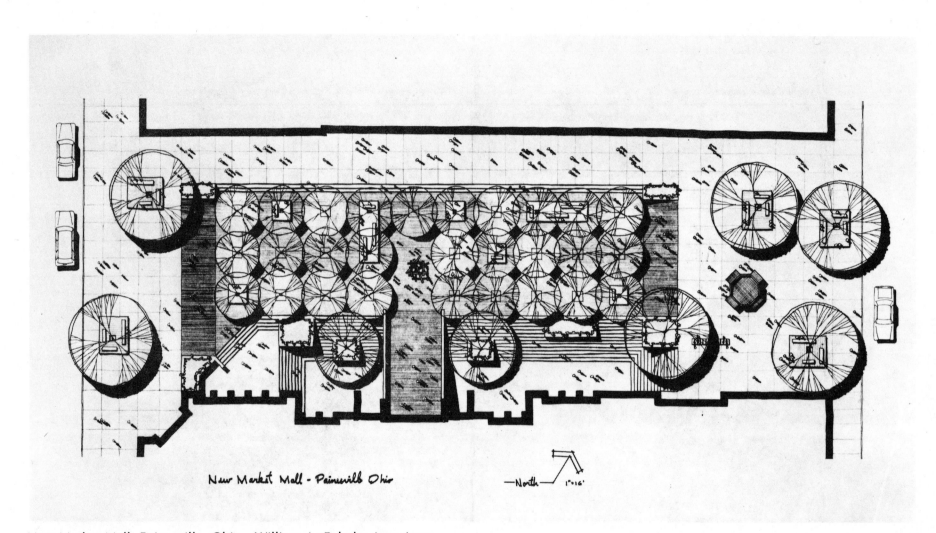

New Market Mall - Painesville Ohio

—North— 1"=16'

New Market Mall, Painesville, Ohio. William A. Behnke Associates,
by Russell L. Butler II. Ink and pencil on mylar.

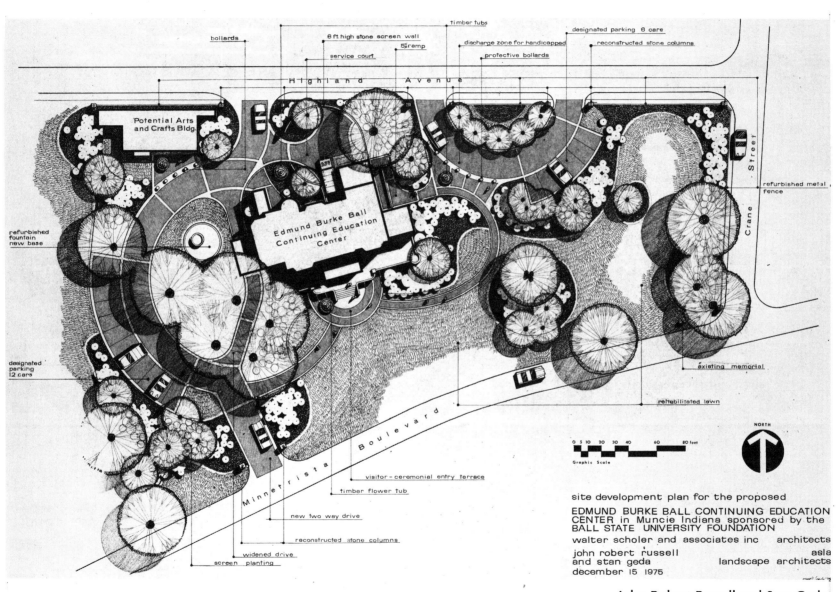

bollards

timber tubs

6 ft. high stone screen wall

5% ramp

service court

designated parking 6 cars

discharge zone for handicapped

reconstructed stone columns

protective bollards

H i g h l a n d   A v e n u e

Potential Arts
and Crafts Bldg.

Edmund Burke Ball
Continuing Education
Center

C r a n e   S t r e e t

refurbished metal
fence

refurbished
fountain
new base

designated
parking
12 cars

existing memorial

rehabilitated lawn

M i n n e t r i s t a   B o u l e v a r d

NORTH

0 5 10   20   30   40   60   80 feet

Graphic Scale

visitor - ceremonial entry terrace

timber flower tub

new two way drive

reconstructed stone columns

widened drive

screen planting

site development plan for the proposed
**EDMUND BURKE BALL CONTINUING EDUCATION
CENTER in Muncie Indiana sponsored by the
BALL STATE UNIVERSITY FOUNDATION**
walter scholer and associates inc   architects
john robert russell   asla
and stan geda   landscape architects
december 15 1975

John Robert Russell and Stan Geda.

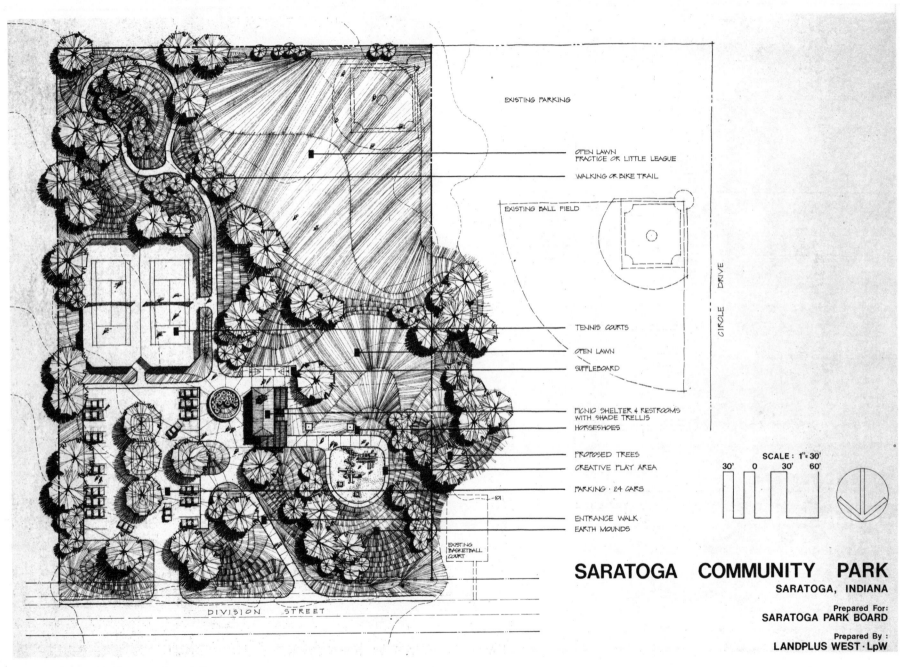

EXISTING PARKING

OPEN LAWN
PRACTICE OR LITTLE LEAGUE

WALKING OR BIKE TRAIL

EXISTING BALL FIELD

CIRCLE DRIVE

TENNIS COURTS

OPEN LAWN

SHUFFLEBOARD

PICNIC SHELTER & RESTROOMS
WITH SHADE TRELLIS

HORSESHOES

PROPOSED TREES

CREATIVE PLAY AREA

PARKING · 24 CARS

ENTRANCE WALK

EARTH MOUNDS

EXISTING
BASKETBALL
COURT

DIVISION STREET

SCALE : 1"=30'

30'   0   30'   60'

SARATOGA COMMUNITY PARK
SARATOGA, INDIANA

Prepared For:
SARATOGA PARK BOARD

Prepared By :
LANDPLUS WEST · LpW

Bruce Alexander/Deane Rundell.

217

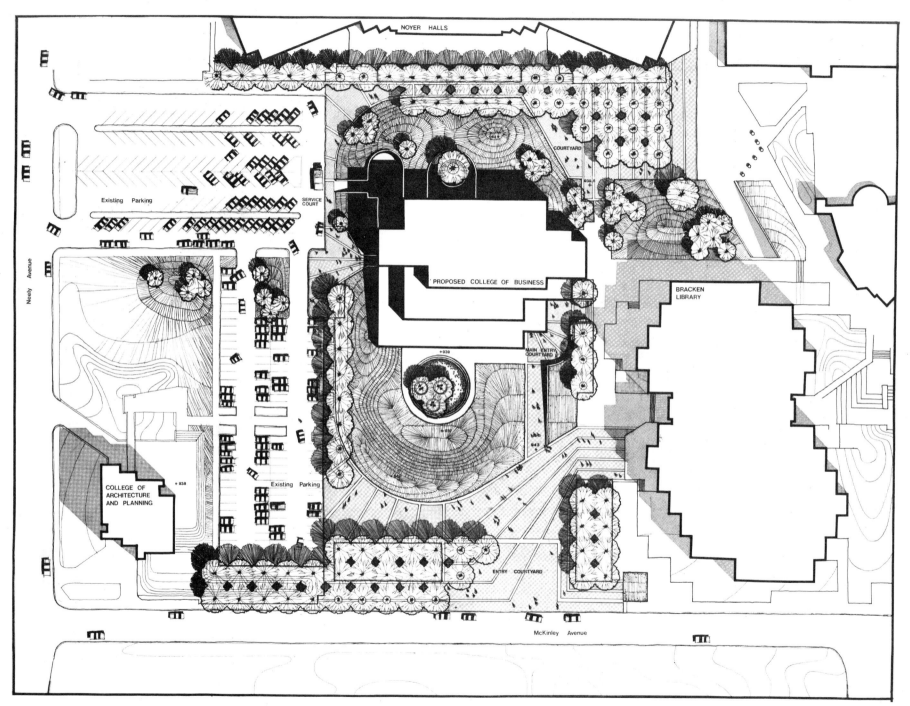

NOYER HALLS

COURTYARD

Existing Parking

SERVICE COURT

Neely Avenue

PROPOSED COLLEGE OF BUSINESS

BRACKEN LIBRARY

+938

MAIN ENTRY COURTYARD

COLLEGE OF ARCHITECTURE AND PLANNING

+938

Existing Parking

ENTRY COURTYARD

McKinley Avenue

218

College of Business, Ball State University,
Muncie, Indiana. Landplus West by Stan Geda.

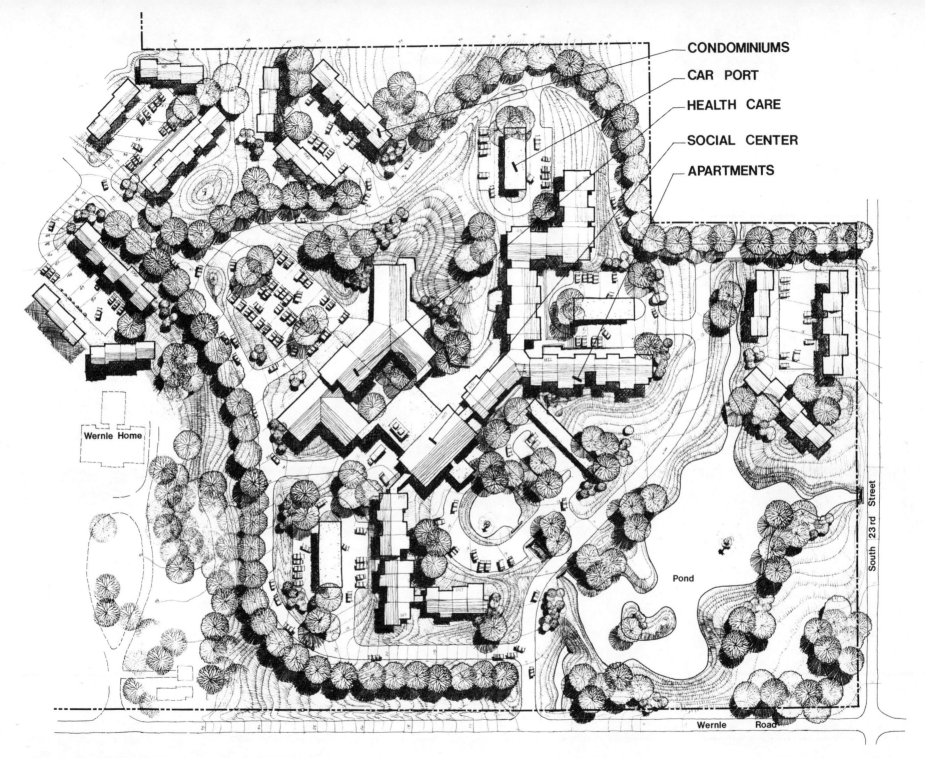

CONDOMINIUMS

CAR PORT

HEALTH CARE

SOCIAL CENTER

APARTMENTS

Wernle Home

Pond

South 23rd Street

Wernle Road

Vista Pines Retirement Community. Landplus
West by Tom Stearns and Stan Geda.

219

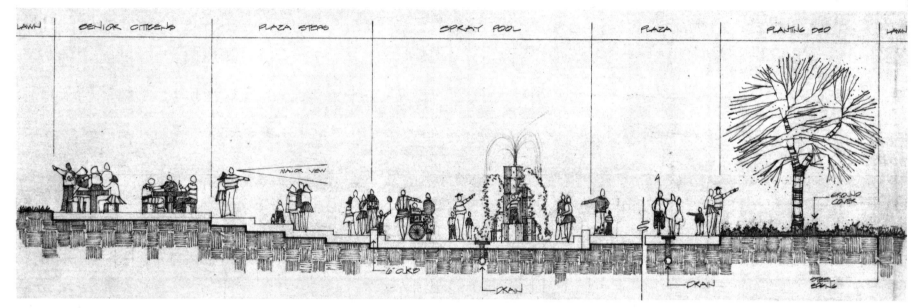

Wynnefield Park, Philadelphia. Donald R. Knox, Inc., by Francis X. Donnelly.

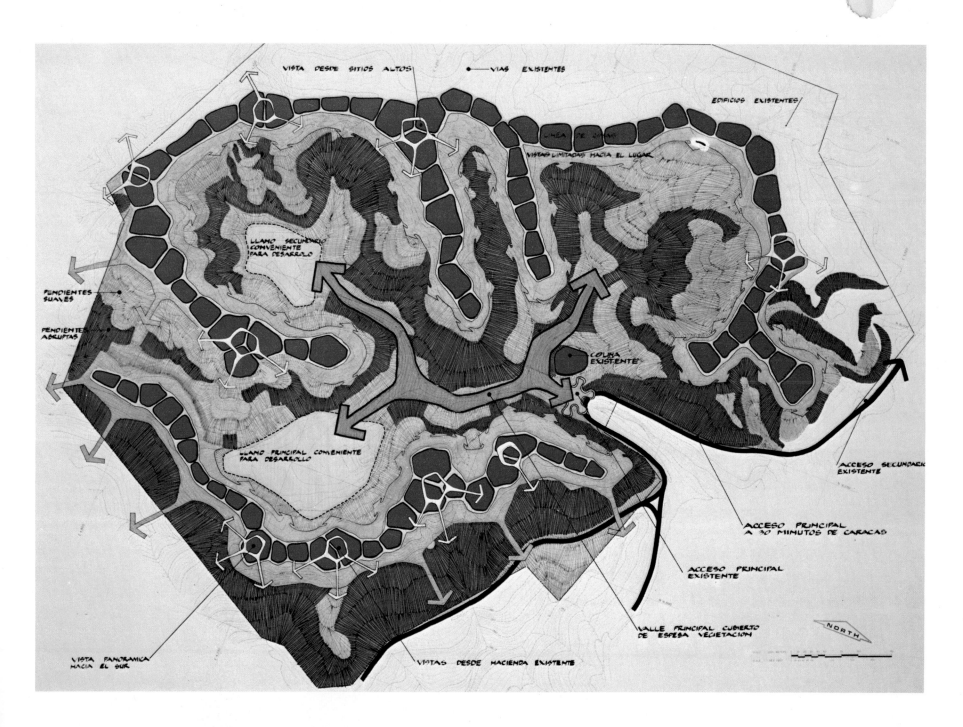

VISTA DESDE SITIOS ALTOS — VIAS EXISTENTES

EDIFICIOS EXISTENTES

LINEA DE LUGAR

VISTAS LIMITADAS HACIA EL LUGAR

LLANO SECUNDARIO CONVENIENTE PARA DESARROLLO

PENDIENTES SUAVES

PENDIENTES ABRUPTAS

COLINA EXISTENTE

ACCESO SECUNDARIO EXISTENTE

LLANO PRINCIPAL CONVENIENTE PARA DESARROLLO

ACCESO PRINCIPAL A 30 MINUTOS DE CARACAS

ACCESO PRINCIPAL EXISTENTE

VALLE PRINCIPAL CUBIERTO DE ESPESA VEGETACION

VISTA PANORAMICA HACIA EL SUR

VISTAS DESDE HACIENDA EXISTENTE

NORTH

Theme Park, Caracus, Venezuela. Edward D. Stone, Jr. and Associates.

221

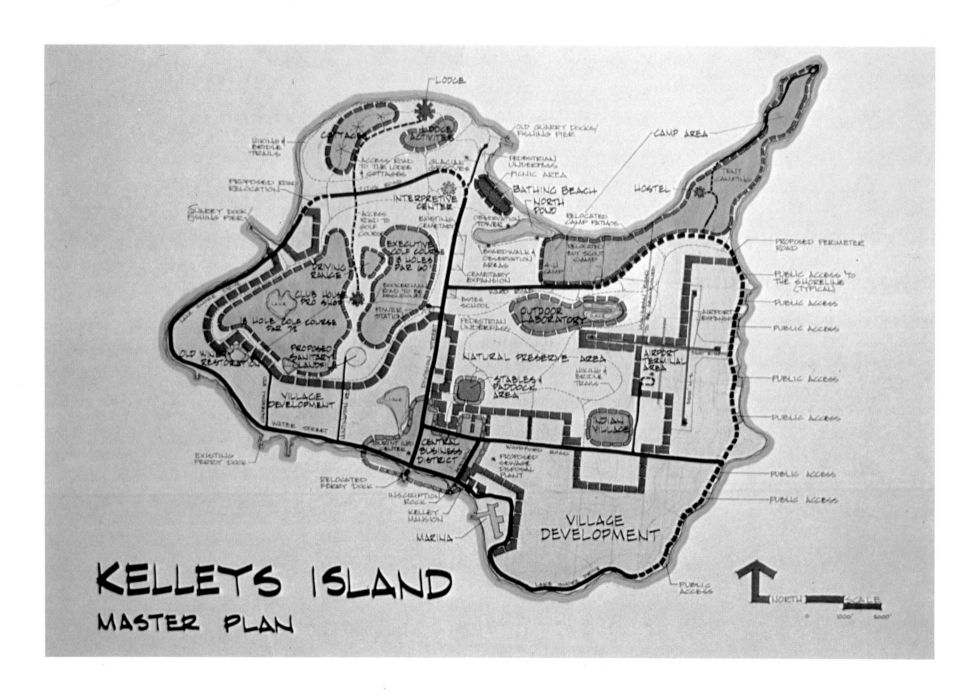

KELLEYS ISLAND
MASTER PLAN

Erie Islands State Park Study. William A. Behnke Associates,
by W. Lee Behnke and Russell L. Butler II. Felt markers on print.

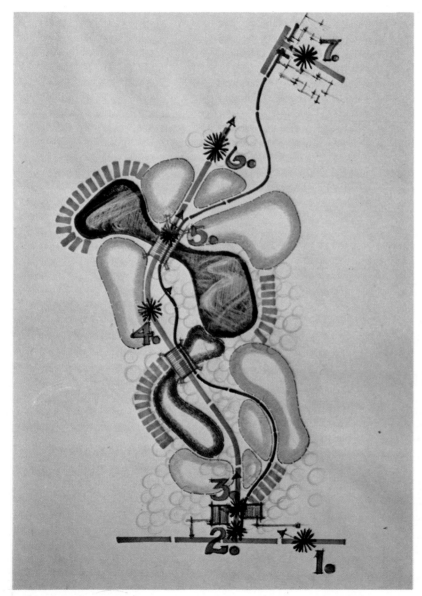

Browning-Day-Pollak, Inc.

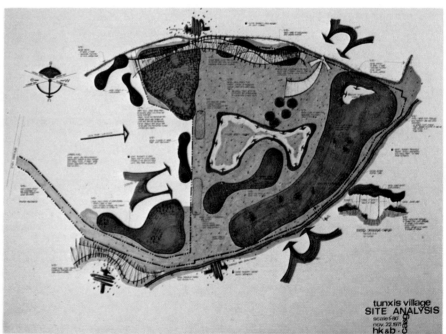

CR3, Inc.

CR3, Inc.

CR3, Inc.

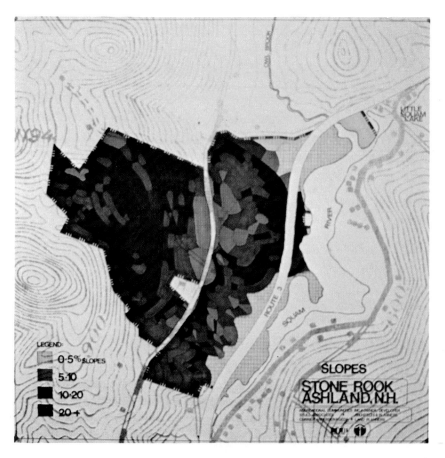

CR3, Inc.

CR3, Inc.

CR3, Inc.

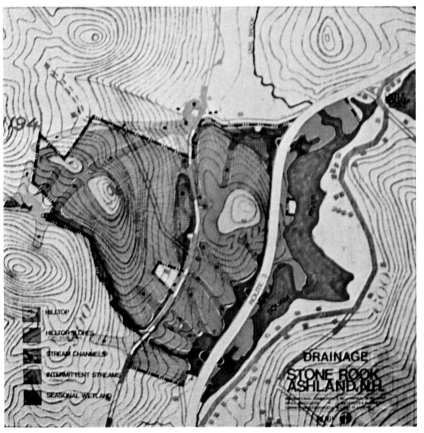

CR3, Inc.

LEGEND

EXCELLENT

GOOD

FAIR

POOR

#BASE-EXTG: SITE CONSTRAINTS

SUITABILITY-HOMESITES
STONE ROOK
ASHLAND, N.H.

CR3, Inc.

PUD-LAND USE PLAN
STONE ROOK
ASHLAND, N.H.

CR3, Inc.

CR3, Inc.

CR3, Inc.

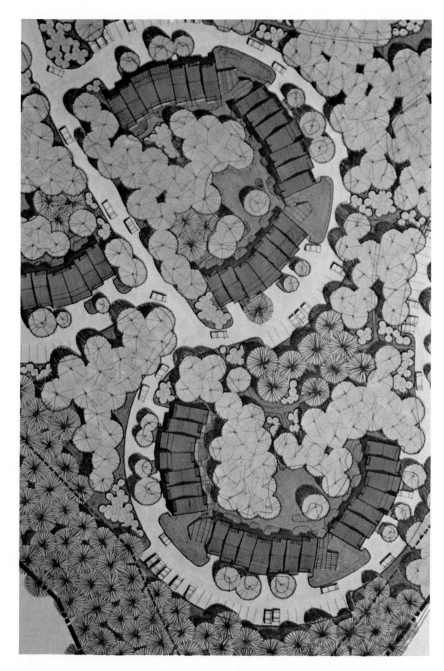

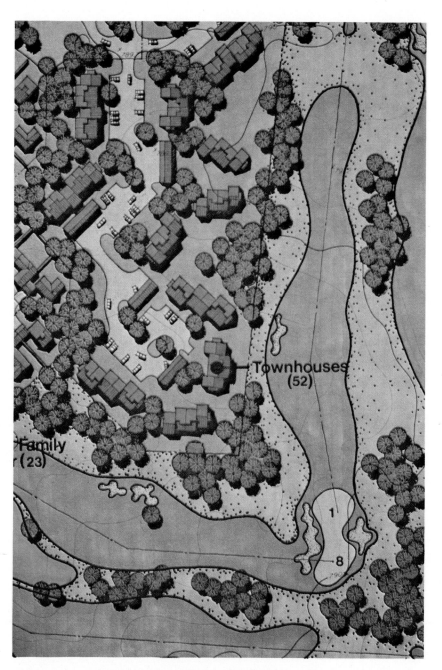

CR3, Inc.

Honeywell Gardens, A Planned Recreational
Community. Landplus West by Deane Rundell.

229

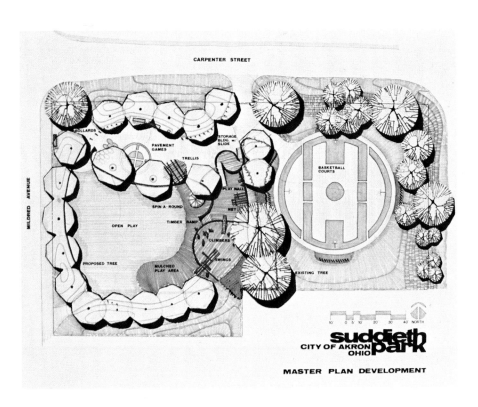

Bonnell & Associates.

Donald R. Knox, Inc., by Francis X. Donnelly.

Edmund Burke Ball Center Continuing
Education Center. Stan Geda and John Robert Russell.

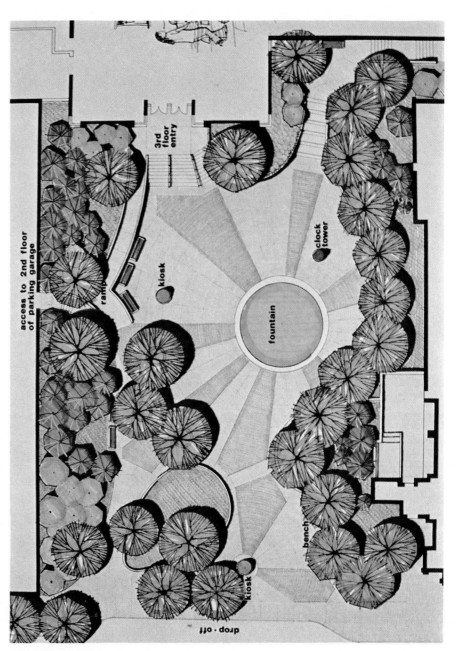

Bonnell & Associates.

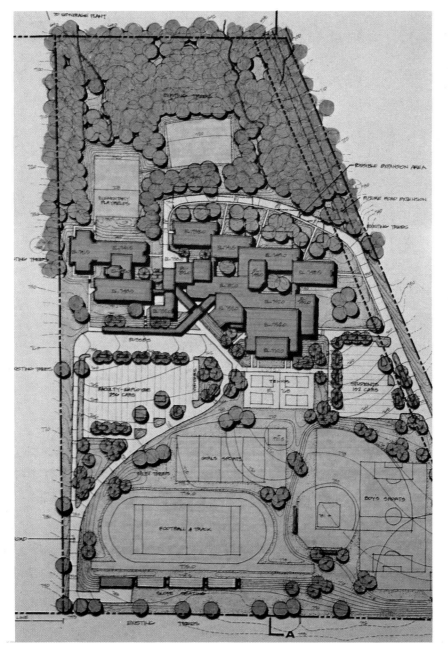

CR3, Inc.

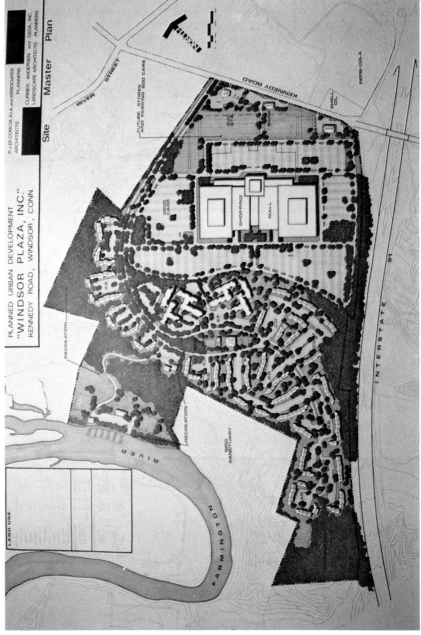

CR3, Inc.

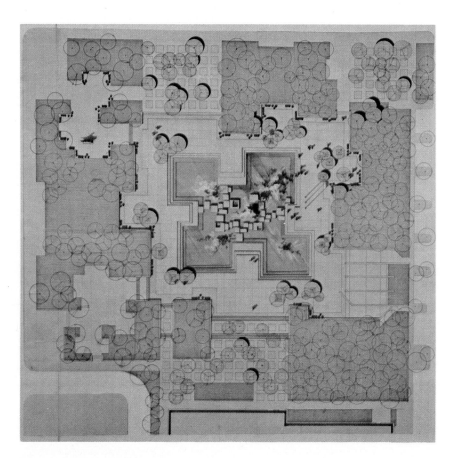

Browning-Day-Pollak, Inc.

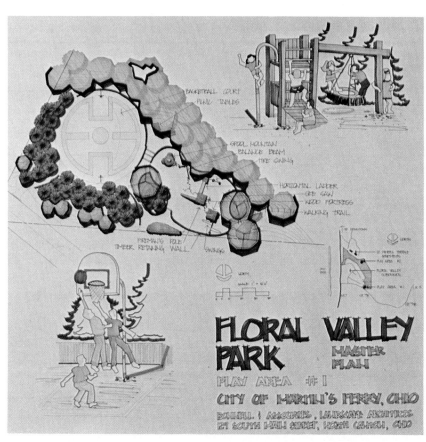

CR3, Inc.

OTHER BOOKS BY THE SAME AUTHOR:

Perception and Environmental Design. 1971

Perspective Sketches. 1972, 1975, 1977

Plants in the Landscape. 1975

ABOUT THE AUTHOR . . .

Theodore D. Walker is Associate Professor of Landscape Architecture at Purdue University. He received a Bachelor of Science degree in Landscape Architecture from Utah State University in 1957, and a Master of Landscape Architecture degree from the University of Illinois in 1967. His professional experience includes three years in a private office in Salt Lake City, six years as Site Planner for Brigham Young University, and 15 years in private practice. He is currently President of Walker, Harris Associates, Inc., West Lafayette, Indiana.

Active in the American Society of Landscape Architects, he has been a Member since 1964. He served as Secretary-Treasurer of the Rocky Mountain and North Central States Chapters and is currently Trustee of the Indiana Chapter. From 1972 to 1974 he served on the Board of Landscape Architectural Accreditation.